London Docklands

London Docklands:
Urban Design in an Age of Deregulation

Brian Edwards

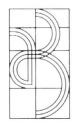

Butterworth Architecture
An imprint of Butterworth-Heinemann Ltd
Linacre House, Jordan Hill, Oxford OX2 8DP

 PART OF REED INTERNATIONAL BOOKS

OXFORD   LONDON   BOSTON
MUNICH   NEW DELHI   SINGAPORE   SYDNEY
TOKYO   TORONTO   WELLINGTON

First published 1992

British Library Cataloguing in Publication Data

A catalogue record for this book is available from the British Library.

ISBN 0 7506 1298 3

Library of Congress Cataloguing in Publication Data

A catalogue record for this book is available from the Library of Congress.

Composition by Scribe Design, Gillingham, Kent
Printed and bound in Great Britain by Thomson Litho Ltd, East Kilbride

Contents

Preface

London Docklands is undoubtedly the bravest experiment in urban design and architecture undertaken in Britain since the demise of the new towns programme in the early 1970s. The regeneration of the eastern corridor of London using free market policies and energies stands in contrast to the sense of municipal endeavour displayed by the formation of new communities such as Milton Keynes. Docklands was an attempt to bring the skills of the market place to a worn out inner city area by a combination of fiscal incentives and planning deregulation.

This book catalogues the processes and products of the first ten years, and seeks to establish certain lessons which may prove useful for other cities facing the redevelopment of redundant dockland areas. In the process a number of more general conclusions can be drawn about the nature of urbanism at the end of the twentieth century. As the controlling mechanisms have been rather loosely prescribed in London Docklands, a number of questions can be asked of contemporary architecture. This book does not pretend to answer all the questions raised, but it does engage in certain speculations which may prove helpful to other cities facing the redevelopment of their docklands.

As someone who went to school in east London within a stone's throw of the Thames, I feel a particular affinity for the area. After two decades working in Glasgow and seeing that city shake off a generation of economic decline and the collapse of its maritime lifeblood, it is heartening to see London following Glasgow's admirable lead in urban regeneration. In my interview with Michael Heseltine (see Appendix III) he too acknowledged the lessons from Glasgow and the important role of an agency or corporation spearheading partnerships with private companies to bring about area renewal. Hence the book draws parallels with other cities facing decline, and this provides part of the justification for having written it from an office near the Clyde as against the Thames.

Addendum

This book was written before the problems of Canary Wharf became public. The lack of infrastructural investment in Docklands as a whole and the Isle of Dogs in particular has undermined the success of a mainly privately funded decade of regeneration. Olympia and York are the principal losers amongst a clutch of development company failures. Progressive housebuilders, Kentish Homes, and innovative developers, Butlers Wharf Limited, have been forced into receivership, and now the world's biggest property company Olympia and York have sought the protection of 'administration'. The business failures simply highlight the need for a measure of town planning to integrate investment in the inner cities. The want of an urban development framework which this book illustrates is one reason for the failure of Canary Wharf and with it the collapse of Olympia and York.

Acknowledgements

My chief debt is to the staff of the London Docklands Development Corporation who, over ten years, have been unstinting in their release of information, their willingness to answer difficult questions, and their help with photographs and plans. Even if these pages are at times critical of the LDDC, staff never ceased to cooperate or failed to offer a timely cup of coffee after a long walk across the wastelands and building sites of Docklands. I am particularly indebted to Barry Shaw, for a time the head of urban design at the LDDC, and now active in the regeneration of the Royal Docks. He put me straight on many matters and pointed me in the right direction when I barked up the wrong tree.

Three architects in private practice have also shared their thoughts and ambitions with me over and above that necessary to placate an inquisitive writer. David Price of Price and Cullen, Piers Gough of CZWG and Tony Coombs of Olympia and York have fired my imagination at times and filled me with enthusiasm for the new city of Docklands. I am indebted to all three and to the countless other architects and developers who have shared a long distance telephone call and often an impromptu visit to their offices.

Finally, I would like to thank my employers at the University of Strathclyde for their support and encouragement. Needless to say any errors of fact and judgements are entirely my own.

Introduction

The reclamation of redundant dockland areas has been a recurring theme of European urbanism over the past decade. Following on from the success of waterfront restoration in cities in the United States such as Baltimore and Boston, many European maritime centres sought the regeneration of their docklands as a major plank of government policy during the eighties. The methods adopted from city to city have varied enormously, but nowhere in Europe has followed such a free market philosophy of urban renewal as London Docklands. In a mere decade, London's redundant Docklands have been transformed from nine square miles of wilderness and dereliction into the third major economic node in the capital.

The main vehicle used by the Conservative government to bring about such a transformation has been the London Docklands Development Corporation (LDDC), established in 1981 under the Local Government, Planning and Land Act (1980) promoted by Michael Heseltine as Secretary of State for the Environment. This Act sought to cut the 'Gordian knot' of planning controls in the inner city and release the energies of the private sector through mainly property-led regeneration. The LDDC orchestrated the renewal of London Docklands, spending about £1 billion in the first ten years on environmental and infrastructure improvements and thereby attracting about £10 billion of private investment. Besides removing environmental regulations such as orthodox town planning, the LDDC enjoyed the benefit of an enterprise zone within the heart of its area at the Isle of Dogs. The fiscal benefits and free market ethos of the enterprise zone quickly attracted international investment of which Olympia and York's Canary Wharf development is the most conspicious. Here alone 75,000 new jobs are promised in a collection of modern blocks and skyscrapers of decidedly American appearance.

For ten years Docklands enjoyed unprecedented growth fuelled by the New Right thinking of the Thatcher government. In many ways London's redundant waterside was well placed to exploit the property boom of the 1980s, especially the emergence of a new generation of high specification commercial buildings. The revolution in information technology during the decade led to a range of new building types and a tendency towards urban decentralization. London Docklands has not only benefitted from these changes, but also provided the City and Westminster with a complementary high technology centre which should allow London to retain its pre-eminence within world money markets. Without the extensive floor space available on the Isle of Dogs, London might well have been usurped by Frankfurt or Paris as the European centre of finance.

The urban experiment called London Docklands has led to the construction of a new city within the wastes of east London, but it is a place not without considerable shortcomings. The traditional view of a city has been violated here: there are no civic squares, no public buildings and few parks, and an uncomfortable relationship exists between transportation and new development. As for the architecture it is often meretricious in character and generally in a state of stylistic competition, with the spaces between the various buildings relegated to car parks or enclosed into private squares. The civic dimension in city making has been ignored by the thrust of free market aesthetics. For all the design pluralism and undoubted energy of the area, London Docklands provides a valuable pointer to the type of city created through the deregulation of the environment.

In may ways London Docklands stands against the tidal flow of European urbanism over the past decade. While the LDDC has sought design freedom, the European trend has been towards extending the embrace of orthodox planning control. The European Commission has successfully introduced a framework of environmental impact assessment in order to encourage member states to treat their cities with greater care. Docklands also stands against the flow of urban design masterplanning fostered by recent examples of urban renewal in Berlin, Paris and Barcelona. Suspicious of civic design frameworks and of carrying out an audit of environmental and social benefits, the LDDC has pursued a blatantly free market approach to regeneration. It is a philosophy which has produced much construction and raised the awareness of the value of design in urban renewal, but it has failed to make a balanced city.

London Docklands undoubtedly displays the architecture of the Thatcher years, and the LDDC was clearly created in the Conservative goverment's image. The area shows a passion for building unmoderated by wider social or environmental concerns. Regeneration has been property-led but few local people have benefitted. The lack of a correspondence between physical renewal and social renewal is marked today after a decade of unprecedented investment. If the LDDC had no strategy for urban design other than belatedly to seek to stitch together a mismatch of development, the same is true of community well-being. Areas such as job training, health care and social housing were, at least in the early years, left to the beleaguered local authorities.

The unprecedented speed and scale of regeneration has encouraged the LDDC to focus its attention upon the neglected areas of civic and community renewal in the plans for the 1990s. In 1996, after a fifteen year life, the LDDC will be disbanded–the task of urban recovery substantially complete. Now there is talk of addressing the problem of urban design and the social divide in Docklands. The impetus for the change of heart has come not from within the LDDC board, but from the developers themselves. Big companies like Stanhope Properties and Rosehaugh recognize that their long term investments require a stable local community, and one of genuine environmental quality. The lesson of the past ten years is that we have to learn again how to plan on a big scale.

This book charts a decade of Docklands redevelopment, looking primarily at the buildings, landscapes and urbanism created. With the breakdown of orthodox modernism and the removal of municipal controls, the area has developed into a plural, fragmented but exciting place. The stranglehold of social welfare planning which had dominated British practice since 1947 was broken by the 1980 Act and given specific direction by a combination of the emergence of urban development corporations (UDCs) and enterprise zones. The effect of the new machinery upon an inner city area is the main thrust of this book. A fresh, youthful and dynamic urbanism has grown up in London Docklands; it has the weaknesses of a frontier town and the contradictions of the age which produced it. But in a certain light, and at a certain speed, few parts of London are as vibrant, varied or refreshing.

If this book charts a decade of regeneration, it seeks also to set the first ten years of LDDC activity into perspective. In many ways Docklands challenges the two foundation stones upon which orthodox urban design rests: the establishment of a public realm, and the harnessing of private development for wider civic purposes. Neither has overconcerned the LDDC. So in place of urban planning Docklands gives us development enterprise, and in place of social gain we find the motor of productivity and profit. What type of urbanism follows from this experiment is largely the basis of this book.

Since questions or urban design are best addressed by an examination of the places created, the book focuses upon the new buildings and landscapes of Docklands. Many developments are fine in themselves; the problem concerns not so much the individual projects (though there are exceptions), more the aggregation of the parts. Hence the architecture of

Docklands is described where it leads on to questions of urban fit and agglomeration. Similarly, only through an examination of the buildings can the case for a healthy design pluralism in the docks be sustained. The balance between buildings and urbanism is of perennial concern to the architectural author. Docklands has the added problem that without a structuring framework, the urban places created are largely a by-product of architectural design. The nature and quality of these places, and the lessons to be drawn from their creation, are of more than passing concern.

Part One
Realizing the Potential of London Docklands

The Evolution of Docklands as a Distinctive Place

1

The Georgian legacy

Docklands as a distinctive landscape evolved largely as a result of the commercial acumen of the trading merchants of eighteenth century London. Until then goods were stored in outbuildings or cellars, trade was transacted within the merchants' houses, and wharves consisted of timber jetties lining the Thames. It was only in the 1790s that attention was addressed to the problem of creating a purpose built dock and transportation system for London's growing shipping and warehousing businesses. As in much of Georgian London, the architecture of commerce and speculation was to leave a substantial mark on Docklands.

The growth of London as a port in the eighteenth century was only grudgingly reflected in new buildings and docks constructed specifically for the purpose. Though trade imports increased from £13 million in 1700 to £34 million in 1790[1] no substantial structures were built to accommodate them, until the Pool of London became so overcrowded that Parliament was moved to enact a succession of Acts allowing for the construction of purpose built docks. West India Dock, which effectively made the Isle of Dogs into a true island, was constructed in 1800, London Dock in 1802, the Surrey Dock system in 1804, and by 1828 the East India and St Katharine Docks had been built. Earlier docks such as Howland Dock built in 1700 (later enlarged and renamed Greenland Dock) and Brunswick Dock in Blackwall of 1789 were too far downstream to meet the commercial needs of London.

The docks show that rare blend of architectural and engineering design characteristic of such areas. The materials were solid and robust; the buildings were monumental in scale, and adhered to a distinctive form of engineers' classicism which placed aesthetic emphasis upon repetition and harmonious

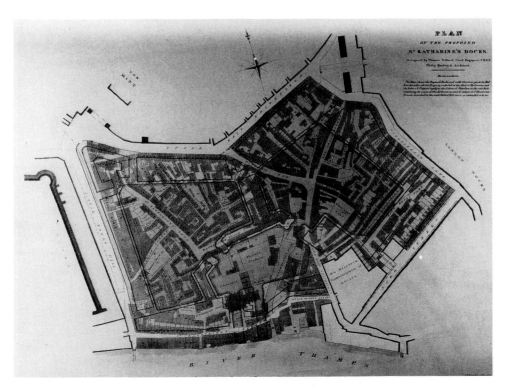

Figure 1.1

Parliamentary plan for the forming of St Katharine Docks. The plans drawn up in 1825 by the engineer Thomas Telford and the architect Philip Hardwick show the removal of many houses as well as the medieval church and cloisters of St Katharine's (photo: Museum of Docklands)

Figure 1.2

Parliamentary plan for the forming of London Docks (1802) (photo: Museum of Docklands)

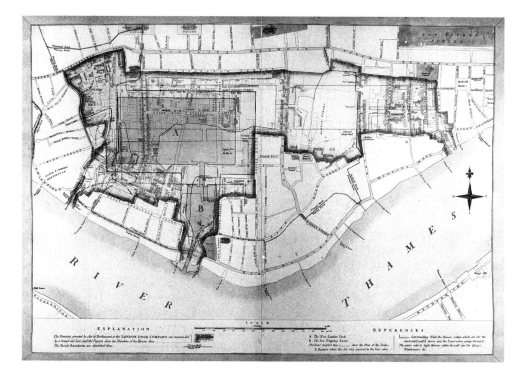

proportions. Those who designed the docks often had a hand in the buildings which lined them, and hence engineers are often credited with the authorship of both the functional and the aesthetic elements.

The various undertakings were generally the result of private Acts of Parliament. Hence Docklands, like much of London, grew out of the entrepreneurial energies of a handful of far-sighted developers. One such was Ralph Dodd, an engineer speculator who not only promoted the extensive Surrey Docks system but planned a new bridge crossing of the Thames, later known as Waterloo Bridge. He and his kind invested in canals, docks, warehouses and bridges. What is most remarkable about the period from

Figure 1.3

View of Surrey Commercial Docks in 1906. This view shows the docks at the turn of the century. Much of the water area has since been infilled with only Greenland Dock (to the right) surviving (photo: Museum of Docklands)

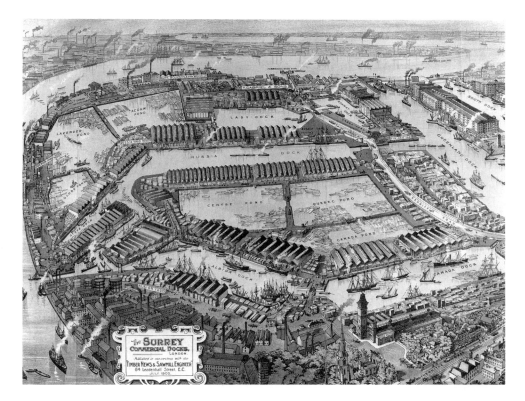

1800 to about 1830 is the speed at which new building types were evolved and constructional methods formulated. Tobacco Dock is typical of the period and thankfully survives just south of The Highway in Wapping. Built in 1811–18 by Daniel Alexander, it features spectacular iron columns which branch out like trees in an attempt to create huge undivided floor areas for the storage of tobacco.[2]

There is much in the surviving warehouse buildings of the docks to indicate that architecture is the servant not just of engineering but of merchandising. Making money has left its mark in Docklands in the same way that displaying accumulated wealth marks the streetscape of the West End. Though too little survives of the total environment which once made the Pool of London the busiest port in the world, the fragments which remain at St Katharine's and St Saviour's Docks give more than a taste of the former splendour.

Segregation by infrastructure

The result of all the dock and warehouse construction was to give the area a character quite unique for London. The dock basins severed the old neighbourhoods of Bermondsey, Blackwall and Wapping, producing distinctive inward looking worlds whose insularity was reinforced by the presence of many foreign sailors. This not only led to a greater sense of community than was often the case in London, but fostered an independence which was later to manifest itself in a less than compliant workforce. The physical isolation of areas like the Isle of Dogs and the Royal Docks was the result of the extensive water basins and the high security walls which extended around each dock system. These walls followed the edges of a largely perimeter road system whose own geometries were dictated either by the Thames or by the docks themselves. Hence Millwall Dock consisted of a long parallel water basin lined by warehouses or sheds and enclosed by walls ten or twelve feet high with gated entrances. The rectilinear configuration of most of the docks stood in contrast to the gently curving walls of the security enclosures and the Thames itself. From the outside the view was of masts and funnels and the rooftops of the many warehouses; inside there were cranes, barrels, crates of bananas and other cargoes waiting to be loaded or unloaded.

If the parallel geometries of the docks contrasted pleasantly with the older irregular landscape of more ancient townships, the scale of the docks was also in marked contrast with that of surrounding houses. The docks and their ships towered above the humble dwellings of the dockers. Only the few public buildings, of which churches were the noblest, moderated the

Figure 1.4

View of the proposed West India Docks in 1802. William Daniell's perspective shows the Thames in the foreground lined by houses with the rectangular basins of the dock system behind. Notice how the docks, warehouses and enclosing walls were treated as one (photo: Museum of Docklands)

overpowering scale of the Docklands landscape. In other Dockland areas such as Liverpool, grand public and commercial buildings lined the river edge at the point where mercantile activity was most intense, but in London Docklands the civic presence tended to prefer the upper reaches of the Thames. Of the churches, only Hawksmoor's splendid and haunting structures from before the period of dock construction could, until Canary Wharf and its neighbours appeared, offer a scale appropriate to these expansive watery landscapes.

If a century and a half of dock construction isolated and fragmented this part of London, it did so in a fashion which has allowed recent administrators such as the LDDC to deal with the area as one. To those within the area Docklands is not however a self-contained world but simply the edge of bigger places such as Southwark, Rotherhithe and Poplar. These neighbourhoods hold on to an identity far older than that which resulted from the arrival of Rennie, Telford or Gwilt. Their roots do not respect the patterns established in the eighteenth century and reinforced in recent legislation. The artificial boundaries of the LDDC make little sense socially or in terms of the bigger community of London, and neither do they respect the financial realities of the market place. But what they do is strengthen the oneness of Docklands and give administrative expression today to a unique landscape created in part by some of the finest engineers and architects of the Georgeian period. That so much has been lost by the destructive forces of war, official vandalism and neglect should not be allowed to colour our judgement. Docklands was created to fulfil the functional requirements of trade, not to give beauty to the capital. That beauty and dignity did occur in good measure was simply the result of building in an age when taste could generally be relied upon.

By the nineteenth century London had developed into a successful plural economy based principally upon mercantile, banking and insurance services at the City and warehousing, shipbuilding, manufacturing and brewing in Docklands. The City and the Port were thus interdependent, with the Royal Mint, constructed in 1818 by Robert Smirke, standing appropriately at their interface. The Thames provided the link between the two worlds, but it was a service channel, not a grand canal along which to build a mansion or civic offices.

The foundations laid in the eighteenth century proved reliable enough in the nineteenth and sufficiently sturdy in the twentieth for Docklands to continue to flourish. Many of the docks were subsequently expanded and new rail and tram services installed, but the basic structure of Docklands imposed in the period 1790–1850 has proved remarkably resilient to economic pressures.

Planning in London Docklands in the twentieth century

As we have seen, the making of Docklands was the result of infrastructure provision rather than municipal planning. The grand projects to construct docks shaped the area from the eighteeneth century onwards and, when a measure of town planning was introduced by the forming of the London County Council (LCC) in 1888, Docklands was already an effective working landscape. The LCC's attentions were directed at slum clearance and street widening, and after 1945 at the provision of social housing for those employed in the industries of the area. Comprehensive planning found expression in the Abercrombie Plan for London of 1944 and the LCC's Development Plan of 1951, but neither had much impact upon the area. Urban remodelling of the Poplar and Stepney areas failed to materialize even with the help of a backlog of wartime bomb damage. Planning activity in Docklands derived not so much from County Hall or the local boroughs, but from the Port of London Authority. The PLA had been established in 1908 and was much engaged up to 1960 upon dock widening, warehouse construction and smoothing out the inefficiencies of a largely eighteenth century industrial landscape.

As tonnage handled began to decline from its peak in 1959 (when over 50 million tons of cargo passed through the docks, or about a third of Britain's seaborne trade), the PLA was forced to infill the docks. This created sites for development which helped the PLA to repay its capital debts to central government. Unfortunately, such was the sharp economic and social decline in the 1960s that redevelopment tended to be for low grade industry, scrap merchants and haulage depots, thus undermining an already degraded physical environment.[3]

Decline focused minds upon a planned approach, and in 1974 the Docklands Joint Committee was established comprising the five riparian borough councils and the Greater London Council. Slightly earlier the PLA had commissioned planning consultants Travers Morgan to prepare development options for Docklands, and they proposed five options: Europa, Thames Park, City New Town, Waterside and East End Consolidated.[4] Now at last visionary proposals were appearing, but the Joint Committee recommended that the infilled docks be used mainly for building houses for local people and for laying out parks. The Docklands were to be consolidated, not drastically changed, and government money not venture capital was to pay for the work. The emergence of the LDDC put an end to locally hatched plans for the revitalization of the area and redirected ambitions back to the Travers Morgan proposals.

The forming of the London Docklands Development Corporation

The Local Government, Planning and Land Act of 1980 sought to change perceptions in Docklands by forming a new administrative body responsible for urban regeneration (the LDDC) and new procedures (enterprise zones). (The main provisions of the 1980 Act, and the action taken by the LDDC as a result, are summarized in Appendix II.) Naturally the Joint Committee found itself stripped of power, especially after the demise of the GLC in 1985. A splinter group–the Docklands Forum–continues to promote planning policies which are based loosely upon the Joint Committee's recommendations. It has published a series of papers critical of the performance of the LDDC–some by former staff of the corporation such as Ted Hollamby.[5] But the power base had by then switched to the LDDC, which has carried out extensive regeneration of the area employing largely free market philosophies in marked contrast to the planned approach of the recent past.

The role of the LDDC board

The LDDC is controlled by a board of thirteen members, each appointed by the Secretary of State for the Environment. Of the board members, some are drawn from industry and others from the world of property development and construction, including Sir Andrew Derbyshire, partner of the London-based office of architects Sir Robert Matthew, Johnson Marshall and Partners. The chairmen of the board of the LDDC from 1981 to 1989 were all property men and hence gave the corporation the expertise necessary in marketing sites, selecting developers, and seeking to control rising land values to the area's advantage. The first chairman, Nigel Broakes (1981–4), was a director of Trafalgar House; Christopher Benson (1984–7) was from MEPC; and David Hardy (1987–90) was from Globe Investment Trust.

Board meetings are closed to the public, and only recently have the deliberations of the planning committee been open to outsiders. This has bred distrust between the LDDC and the London boroughs on the one hand and between the LDDC and local community groups on the other. Recent moves towards meeting social housing and training programmes have oiled troubled waters, though the economic downturn from 1990 has tended to undermine the good intentions. The main benefit of a property dominated LDDC board has been to attract many of the big commercial developers to the area, and to put little in their way when grand schemes were being hatched.

The board directs the officers of the LDDC through a chief executive who in turn is responsible for the eighty or so full-time staff of the corporation. The intention has always been to run the LDDC with a small team of staff, using consultants wherever possible. The in-house teams of architects, planners, engineers etc. are divided between a central office which coordinates activity and monitors the performance of regeneration, and four local offices at Wapping, the Isle of Dogs, Surrey Docks and Royal Docks. The area offices are more action-led than the central office, and enjoy a certain autonomy.

Eighty full-time staff is a small establishment for an area of 5000 acres, a resident population of 55,000 and a working one of about 100,000. It is also pretty slim when set alongside the £850 million of public money put into Docklands in the decade from 1981 and largely coordinated by the various area teams. Some would see the decision making structure of the LDDC as a model for Britain's local government: board members appointed by central government using the minimum of full-time staff and the maximum of private consultants.

Under the LDDC's first chief executive Reg Ward, the landscape of Docklands changed more than over the prevous fifty years. Ward, a former tax inspector and high ranking local government officer, worked wonders for Docklands, whilst apparently running rings round the Department of the Environment and the LDDC board.[6] Ward described himself as a 'romantic dreamer with both feet firmly in mid-air'.[7] He achieved miracles for Docklands, though people are now asking whether they were the right miracles: Canary Wharf owed much to Ward's persuasive style and love of limelight. In 1987 when his sixtieth birthday was reached the board did not extend his contract, though he was anxious to stay on.[8]

Ward was replaced by the architect Michael Honey. Honey, like Ward,

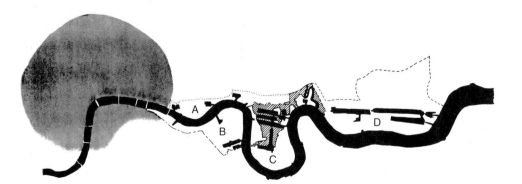

Figure 1.5

Area of Docklands placed under the control of the LDDC in 1981. The shaded area to the left shows the commercial heart of London, the hatched area the enterprise zone. Dock areas: (A) Wapping and Poplar, (B) Surrey Docks, (C) Isle of Dogs, (D) Royal Docks

emerged from within the ranks of local government, and brought a widening of perception to the problem of Docklands. Two distinct benefits flowed from his appointment: urban design was at last recognized as a problem, and bridges were built with the local community, particularly in the field of social housing provision.

The chief executive of the LDDC manages his staff through two different kinds of division. One deals with topics such as development, projects and finance, and the other with specific area responsibilities such as the Isle of Dogs. Each major task is under a director answerable to the chief executive and hence to the board. In 1991 plans were announced to merge the area teams into four new divisions formed by a rationalization of the earlier functions. Hence, the area teams face greater control from the centre, a situation which may lead to a loss of local diversity in Docklands. Another result of the management review was to refocus attention upon the Royal Docks so that it could develop in a fashion which complemented the increasingly office dominated Isle of Dogs. The latter may well have been in response to criticisms by the House of Commons Employment Committee, which reported soon after Honey's appointment that 'UDCs cannot be regarded as a success if buildings and land are regenerated but the local community are by-passed and do not benefit from the regeneration.'[9]

Problems with funding infrastructure

The trend towards accountability at the LDDC has coincided with a series of battles with central government over support for transport in Docklands. The experiment in enterprise architecture had not been matched by a corresponding provision in public transport. The Docklands Light Railway was fine for the first wave of regeneration, but hopelessly inadequate for the 15,000 people per hour needs of schemes such as Canary Wharf. Similarly, road provision was proving inadquate even as early as 1985, yet the Department of Transport refused to invest on the scale required. The situation deteriorated and in the early 1990s it was taking ninety minutes to get off the Isle of Dogs by road. Construction to ease the problem had to be met out of the LDDC's account, not the Transport Department's, thereby adding further disquiet.

Docklands is undoubtedly the victim of its own success, but it also demonstrates the shortcomings of New Right policies for the inner city. If the LDDC is to broaden its horizons to encompass community, educational and social concerns, then it must not be overburdened by massive investment in areas such as transportation which most countries provide from central funds. The want of central government investment in Docklands may yet push the LDDC board and its chief executives into the same conflicts as those experienced by the local authorities. Honey, having paved the way for a more rounded Docklands, resigned after two years, and was replaced by a former civil servant Eric Sorensen.

With disquiet in the air, the Chancellor of the Exchequer John Major moved in his autumn statement of 1989 to double to £1 billion over five years the grant to the LDDC. The main objective was to try to prevent Docklands becoming an inaccessible island of overdevelopment in East London.[10] The LDDC's own inability to pay for road and rail construction stemmed largely from the slump in land prices, which meant that the corporation was not able to make massive profits as it did up to 1988 on the sale of land. Hence, reluctant chancellors have been forced to make greater provision for the construction of roads etc. to placate developers such as Olympia and York, and to keep the credibility of Docklands alive. Docklands is increasingly seen as a personal monument to Margaret Thatcher, just as the grand projects in Paris, such as La Défense, are monuments to President Mitterrand. What is striking, however, is that the French monuments have been in the form of architecture funded by the government, whilst the British architectural monuments have been paid for by private developers with the state paying only (and with a measure of meanness) for the transport links.

Heritage as development lure

Except for the water, warehouses and historic churches, there is not a great deal which gives Docklands its sense of place. The new buildings are often indifferent to place; in fact 'placelessness' describes much of the environment of London Docklands. Those things which establish place are invariably inherited from the past, be they historic buildings, interesting old neighbourhoods, or industrial relics such as cranes, wharfs and dock basins. A heritage industry has grown up in Britain over the past fifteen years, partly to serve urban tourism and party to give a sense of place to areas undergoing much change. The nineteenth century architectural writer John Ruskin saw historic buildings as society's memory and put forward theories to guide the restoration of old buildings[11]; but today, in areas such as Docklands, conservation is concerned as much with marketing as with simple preservation.

The idea of memory is, however, particularly important in neighbourhoods which are changing their identity or social base, and this is one reason why the LDDC has been so generous in the provision of funds to restore Docklands architectural heritage. The corporation has, however, been less than keen to treat industrial remains with equal generosity, particularly those not scheduled as official monuments. Archaeology and historic buildings have not only enjoyed considerable financial support, but also appeared prominently on LDDC promotional literature for the area. Heritage, in fact, has proved a very marketable commodity for the corporation.

When one visits the area it quickly becomes obvious that churches and structures associated with former Dockland activity (warehouses, shipyards, wharves etc.) are the principal heritage resource. Though there are fine groups of eighteenth century houses and the occasional medieval pub, the area's heritage is clearly split between the world of ecclesiastical structures and that of industrial ones. In a sense it is divided between high and low art, or between the interests of architectural historians and those of industrial archaeologists.

Economic decline in London Docklands since the 1960s led to considerable neglect of the fabric of the area. Though the decline was spectacularly reversed after 1981, much remained to be done in terms of restoring and rehabilitating older buildings and finding new uses for them. Through grant aid by the LDDC to historic buildings (£4.5 million in the period 1981–7[12]) and environmental improvements in conservation areas (£1.5 million in the same period) the backlog of neglected work was addressed, but the effect has been to concentrate overmuch on individual buildings at the expense of their setting. Churches have been painstakingly restored, but their immediate environment has remained untouched or become altered out of recognition. Memory extends beyond the individual monument to encompass fragments of neighbourhood in which the old buildings sit – both physically and socially. If a historic building's visual frame of reference is left to decay or becomes altered in a fashion which destroys important relationships of scale or detail, then the currency of memory is devalued. This is the problem with much of London Docklands.

For historic buildings to survive the question is generally twofold: first, whether funds can be found to carry out the necessary repair or maintenance; and second, whether the building can continue to support present activity or accommodate a new sympathetic use. Areas which change rapidly, such as Docklands, throw existing buildings quickly into obsolescence, but at the same time generate new uses to place in the redundant shells of those buildings which are to be preserved. In Ruskin's time new

Figure 1.6

Restored church of All Saints, Poplar. One of several landmarks restored with grant aid from the LDDC (photo: Brian Edwards)

uses were not at issue; the question was smply how to carry out correct and faithful restoration, thereby preserving the memory intact.

In Docklands, however, whilst restoration has generally followed the principles of the Society for the Protection of Ancient Buildings (SPAB) – the result largely of Ruskin's strictures as modified by William Morris – the market-oriented world of the LDDC has led to some unsatisfactory conversions. At Tobacco Dock, Terry Farrell has carefully restored the Old Skin Warehouse and placed within it shop units which are obviously of recent origin (though sympathetically treated), but the wider environment is filled with plywood replica sailing ships which add an unwelcome and compromising Disney-like air. One could argue that much of Docklands has the feel of a theme park, yet historic buildings, especially when they are grade 1 listed as here, must maintain their integrity.

Questions of appropriateness also arise particularly with regard to the conversion and extension of Hawksmoor'e St-George-in-the-East by Price and Cullen. It was bombed in the last war and is now a mere shell alongside The Highway, and the proposal to build workshops and houses in its grounds raises difficult moral issues. Without nearby occupation the building is more subject to vandalism, but low rise housing within the curtilage of the church disrupts its sense of sanctuary and weakens its monumentality. Though the church itself is not violated, its relationship to the street and the immediate world of this part of east London is important. The argument is compounded by a long tradition of housing acting as a foil to the church, but the beauty and pathos of Hawksmoor's tower demands it be seen as an isolated monument.

Warehouse conversions in Docklands

There is always a price to pay in terms of loss of character for the change of use of an historic building (though there should never be character loss in pure restoration). How this character price is to be paid and by whom is important. The LDDC has acted largely as an honest broker between the development community and those intent upon restoration, particularly English Heritage. Grant aid has been employed to direct sensitive developers towards important buildings, and space standards have been relaxed to achieve the type of heritage-led conversions which many local groups desire. With regard to loft conversions or the adaptation of nineteenth century warehouse buildings, heritage has been grasped with an enthusiasm rare in Britain. To possess a few cast iron beams or a projecting gantry crane has become the height of fashion for some in this part of London. These elements, usually mere fragments of a bigger whole, are lovingly displayed within the living rooms or bedrooms of countless loft conversions, particularly in the area of Wapping Pier Head and St Saviour's Dock. They demonstrate the lure of heritage and the increasing shift away from conservation as a community enterprise towards conservation as private wealth. The ownership of such flats is seen by many as a kind of connoisseurship, and the more industrial fragments possessed the greater the sense of trophy. No wonder such flats figure frequently in television commercials (usually for credit cards or lager) and no wonder too that CZWG has deliberately incorporated pseudo masts in The Circle near Tower Bridge as a play upon this theme.

Warehouse conversion generally offers only one way to expand – upwards. The popularity of penthouse flats and the spectacular views along the Thames from riverside warehouses have led to some unsatisfactory rooftop additions. The problem is partly aesthetic, and partly concerned with protecting the interesting roof structures of many of the listed warehouses. Gun Wharves, Hays Dock, Butlers Wharf, St Saviour's Wharf and Brandram's Wharf in Rotherhithe are all examples of attic storeys added to listed warehouses without historic precedent.[13]

The conversion of listed warehouses has had the benefit of creating mixed use development in areas where single land uses and repetitive buildings are more common. The structural complexity of some of the older buildings has resulted in a mixture of office, studio, apartment and penthouse accommodation within the same block. Elsewhere converted property has provided much cheaper accommodation for start-up companies than in the new, highly serviced buildings. This has resulted in greater social diversity, as well as welcome visual variety. An example is the Quadrangle Building of 1824 near the entrance to West India Dock converted recently to the Cannon Workshops. As a general rule the conversions nearer to the centre of London are mainly for office use, those in the central Dockland areas and

along the riverside for residential use, and those further afield for light industrial or retail use. Whatever the conversion, retained buildings are a welcome exception to the general rule of new building.

Providing legibility through conservation

If Dockland heritage has been too easily compromised for the likes of English Heritage or the Royal Fine Art Commission, the character benefits have flowed mainly in the direction of commercial advantage as against social gain. This is hardly surprising given the nature and objectives of the LDDC, but one great opportunity was missed at the outset of operations. Dockland's historic buildings and industrial archaeological sites could have been made more visible and accessible to the public. Much of interest remains hidden from view or within the private ownership of companies or individuals. A strategy of guaranteed access and greater visibility would have benefited the redevelopment of the area. For example, the great eighteenth century churches could have become terminating points for axial vistas, thereby giving new development greater coherence and at the same time strengthening the bond between old buildings and new. Such vistas would also have given the new areas, such as the Isle of Dogs, a sense of directional differentiation and civic scale. One lesson of the nineteenth century was that urban renewal could be employed to make historic buildings more visible, to disencumber them of lesser buildings and hence improve their

Figure 1.7

Conversion of riverfront warehouses below Tower Bridge. The warehouses not only provide an opportunity for mixed use conversion but give a context for the design of new buildings (photo: Michael Squire Associates)

immediate setting, and as part of the process to stitch them back into the fabric of modern life. Here the LDDC has been sadly unimaginative.

The hype generated by the corporation in the mid 1980s claimed that London Docklands was the biggest exercise in urban development in Europe, yet the corporation failed to draw lessons from comparable remodelling either in the nineteenth or more relevantly in the twentieth century. The late seventies and early eighties provided visions of urban change in Germany and France which could have informed action in London. The competition to redevelop Les Halles in Paris for instance attracted much comment in professional journals, as did the remodelling of Berlin through the Internationale Bauausstellung (IBA). Both sought to model the reconstruction of the area around the geometric or aesthetic dictates of existing monuments, and both appreciated that major historic buildings need a preeminent position in any new urban hierarchy. Having drawn parallels with Europe in its publicity material, it is a shame that the LDDC did not seek to learn from Europe's experience. For London Docklands is not such an exceptional place, apart from the splendid and massive Hawksmoor churches and the existence of the Wren inspired Greenwich axis which (at least by extension) crosses the Isle of Dogs to St Anne's Limehouse. The reluctance to impose an order which derives from these monuments undermines the good work of the LDDC in funding simple building restoration. It also suggests a lack of familiarity with the writings of the influential urban theorist Aldo Rossi, whose book *The Architecture of the City* argues for a clear relationship between public monuments and private buildings.[14]

A similar argument could be employed for the major dock basins and the River Thames itself. These are, however, as much landscape as townscape resources and, being large voids within the urban fabric, raise issues of

Figure 1.8

St-George-in-the-East church. The opportunity to open the splendid Hawkmoor churches to view by using them as terminations to development axes was not taken by the LDDC. As a result they remain often hidden from view within the wider townscape (photo: Brian Edwards)

containment and edge continuity rather than skyline punctuation or vista termination. However, the reluctance to establish an urban framework here results in an inability to comprehend fully the watery structure of the area, or to enjoy the decaying machinery of the dock basins with any understanding of their relevance. For even if access is available, their setting is often marred by overlarge office buildings or underscaled houses with pretensions of Dickensian prettiness. The honest, robust industrial landscape of the docklands has not survived piecemeal redevelopment. Only in Greenland Dock, thanks to a development plan prepared by Conran Roche, do these issues appear considered, and here the containment by buildings seems undersized for the extent of the water. Elsewhere, industrial remains such as swing bridges and warehouse archaeology have a largely haphazard relationship to the new landscape of Docklands.

One of the finest groups of warehouse buildings is the sugar warehouses alongside West India Dock. Owned by the LDDC, they are soon to be converted to flats, restaurants and related leisure uses with the retention of the historically important structure of cast iron columns and massive timber floors. The intention here is to create a large tourist development around the collection of listed warehouses and stores and the Dockmaster's House in a fashion already established at Tobacco Dock; only a short distance away, however, Canary Wharf rises to its full fifty storeys thereby destroying the setting of the splendid group though not actually damaging their fabric. In New York abrupt discontinuities in scale and date are commonplace and part of the city's charm; in the Isle of Dogs enterprise zone the same qualities will soon prevail. Other cities would perhaps have stepped the skyline to frame the inherited monuments; in Docklands the approach is rather more collage than urban design, or at least aggressive collision.

Disjointedness, however, is better than the demolition which marked the decade before the setting up of the LDDC. Ken Powell, former chairman of Save Britain's Heritage, has said that the demolition of London's docks was a scandal that has never been adequately explained.[15] Much of St Katharine Docks including three warehouses designed by Telford and Hardwick were demolished, and in London Docks five massive bonded blocks by D.A. Alexander were lost. Today they would all have been converted to new office or residential use or even moved to a better location as with Spice Quay.

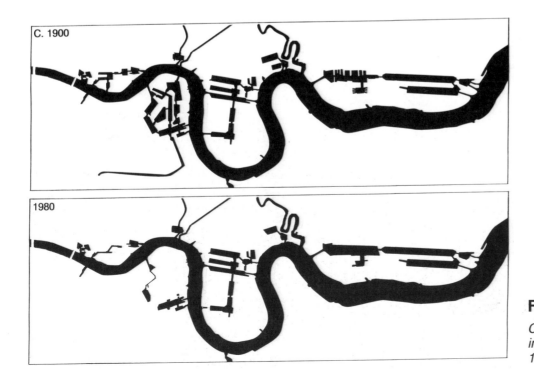

Figure 1.9

Comparison of the water areas in docklands in c.1900 and in 1980

Part of the blame lies with the Docklands Joint Committee which argued in 1976 that the cost of warehouse conversion made it 'irrelevant to the people in greatest need'.[16]

Extensive areas of dock basin were also infilled during the 1970s, particularly in Wapping and Surrey Docks. Some basins are now mere channels, treated as shallow canals to facilitate storm drainage and create the pretence of a little Venice. The loss of historic warehouses is nearly matched by the loss of the water itself, which is after all what makes Docklands different from other parts of London. Little regret has been expressed at the infilling of the docks, yet their loss is as much a reduction of character as the demolition of a warehouse or a church. Even today the constructing of buildings over the water is condoned, yet the relationship between water basins, dockside warehouses and quayside walks is the essence of Dockland character. Sadly, heritage concerns in Docklands places less weight on industrial than architectural monuments, and is happy to preserve the latter when the former is what really constitutes cultural memory to most ordinary people.

Social memory through conservation

One area where social memory has been preserved is in the Chapel House conservation area on the Isle of Dogs. This is made up largely of public housing built as cottage styled terraces by Poplar Borough Council in the 1920s and 1930s. With its Queen Anne inspired details and tree lined streets, this estate of houses stands in marked contrast to the nearby high rise council blocks of the 1960s. Preservation here is a timely reminder both of the role of the welfare state in housing provision in twentieth century Britain and of the tradition of modest terraced houses which marks the Englishness of inner city housing. Many of these houses are now in private ownership (as a result of the right-to-buy policies of the Conservative government) and are usually marked by changed window and door details.

Except for those formed around early council housing estates, the conservation areas of Docklands do not generally consist of whole neighbourhoods. Instead, they are slivers of townscape along the Thamesside or pockets of land around churches. Hence the vast bulk of the seventeen conservation areas are little vestiges of city, not in any sense areas which encompass whole communities of people or their buildings. The sense of heritage protection by fragmentation, evident in the treatment of certain individual buildings, is repeated in the preservation of the urban fabric. Such an approach reinforces the view that urban collage, as against genuine urban design, has been the effect of the policies of the corporation. Conceptually, of course, collage is open and flexible, making no demands upon a correspondence of scale or style, unlike urban design which seeks to establish patterns and comfortable relationships. This flexibility has been used by developers to advantage: heritage in Docklands has become part of their world, subsumed within market forces and marketing policies.

Notes

1 John Summerson, *Georgian London* (Barrie and Jenkins, 1969), p. 252.
2 *Docklands Heritage: Conservation and Regeneration in London Docklands* (LDDC 1989), p. 25.
3 Ted Hollamby, *Docklands: London's Backyard into Frontyard* (Docklands Forum 1990), p. 7.
4 *Ibid.*, p. 8.
5 Ted Hollamby was former chief architect and planner at the LDDC and resigned in 1985 over the Canary Wharf proposals.
6 Christian Wolmar, 'The new East Enders', *The Weekend Guardian*, 8–9 April 1989.
7 *Ibid.*
8 Personal communication with author, August 1991.
9 Quoted in 'Public Eye', BBC2, 27 April 1991.

10 Christian Wolmar, 'Crisis of confidence rocks Docklands dream', *The Independent*, 4 January 1990, p. 5.

11 John Ruskin, *Seven Lamps of Architecture*, (George Allen 1886), especially the 'Lamp of Memory', pp. 176–198.

12 *Docklands Heritage*, p. 80.

13 These are listed by Paul Calvocoressi in his admirable essay *Conservation in Docklands: Old Buildings in a Changing Environment* (Docklands Forum 1990), p. 15.

14 Aldo Rossi, *The Architecture of the City* (MIT Press 1982), p. 29.

15 Calvocoressi, *Conservation*, p. 6.

16 *London Docklands Strategic Plan* (Docklands Joint Committee 1976).

2 Docklands: a Regenerated Place or the Landscape of Speculation?

In the mid 1970s the view from the top of a no. 5 bus as iit drove eastwards into Docklands from Tower Bridge was a profoundly depressing experience. Urban dereliction marked nearly every stop, and the view over the rooftops to the old dock basins of Shadwell and Millwall showed the near terminal state of advanced obsolescence. The combined pressure of changing trade patterns, technological innovation and an inflexible labour force had brought about closure on a huge scale, starting with the East India Dock in 1967 and finishing with the Royal Docks in 1981. Dock closure was accompanied by an inevitable cycle of social and economic decline, and most noticeably a deterioration in infrastructure, public transport and housing.

In 1981 the situation was as hopeless as at any time since the Blitz. Docklands had become isolated both socially and physically. The high walls which enclosed the old dock basins remained, giving the appearance of a divided city. There was a measure too of social isolation bred of years of entrenched industrial relations attitudes and a high dependence on relatively isolated council housing estates. Docklands remained, two years into the Conservative government's reign of office, the great domestic challenge.

Earlier attempts to regenerate the area had failed to attract the interest either of central government or of the great financial institutions right on the area's doorstep in Threadneedle Street. The London boroughs of Southwark, Tower Hamlets and Newham had prepared plans, some visionary and ambitious, especially that of Southwark whose development proposals for Surrey Docks were the basis for later LDDC plans. The nine square miles of decaying Docklands, housing 55,000 people of whom 85 per cent lived in council houses, was according to the Secretary of State for the Environment 'the greatest challenge of our time'.[1] To meet this challenge the 1980 Act introduced UDCs and enterprise zones into the local political arena. There was naturally a great deal of mistrust between the new agency of change and the old establishment order. The Greater London Council (abolished in 1985) and the various Dockland boroughs found cooperation with the LDDC difficult, especially as the corporation's first chairman Sir Nigel Broakes of Trafalgar House was a champion of free market economics.

Compared with the other ten UDCs – Merseyside was established in 1981 and the remaining nine in 1987 – the LDDC had considerable advantages. Being located in the capital city was, of course, a major benefit, and finding itself only a couple of miles from the financial institutions of the City of London proved of great advantage, especially in the second phase of regeneration which followed the deregulation of the Stock Exchange in 1985. The location and financial advantages should, however, be set against the long term decline of the area, the problem of poor industrial relations, a heavily polluted and neglected environment, and the tendency of twentieth century London to move forever westwards.

One advantage of recent regeneration of Docklands has been the pressure taken off older areas of central London for redevelopment. Had the office space of the Isle of Dogs been built in the City of London and the West End, the traditional pattern of streets and a skyline still partially preserved would have been lost or drastically altered. Docklands has provided London with essential breathing space; it has allowed the capital to pursue its policy of urban conservation and redevelopment which is largely dictated by context. In this sense Docklands is the La Défense of London, and has helped the 'Square Mile' in particular to preserve its considerable townscape assets.

The constraint on development imposed by the planning authorities of Westminster and the City of London has been part of a largely unstated regional policy which has in its turn encouraged massive redevelopment not just in Docklands but at King's Cross, Spitalfields and around Liverpool Street station. These new satellites have begun to alter the face of London, and promise to give the city some memorable new buildings and urban spaces. What makes Docklands and particularly the Isle of Dogs more interesting, however, is the deregulation of planning in this area, and hence we can begin to examine what the architecture of unfettered enterprise looks like. For unlike King's Cross and the other areas, regeneration in Docklands has not been accompanied by rigid land use controls or the spatial parameters of a traditionally conceived master plan. A combination of massive wealth and a political indifference to development control has made the docks a fascinating experiment in a new urban order.

In many ways the Isle of Dogs marks the end of two centuries of British town planning; it concludes a chapter which began with the making of the great estates of Georgian London, extended through the municipal pride displayed in Victorian public buildings and parks, and continued to the utopian social visions of architects and planners at the Greater London Council in the immediate post-war period. Docklands, and particularly the Isle of Dogs, brings to an end the assumption that urban development must serve wider social or environmental ends.

What is perhaps remarkable is the sheer architectural energy which has resulted from the experiment. That the energy does not always pull in the same direction is hardly surprising, but the display of ideas and images in the various buildings constructed is as rich as elsewhere in London. The experiment suggests that control and regulation are not the only course to architectural richness – that freedom itself produces urban diversity. There are limits to the approach, especially when public assets such as historic buildings and the waterside become involved, but as a general rule the new machinery of the 1980 Act has proved remarkably successful, especially for the development of a new architecture in London Docklands.

One question concerning commentators in how transferable is the London Docklands experience to other cities. The remaining urban development

Table 2.1 Urban development corporations in England and Wales

	Year of designation	Area at designation	Population at designation	Employment at designation	Water edge situation
Merseyside*	1981	350	450	1,500	Dockside, river, sea
London Docklands	1981	2,150	40,400	27,213	Dockside, river
Trafford Park	1987	1,267	40	24,468	Canalside
Cardiff Bay	1987	1,093	500	15,000	Estuary, sea
Black Country*	1987	2,598	35,405	53,000	Canalside
Teesside	1987	4,858	NA	NA	Riverside, estuary
Tyne and Wear	1987	2,375	4,500	40,115	Riverside, estuary
Central Manchester	1987	187	500	15,300	Canalside
Leeds	1987	375	800	NA	Canalside
Sheffield	1987	900	NA	NA	Riverside
Bristol†	1987	420	NA	19,500	Dockside, river

*Extended in area in 1988.
†Reduced in area in 1989.
NA: not available.
Source: adapted from Stephen Potter, 'New town statistics', Town and Country Planning, November 1988, p. 297.

corporations are disadvantaged by location (except perhaps that in Bristol) in terms of the new Europe of the nineties, and do not enjoy the LDDC's proximity to a world centre of finance. Table 2.1 shows the land areas of the various UDCs, their population and the number of people .employed. It is evident that the LDDC was quite exceptional in size of area and population until the Black Country was designated in 1987. With only the Merseyside Development Corporation to compete with for six years, the LDDC was able to win a lion's share of government grants, even without a project such as the Garden Festival which had become the flagship of Merseyside regeneration plans.

The government paper of 1987, *Action for Cities*, described the UDCs as 'the most important attack ever made on urban decay'.[2] Judging by the date, the claim was based upon the experience of the first generation of UDCs which as explained was rather dominated by the LDDC. What the paper sought was the combining of private sector wealth and enterprise with those of freely composed UDCs to bring about urban renewal in the entrenched inner cities of Britain. These were (except for London Docklands) largely outside the influence of the Thatcher revolution, and still heavily controlled by the local authorities.

Though the differences are great between the eleven UDCs, there are three conspicuous administrative similarities: all are within Labour controlled areas, all contain large areas of industrial land, and all contain extensive parcels of land in some form of public ownership. Hence, bodies such as the Coal Board, the Docks Board, British Rail and local authorities had land which could easily be transferred to the ownership of the UDCs.[3] These factors, coupled with the power of compulsory purchase, have led to marked antagonism between the new development corporations and the old order of labour controlled councils and inflexible, land hoarding agencies. But one further factor is found in common in all UDCs, and that concerns the presence of water (see Table 2.1). Each area has some waterfront, seaside, canalside or riverside land which could be turned into up-market development of one form or another. What has tended to happen is that the prime sites have become not social housing but private housing, and the water not public recreation but private marinas. Although these developments have become flagships to promote a new image of their respective areas, the over-privatization of waterside land has become one of the chief sources of local conflict.

After ten years the main lesson of Docklands concerns the need for developing a new kind of opportunist plan, a framework for bringing about a measure of environmental fit between the various parts. There is not a great deal of difference between regeneration in the Mersey Docks and London Docks: both have tended rather more towards urban disaggregation than civic design. Throughout the UDCs there is a consistent mismatch between the various building elements, and between the old monumental structures of the docks and the new lightweight, often retail buildings of present needs. This mismatch stems at least in part from the dismantling of traditional planning powers and their replacement by a new market aware authority operating with at best sketchy development frameworks.

How urban development corporations operate

The approach of the UDCs is more akin to that of the new town development corporations than the local authorities. A smallish team (forty to a hundred) of full-time professional staff – architects, planners, landscape designers, lawyers etc. – is supplemented by outside consultants, many of whom are renowned in their profession (Sir Richard Rogers has been employed at London's Royal Docks, and James Stirling at Liverpool's Albert Dock). Once the full-time teams are in place, a development framework is prepared and used both to promote the UDC as an agent of change and to

Figure 2.1

South Quay Plaza in 1987. This building changed perceptions of Docklands from a landscape of low rise business parks to one with urban ambitions (photo: Brian Edwards)

make potential developers aware of available sites. In parallel, infrastructure improvements are carried out in the form of landscaping of eyesores, construction of new roads or the installation of light railways systems.

Once a system of new roads and services such as advanced telecommunications is in place, the UDCs seek the early development of a flagship scheme such as *The Daily Telegraph*'s South Quay Plaza at the Isle of Dogs. These bring welcome investment in their wake and much publicity, which is then turned to advantage by the well oiled public relations machinery of most of the development corporations. Unlike new town corporations, the UDCs do not have a guaranteed market of house builders or commercial developers, and hence self-publicity becomes an essential, if locally despised, activity.

One can begin to understand the importance of environmental quality in this market-oriented world. The red brick roads and pavements of the enterprise zone, the avenues of plane trees, and the quality of detailing on the dockside walkways are as important as the colour brochures so enthusiastically produced. Each of the UDCs has followed a similar path, though one suspects that the model of the LDDC has been aped rather uncritically.

Government investment in London Docklands has been well ahead of other UDCs (Table 2.2), partly in order to keep apace of the level of private investment in the area. Generally speaking grant aid to the LDDC has been ten times that of the remaining areas. Grand aid to the UDCs has also been well ahead of government assistance to other inner city areas; in fact financial assistance to the LDDC in the period 1989–92 was nearly twice that of the whole urban programme for the rest of the UK.[4] The favoured status of London Docklands is attributed to the huge infrastructural investment required in roads and railways to provide a framework of public services to support massive private schemes such as the £3 billion Canary Wharf project. But as other UDCs have seen the government willing to invest heavily in the LDDC, they too have begun to harbour ambitious plans of their own such as the barrage at Cardiff Bay and a river crossing over the Tees. Critics have begun to ask whether such investment will alter the traditional

Figure 2.2

Albion Channel in Surrey Docks. This canal, formed as a connection between Canada Water and Surrey Water, was restored and landscaped by the LDDC prior to development taking place (photo: Brian Edwards)

pattern of our cities with consequences for the wider regional economy. For the architects and engineers of the docklands it represents great opportunity and the chance to make the relatively derelict watersides of most British cities more available for public use, housing and retail development.

Given the advantage of a ten year exemption from local rates, freedom from land development tax and relaxation of planning controls, those areas which contain an enterprise zone have benefits additional to those already listed. But again the conflict between physical renewal and social development arises. Many in the local authorities argue that economic recovery by itself will not benefit local people unless a framework of training is put in place. As a general rule the inner city tends to suffer from poor educational achievement, and hence the jobs created within areas like the Isle of Dogs enterprise zone do not help nearby residents. The lack of a parallel training programme has tended to isolate the new developments socially with possible long term consequences. The haste with which building development has proceeded under these tax and financial benefits has tended to lead not just to an environmental disjointedness but also to a social one.

Table 2.2
UDC grant aid 1989–92
(£ million)

	1989–90	1990-91	1991–92
London Docklands	256	322	225
Merseyside	23	24	25
Black Country	31	32	33
Teesside	36	38	36
Trafford Park	17	29	30
Tyne and Wear	36	38	36
Bristol	5	10	7
Central Manchester	11	14	16
Leeds	8	14	8
Sheffield	10	19	13
Cardiff Bay	29	31	34

Source: DOE and Welsh Office.

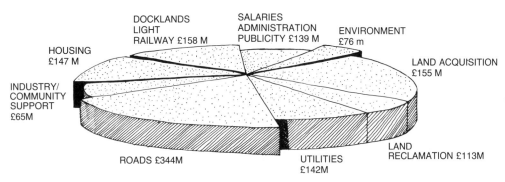

Figure 2.3

Investment by the LDDC 1981–91. Withdrawn segments represent main influences on urban design; the importance given to road construction is evident

In purely financial terms Docklands has been an undeniable success. In its first ten years the LDDC invested about £1 billion in roads, the Docklands Light Railway (DLR), land reclamation, housing etc. and attracted about £9 billion of private funds, nearly half of which was from the Canadian developer Olympia and York. The investment gearing is admirable, though the distribution of LDDC money into the various sectors highlights the root of many of the current problems.

The LDDC as an agent of change

The preamble to the 1980 Act talks of 'relaxed controls' coupled with the formation of 'corporations to regenerate urban area'.[5] Under the legislation, UDCs are given specific powers to bring land and buildings into effective use, create an attractive environment, develop industry and commerce, and to ensure that housing and social facilities are available to encourage people to live in the area.[6]

An enterprise zone[7] such as that on the Isle of Dogs is really the opposite to a conservation area; it is a zone where development is encouraged and where planning constraint is virtually non-existent. Where enterprise zones were designated, planning authorities had to modify their local and structure plans to accommodate the anticipated flood of development. In London Docklands this has been one of the sources of conflict between the LDDC and elected planning members within adjoining London boroughs.

Freed of any form of aesthetic constraint within the enterprise zone and guided by the ambitious proposals for area regeneration emanating from within the board of the LDDC, Docklands enjoyed a boom in construction. But if the erection of buildings flourished, so too did a new enthusiasm for design. The entrepreneural spirit fostered by the Act promoted, indirectly at least, a flowering of design within the wilderness of Docklands. Though not everybody liked the new freestyle classicism of the office blocks or the quirkiness of some of the housing, it was quite a change from the air of dereliction which preceded it.

The transformation of redundant inner city dockland areas has been a recurring feature of Western cities since the last war. In both America and Europe the changing pattern of transportation of goods by shipping, accelerated by containerization in the early 1960s, threw many traditional dockland areas into obsolescence. From Boston to Hamburg, Liverpool to San francisco, and Glasgow to London, a productive landscape of dock basins, bonded warehouses and simple storage sheds suddenly became redundant. The answer generally was to seek to retrain the workforce, tidy up the areas and foster tourism. For Boston and San Francisco tourism proved a successful catalyst for regeneration, but in London and Liverpool the scale of obsolescence required more comprehensive measures.

The UDCs and enterprise zones of Britain's run-down docklands are part of more ambitious proposals for area regeneration. Though tourism in London Docklands has been important, especially at the margins of the area such as St Katharine Docks and across the river at Butlers Wharf, more substantial economic revival has been the result of deregulating the London Stock Exchange. The opportunity created for inner city, middle class house building along the Thames and around the old dock basins has matched economic recovery with environmental upgrading.

Docklands as a landscape of opportunity

The two main investment activities in Docklands – office construction and house building – have created both a new physical landscape and a climate of optimism (at least until the recession of 1990). Office building has sprung up on the land adjoining the main docks on the Isle of Dogs. Much of this commercial architecture is pleasantly brash and assertive. Generally speaking the new landscape of offices around Millwall Dock is not the prestige architecture of headquarters buildings but speculative office space. As such it is commercial architecture at its most speculative, a mere device for making money. This element of naked commercialism has led to the development of an office vernacular already present in other parts of London. But in Docklands it has taken on a new dimension of visual excitement which derives from an unashamed love of scale and colour in proximity to a spectacular water-filled landscape.

Housing too has evolved to meet new market opportunities. The need to widen housing tenure and extend the range of housing type and choice has resulted in some entertaining domestic architecture. Much new housing has been architect designed, prompted both by the LDDC which has been anxious for its 'exceptional place' philosophy to be matched by some exceptional building, and by housing developers who learned through the eighties that 'design' paid. With the LDDC and ordinary developers committed to the belief that good design helps sell places and buildings, there has been a remarkable influx of design talent into Docklands. The employment of younger designers by housing developers, of which Kentish Homes's patronage of CZWG was by no means exceptional, means that Docklands is remarkable today for sheer variety and gay abandon within the residential field.

Housing has brought new people into Docklands, thereby aiding the regeneration of the area. The Englishness of some recent housing in Docklands stands in marked contrast to the international aesthetic of the office developments. In fact, English design talent has been employed almost exclusively within the domestic field, but not for the major office buildings such as Canary Wharf. Here American architects are preferred, creating in the process sub-Manhattens in Millwall. Hence the result of the 1980 Act has been to create a landscape of contrasts: an office block world which could be in Los Angeles, and new residential neighbourhoods which could be transplants of Kentish Town.

A flowering of design?

If the Act sought regeneration then it has been singularly successful in spite of the downturn in the property market from 1989. An unexpected result has been the flowering of design talent and the remarkable contrast in the approach to building from one part of Docklands to another. This had led to a kind of museum environment where each development is a separate world, evolved from a slightly different thesis. One can spectate at Docklands in the same way that museum visitors gaze upon exhibits. Each part has a relevance within the changing values of the age, but few parts seem to fit well together.

The disconnections in Docklands are a result of the abandonment of traditional planning and the parallel loss of an aesthetic consensus amongst designers. Design has moved away from its social/utility axis to one which

Figure 2.4

View of the Isle of Dogs from Millwall Docks. The disjointedness and lack of townscape legibility is largely the result of deregulation, though each building has its own integrity and relevance. The view shows the limitations of using architecture alone as a measure of regeneration (photo: LDDC)

places style and added value at the new rotated poles. Added value through design has allowed both office and residential developers to broaden the appeal and enhance the marketability of their schemes through the deliberate choice of designers. Hence an office speculator wishing to attract American corporate clients to his building naturally chooses an American architect and one whose buildings are already well known back home. Design is, therefore, part of the packaging and an important element in image promotion.

The same is true within the housing field. Certain designers create the type of housing which appears in fashion and architectural design magazines, and hence appeals to the very people attracted by the design and lucrative service jobs of Docklands. Such housing would look alien in Richmond or Hampstead, but fits well into some of the more dynamic and style-conscious areas near to say the Design Museum.

There has, therefore, been a marked shift in the use of design in Docklands. The area represents the first real exercise in design-led urban renewal in the UK, with all the superficiality and limitations that the approach implies. There are clearly drawbacks in the approach, but advantages too, especially if the external design world is enjoying one of those interesting transition periods which always accompany the breakdown of orthodoxy. The decade 1980–90 was one such period, in which order gave way to experimentation. The old world of modernist functional theory has cracked to let in the light of design voyeurs who have made quite a mark in various corners of Docklands.

If design has aided the regeneration of Docklands, it has not greatly benefited ordinary people. The housing is generally beyond the reach of the indigenous population, and the jobs within the offices are inaccessible through want of skills. Design has therefore only indirectly helped local people, and here mostly through enhancing their own property values. The next decade may see the so-called trickle effect of benefit flowing downwards, but in the meantime resentment against the LDDC, and all the building it has generated, had led to a measure of distrust regarding design. Graffiti and billboards in the area produced by residents' groups have on occasion attacked design with almost as much vehemence as they decry other displays of wealth. If the LDDC has a challenge ahead, it is to re-

Figure 2.5

Prince's Tower, Rotherhithe. Designed by Troughton McAslan for a site facing the Thames below the Design Museum, this building provides a welcome landmark to the river in a crisp modern style (photo: Peter Cook)

establish the social dimension of design and to rescue the process from that merely of money making. For the government, the new task is how to finish what has been started, and how to extend the UDC model to other areas of east London.

London Docklands and trend planning

Of all the areas of Britain, none better represents the use of trend planning as a vehicle for facilitating urban change than London Docklands. Trend planning is a form of market-led planning which gives free reign to the developer and relegates the town planner to simply oiling the machinery of public investment to the developer's advantage. Market-led planning took three distinct forms during the Thatcher years: trend planning, leverage planning, and private management planning.[8] Trend planning has certainly been the most predominant, especially on the Isle of Dogs, but leverage planning – where public money is geared to attracting private investment – has also been vigorously employed. Our third example, private management planning, typifies the approach of Olympia and York at Canary Wharf.

The distinctions between these different forms of market-led planning are, however, rarely clear. The St Martin's Development Company responsible for London Bridge City has taken advantage of all three approaches and in the process established a level of cooperation between private and public interests which other major developers have sought to emulate. The development of distinctive typologies within the new field of market-led planning has, to some extent at least, been as a result of experiments undertaken in London Docklands. For of all the UDCs in the UK, the LDDC has been the best funded and the most loosely constrained. Recent developments in other UDCs, notably at Cardiff Bay, have sought to extend the LDDC's experiments of different approaches to market-led planning in inner city areas.

Market-led planning has opened fresh opportunities for the town planner who hitherto was largely employed within public administration. As a consequence new skills have had to be acquired in fields such as development finance and urban design. This diversification of professional employment has led to a broadening of philosophical approach which may well prove one of the lasting benefits of the LDDC's advocacy of market-led urban renewal.

The development process in London Docklands

According to Barry Shaw, former head of urban design at the LDDC, what marks the problem of the inner cities in Britain is the lack of a consensus both politically and in terms of urban design.[9] Political pressure for reform of the inner city has often led to decisions which go against the presiding local view, and contradiction and compromise are the inevitable results for planning and design.

The development process adopted by the LDDC has leant heavily upon the promotion of the Docklands area as a desirable place to live and work. The LDDC has power of development control within the designated area but only for proposals deemed not to be in the national interest. The 1980 Act charged the LDDC with the regeneration of this part of east London; thus although development proposals can be, and often are, against local interests and damaging to the local environment, they cannot easily be thought contrary to national priorities such as the regeneration of the inner cities or the stimulation of the economy. This has remained a dilemma for the LDDC and is the source of much conflict with the London boroughs, who have retained certain planning powers within the area. The LDDC has powers to control development, but no corresponding responsibility for plan making. As a consequence the corporation's prime influence has been as land owner using the assets of the former PLA. It has worked loosely within the framework of inherited plans (though it has not always agreed with them) whilst

Figure 2.6

First generation business architecture on the Isle of Dogs. Built in 1985 this pleasant development of green coloured business units known as Great Eastern Enterprise was designed by Howell, Killick, Partridge and Amis for a site facing Millwall Dock (photo: Brian Edwards)

granting permission for development which often runs counter to their under-lying spirit. Shaw and others within the LDDC worked previously for the London boroughs involved in Docklands, helping to draft plans whose polit-ical aspirations were undermined by the national interest as perceived from the centre.

The corporation, under its energetic if enigmatic first chief executive Reg Ward, sought the attraction of development not its control.[10] The view existed

Table 2.3 Development phases in London Docklands

Planning 1981–84	Marketing 1985–87	Construction 1988–91	Remedial 1992–96
Infrastructure provision	Increased infrastructure provision	Construction of many prestige developments such as Reuters, Canary Wharf, *Daily Telegraph*	Solving the public realm problems, especially Thamesside and disjointedness of Isle of Dogs
Environmental improvement	Attraction of flagship developments	Addressing mismatch between scale of building and infra-structure provision	Investment in social housing, education and leisure facilities
Heritage conservation	Appointment of named consultants and developers	Recognition of the social dimension	Shifting the emphasis to the Royal Docks
Marketing of area in UK	Marketing of area internationally	Extensive use of architectural competitions to raise level of design	Construction of new river crossings Construction of extra transport provision Extention of LDDC model to lower Thames

then, and still prevails, that planning is good at controlling growth in areas like the London Green Belt, but poor at promoting it within the run-down inner cities. Hence, the LDDC marketed London Docklands with the same enthusiasm employed by the Conservative government in the sale of national assets such as British Telecom. Docklands was called 'the water city of the twenty-first century' and the planned regeneration programme was the biggest in Europe. In this market-led approach to area renewal, plan making and development control had low priority.

The first wave of development activity (1981–5) was replaced by more ambitious proposals, many financed by international banks convinced that Docklands would be a good location within Europe after 1992 (Table 2.3). Again hard selling rather than traditional town planning was at the centre of LDDC activity, and naturally the government was delighted when the LDDC finally landed the big fish of Canary Wharf in 1987. But sceptics remained, some within the ranks of the LDDC and some amongst increasingly reluctant residents of the area who, having been attracted by the new housing on offer, then found their homes a millstone around their necks as house prices fell in London. Investors in Docklands, whether newspaper publishers, property developers or residents, were forced to take a long term view.

The making of Docklands into London's third node of economic activity

Having made Docklands into a third node of economic activity in London (after the City and Westminster), the LDDC is naturally sanguine about future prospects. It looks back over a decade which has seen 15 per cent of London's office space provided in Docklands (with proposals for a further 10 per cent), a major commitment to extend public transport services eastwards to the area, an inward investment of £4000 million creating about 100,000 jobs on the Isle of Dogs, and a shift from 96 per cent council housing to nearly 50 per cent private housing.[11] All this has been achieved without the cumbersome and expensive machinery of town planning; in fact, market research, marketing and development incentives have achieved in ten years what planning failed to deliver in over forty.

A departmental memorandum issued as early as 5 February 1982 stated unambiguously that the corporation was to make its views known by 'issuing policy statements' in order 'to give an early indication of its general views to guide would-be developers'.[12] The emphasis was clearly upon promoting development as against its control, and the local authorities were obliged to take such policy statements into consideration when preparing their statutory plans. The commercial exploitation of the wastelands was made inevitable by the constitution of the LDDC board. Hence opportunity planning replaced statutory planning, marketing replaced political validation of policy, and in the end development replaced grand intention.

Quality and variety in the details

At the outset of operations the LDDC analysed why high tech companies were drawn to the countryside, and sought to create a similarly attractive landscaped environment within the inner city. The Isle of Dogs was paved in brick, heavily landscaped around refurbished dock basins and given an enterprise zone as a lure to investors. The details of road and pavement design, of street lighting and seats, were carefully chosen to create the very opposite of the rust-belt appearance which had dogged the development ambitions of the borough councils. It is to its credit that, given the political climate of the Thatcher administration and the initial uncertainty over the success of operations, the LDDC sought to adopt design standards higher than generally found in the inner city and largely absent from the portfolio of activities undertaken by the other British UDCs.

We find in Docklands at the outset of operations a search for excellence in building materials and landscape details, both apparently against advice at the time. The policy was to insist upon the best quality of materials which could be afforded, and, as wealth has flowed into the area especially since 1985, the standard of construction and finishes has risen. The method is not unlike the creation of eighteenth century London where the leaseholds were granted subject to conditions regarding the finish to the house and the design of windows, doors, railings and pavements. The corporation also set an example to others in the way roads were detailed and in the design of public utility structures such as the pumping station by John Outram on the Isle of Dogs. What the corporation did not do (and could not under the Act) was to become a major developer itself. Georgian London grew upon the example of excellence established by squares built by the land owning aristocracy, these both providing an incentive to construct houses in the adjoining streets and establishing a design standard for others to follow. However, the attention shown by the LDDC to the details and quality of building materials goes some way to mitigate the reluctance to engage upon urban design structuring (at least on the Isle of Dogs) and carry out commercial building itself.

Graffiti and vandalism are surprisingly scarce within London Docklands. Only in the council housing estates which embarrassingly line the route of the DLR from Tower Gateway to Limehouse is the environment greatly abused. The reason given for this is the corporation's policy of seeking quality of finish at every opportunity.[13] Researchers have confirmed the argument on countless occasions, but most inner city authorities cannot afford the standard of materials employed in Docklands. Hence the Isle of Dogs and Surrey Docks do not generally display the battle-hardened characteristics of other parts of central London. Instead, marble, stock brick and polished granite adjoin public routes with barely a blemish. Critics will point to the army of security guards patrolling the prestige developments, but a mixture of design in high quality materials and good surveillance of private and public space appears an effective solution to this perennial problem.

One important power possessed by the corporation is that of compulsory purchase. Compulsory purchase orders (CPOs) have been employed to parcel together sufficient land to allow the bigger projects to go ahead, and to ensure a measure of public amenity. Lengths of riverside walk and viewing slots of historic buildings have been created by the judicious, if scarce, use of CPOs. But without this important power the regeneration of Docklands would not have proceeded so smoothly. There is a price, however, for this administrative convenience. Too many idiosyncratic corners of Docklands have been swept aside in the name of land packaging, especially in and around historic areas. As a result the character of Docklands has been eroded – a character that derives not from set monuments but from the agglomeration of lesser pieces of townscape. The effect of CPOs has also been to allow single materials to spread across large areas of Docklands. For example, brick paving extends into many corners and glass gridded office fronts face roads without interruption. Though the materials are admittedly of high standard and generally well detailed, the tendency has been towards the aggregation of big units of townscape at the expense of smaller ones.

In an age when planning has begun to relax its land use orientation, Docklands presents a picture where quality of environment is considered as important as economic or social gain. The idea of social gain gathers currency in Docklands only at the edges, in places like Rotherhithe or Poplar. Elsewhere the coalition between economic regeneration and an enhanced environmental standard makes for a happier marriage. One factor in this equation has been the consistently competent performance by the LDDC's own landscape team, and on occasions the admirable support provided by landscape and urban form consultants. Since the outset the corporation has maintained a small team of landscape architects who, working with a relatively narrow palette of materials, have brought much beauty to the area.

The engineering brick and granite edged canals and dock basins, the delicate willows and sallows of the ecological park at Stave Hill, the avenues of London plane trees around Millharbour, and the choice of seating and railings at Hays Wharf, all give Docklands a distinctiveness lacking in many newly created communities.

From the outset the corporation placed landscape design at the forefront of operations with as much enthusiasm as it suppressed urban design. One only has to compare Cullen and Gosling's townscape proposals for the Isle of Dogs (which were shelved in 1982 as too radical) with the adopted landscape plan for the Royal Docks by Gillespies to realize where the priorities lie. The Conran Roche plan for Greenland Dock sits between these two, and not surprisingly the landscape elements have been adopted whilst those which deal with urban design appear at times to be ignored, especially with regard to the height of Baltic Quays.

The role of architectural competitions

If a commitment to high quality landscape design is a commendable feature of ten years of LDDC activity, the same is equally true of the use of architectural competitions for the selection of developers. The policy of seeking to attract the best developers has frequently entailed the use of competitions to set quality of design alongside financial tenders for the site. As the LDDC owns much of the land it has two interests: how to gain the most financial reward for the site, and how to attract the best architecture to the area. In fact the system employed by the corporation seeks a balance between monetary return and aesthetic standards. Combined design and tender competitions allow this practice to flourish, since smaller developers are not set against the big players of the development community on financial terms alone. The results can be spectacular if a little shocking, as a walk near Shad Thames illustrates, but there is no doubting that London Docklands has been responsible for the emergence of a whole new generation of design talent. If the area babbles to us like music on the air waves, as Michael Ignatieff cleverly put it,[14] then the new tunes are the result of the design enterprise of the LDDC. The developer competition has not only fostered new design talent, but also helped to educate builders and investment companies in the importance of design.

Docklands has a healthy mixture of established practices working for well known developers, and upstart architects barely out of college employed sometimes on developments they have funded themselves. The relaxation of the code of professional conduct by the Royal Institute of British Architects (RIBA) in 1984 (which encouraged the emergence of developer architects) coincided roughly with the regeneration of Docklands to each party's advantage. If there is a healthy design pluralism in the docks it is partly as a result of the corporation's employment of the architectural competition.

In about ten years a city the size of Oxford has been created out of the wilderness of decaying cranes and neglected dock basins. But it has taught a simple lesson: urban design cannot be relegated to market forces quite as easily as the aesthetics of buildings. Even if the argument for urban collage described in Chapter 10 is accepted, the case for urban design transcends the fashionable interest in collision geometries and urban fragmentation. The wholeness of cities depends upon an underlying order – a respect for public monument as well as private building, and for civic space as well as private promenade. Shaw too understands the arguments and the limitations of what has been built to date. To his credit he formed in 1990 the Docklands Urban Design Advisory Group, independent of the LDDC though serviced by it. Whatever the outcome of the group's deliberations, urban design now has an avenue by which it can influence development decision making at the LDDC. After ten years of renewal in Docklands during which, as even the Minister for the Inner Cities admitted, certain building projects fell short of excellence and provided useful lessons to draw on,[15] the machinery is at last in place to bring critical insights to bear upon the nature of the urbanism being created.

Dockland regeneration as a world phenomenon

Although London Docklands was the largest urban regeneration programme of the 1980s, other cities in Britain and around the world have grappled with the problem of redundant docklands. Table 2.4 shows how some of those cities have tackled the problem of bringing new life to obsolete docks. It is

Table 2.4 London Docklands and other dockland regeneration programmes

Place	Area (mile²)	Urban design framework	Approach	Funding	Comments
London Docklands	8.5	No	Government sponsored urban development corporation with relaxed planning controls	Mostly private	Said to be largest docklands regeneration programme in world Much new commercial architecture
Liverpool Docks	2.5	No	Government sponsored urban development corporation	Mixed public and private	Mostly led by landscaping Extensive heritage resources Garden festival employed
Glasgow Docks	2	No	Government funded renewal programme with 'national' facilities	Mostly public	Much infilling of docks and siting of exhibition buildings Garden festival employed
Salford Quays, Manchester	2	Yes	Government sponsored urban development corporation	Mixed public and private	Mostly led by housing with large retail park
Baltimore Harbour, USA	0.4	Yes	Public/private partnership through an enterprise development company	Mostly private	Led by tourism and retail
Darling Harbour, Sydney, Australia	0.4	Yes	Government agency with relaxed planning controls	Mostly public/private partnership	Tourist, museum and exhibition buildings in landscaped park
Barcelona Docks, Spain	3	Yes, traditional master plan	City and regional government initiative through urban development corporation	Mostly public	Led by Olympic sports facilities with spatially structured urban plan
Genoa Docks, Italy	0.5	Yes	City and port authority initiative	Mostly public	Led by tourism and exhibition centre

Source: based partly upon articles in the *Architectural Review*, April 1989; Città d'Acqua, Centro Internazionale Symposium, 23 January to 9 February 1991.

largely outmoded infrastructure and new technology which have led to the decay of docklands in almost every maritime city. The containerization of cargoes and the increasing use of air freight have combined to make older, inner city docklands superfluous to national economies. As the pace of economic change quickened in the sixties and seventies, the traditional dockland landscapes of cranes, warehouses and enclosed wharves became emptied of cargoes and activities. Older industrial cities such as Liverpool and Hamburg felt the cruel impact of departing harbour functions first, but soon Third World and regional centres found themselves isolated from the trading links which had provided their lifeblood.

Various approaches have been adopted in the regeneration of docklands, with regard to both the new uses attracted to the areas and the methods employed to bring about economic recovery. The hand of government is always present but to an extent that varies greatly, as does the level of partnership with private interests. London Docklands is perhaps the most market-led regeneration programme of redundant docklands anywhere in the world, and it also represents the greatest relaxation of municipal planning powers. Other cities have struggled with the politics of dockland regeneration to the point where the debate about winners and losers has stifled investment. For example, urban renewal in the port area of Copenhagen was hampered throughout the seventies and eighties by a failure to reach a consensus on what should happen. Confusion and political disagreements within the city council led the Danish Minister for the Environment to order a freeze on building in 1988. An earlier design competition for the port area had not brought about a coalition of interests as planned, but merely exacerbated the conflicts between developers and local residents.[16]

Similar political and social conflicts have occurred in Genoa, where Renzo Piano has prepared ambitious plans for a metro extension, theatre and exhibition buildings to celebrate the 500th anniversary of Columbus's transatlantic voyage from the city. While Piano was hatching his plans for the dockland areas, the American architect and entrepreneur John Portman was invited by the city council to submit proposals for a hotel and other buildings. The two schemes had little in common, not only in terms of architectural content but more importantly with regard to social objectives. Here, as in Copenhagen, political in-fighting may jeopardize regeneration.

The British pattern of appointing a development agency responsible for overseeing dockland regeneration was adopted at Darling Harbour in Sydney. The advantage of a single government supported development corporation is obvious, especially when local political conflict exists. An Enterprise Development Corporation formed in 1984 on the joint initiative of the Darling Harbour Commission and an American developer was subsequently given exemptions from planning control in a fashion which closely parallels that on the Isle of Dogs.[17] Subsequent development to a master plan prepared by a project design directorate of local officials cut through the political uncertainty. The earlier plans for a largely public investment in cultural and leisure facilities became watered down to one of a mix of commercial and civic buildings, but the idea of an open plaza along the waterfront enjoyed by all remained. Darling Harbour shows the importance of partnership with a committed developer; the earlier plans failed to attract commercial interests and with them a rich mix of shopping, restaurant and leisure facilities. The Enterprise Development Corporation brought action in its wake; some was undesirable, such as the demolition of historic buildings and the relegation of the Maritime Museum to the edge of the area, but as public space the harbourside has now become occupied and enjoyed. The master plan coordinated investment and structured the space, though the architecture remain unregulated. Compared with London or Liverpool, Sydney has a small area of redundant docklands, but the architectural response and the mixture of private and public buildings set in a paved esplanade could prove a useful model elsewhere.

In Barcelona a formal masterplan was also adopted for the regeneration of its harbourside. Prepared by architects Martorell, Bohigas, Mackay, the plan for an Olympic village and other developments builds upon the city's long tradition of highly structured urban plans.[18] The harbourside is an extensive area of part used and partly redundant land between the Old Town of Barcelona and the Mediterranean. The coordinated strategy for the area's regeneration is in marked contrast to London Docklands. Investment in Barcelona has been mainly publicly funded (and this mostly from regional sources through an urban development corporation) on the expectation of handsome returns during the 1992 Olympics and with an eye to long term social development.[19] The masterplan seeks to provide a framework for the various developments, both in the village and elsewhere. The Olympic village has a central pedestrian street modelled on the city's tree lined avenue Las Ramblas, around which are grouped a well defined collection of urban blocks containing housing and administrative buildings – quite different from the structureless sprawl of London Docklands. Within the city new squares are being created and old ones revamped, and the poor definition of external space in recent social housing developments in the suburbs is being improved by the construction of new enclosing buildings.

The benefits of a development corporation are considerable if speed of change and commercial activity are to be encouraged. The losers here are likely to be local residents, and the gainers will be big corporations and by implication central government. As in Sydney, Baltimore and London, the development corporation or enterprise agency is most likely to succeed if it is unencumbered by a traditional masterplan and enjoys exemptions from normal planning controls. The resulting environment may not prove particularly cohesive (either physically or socially) but regeneration is likely to be both quick and comprehensive. The alternative approach is to employ public or government money linked to a structured development plan and with ambitions towards social, cultural or community well-being. Here political validation may underpin every development, but the risks of architecture and urban design falling prey to party politics may stifle progress, as witnessd by the redevelopment of Copenhagen docks. Barcelona stands as an example of a marriage between urban design and a search for regional or Catalan expression through the vehicle of the Olympic Games.

Notes

1 Quoted by Reg Ward in 'London: the emerging Docklands city', *Built Environment*, vol. 12, no. 3, p. 117.

2 Quoted in *The Docklands Experiment* (Docklands Consultative Committee 1990), p. 73.

3 *Ibid.*, p. 75.

4 *Ibid.*, p. 76.

5 The Local Government, Planning and Land Act 1980: Preamble.

6 *Ibid.*: see Section 136.

7 *Ibid.*: see particularly Schedule 32.

8 T. Brindley, Y. Rydin and G. Stoker, *Remaking Planning: the Politics of Urban Change in the Thatcher Years* (Unwin Hyman 1989).

9 Barry Shaw, Lecture to the Urban Design Group, Liverpool, 20 September 1990.

10 Richard Evans, London Docklands, *Financial Times*, 1 October 1986, p. 27.

11 *Corporate Plan 1989* (LDDC).

12 Department of the Environment, 5 February 1982.

13 Shaw, Lecture to the Urban Design Group.

14 Michael Ignatieff, '3 Minute Culture', BBC 2, 1988.

15 *London Docklands Architectural Review* (LDDC 1990), p. 3.

16 Kim Dirckinck-Holmfeld, Copenhagen complications, *Architectural Review*, April 1989, pp. 78–83.

17 E.M. Farrelly, 'Out of the swing of the sea, darling', *Architectural Review*, April 1989, p. 64.

18 For more information see Peter Buchanan's excellent article 'Boost for Barcelona', *Architectural Review*, April 1989, pp. 74–77.

19 *Waterfront* (Centro Internazionale, Città d'Acqua, Venice 1991), p. 30.

3 Planning the New Infrastructure of London Docklands

Up to 1987 investment in new roads and the light railway system was generally in tune with the needs of business attracted to Docklands. The LDDC chief executive at the time, Reg Ward, stated confidently that his obligation to those who had invested in the area had been met by the new communications infrastructure then in place.[1] By July of 1987 this consisted of the Docklands Light Railway (DLR) from the Tower and Stratford to the Isle of Dogs, the London City Airport, and the beginnings of the extension of Britain's motorway network into the area (in the form of the M11 extension to Beckton). It also included private information systems such as fibre-optic networks and land–satellite relay stations, and an extension of the Stock Exchange computer to St Katharine Docks. Ward may have been right to make such a claim in 1987, but by 1991 the success of Docklands in terms of new buildings far exceeded the capacity of the transport system to service them.

The intensity and extent of construction exceeded expectations and, without a planning framework to anticipate and cater for the growth, there has been an inevitable mismatch between the completion of buildings and the provision of public services. Instead of the car being a symbol of freedom in Docklands, it has become an instrument of captivity. Office workers on the Isle of Dogs, fleeing from their desktop computers at 5 p.m., find themselves trapped in traffic jams at Marsh Wall or queuing to board the overcrowded carriages of the DLR. Even the London City Airport at the Royal Docks cannot cater for real international travel because of noise and environmental limits. The deregulated environment finds itself strangled by the measures of its own success – the superjam.

The projected office population in Docklands of 100,000 by 1995 will have to face the prospect of an even more congested and inadequate transportation network. Only after the completion of the Jubilee Line extension from Green Park to Waterloo and thence to Canary Wharf and Stratford will any relief occur. Olympia and York, who have promised to contribute £400 million towards its anticipated £1 billion cost, expect it to open in 1995. By then the Jubilee Line and the DLR will have a combined capacity of 100,000 passengers per day into the Isle of Dogs.

The working population on the Isle of Dogs is expected to have grown from 40,000 in 1990 to 130,000 by 1999. Of these some 50,000 will be employed at Canary Wharf alone. In 1990 about half the workforce on the Isle of Dogs arrived by car or taxi and about 40 per cent by the DLR. As public transport is improved or extended during the 1990s it is anticipated that 60 per cent of the workforce will arrive by rail, with those travelling by car reduced to 20 per cent. It is worth noting that parking space at Canary Wharf and other large developments caters for only about 10 per cent of the working population, the presumption being that public transport will be utilized. Whether public transport is provided on time and to an acceptable standard remains to be seen. Even if car usage can be reduced to 20 per cent of the working population there still remains the prospect of getting 20,000 cars on and off of the Isle of Dogs at peak time. This reality focused minds wonderfully at the Department of Transport and led to pressure upon Cecil Parkinson, the minister then in charge, to allocate additional funds for Docklands infrastructure. In fact in May 1990 Parkinson was able to announce £3 billion already spent or committed on improving Docklands transport infrastructure.[2]

[handwritten margin note:] UNDER CONSTRUCTION DEC. 1994.

Government was moved to introduce the Bill for the Jubilee Line extension after pressure from developers, principally Olympia and York. The belated response from the Department of Transport was not unlike the resurrection of the concept of urban space planning: both required a demonstrable failure to have occurred before action was taken. So linked are matters of infrastructure planning and urban design that the two can now be tackled in partnership. With major development now firmly in place, urban space making and the insinuation of a modern transportation system can be coordinated and slotted into the spaces between or beneath the buildings. Hence, the 1990s will see the provision of a 'capital web' of public services which, assuming adequate government investment, will begin to give order and structure to the spaces between existing developments.

The concept of capital web (see Chapter 5) presupposes an appropriate level of public investment in services. The superjam and the dangerously crowded DLR have alerted administrators to the need for a robust supporting structure of transportation provision. There are signs that the concept of a coordinated transportation strategy for the city may yet re-emerge. London as a whole is increasingly compared unfavourably with Paris, which has invested heavily in public transport, civic spaces and 'grand projects'.[3] London may be on the verge of a return to metropolitan planning, with all that entails for investment in public services and a corresponding concern for matters of civic design. In many ways the Docklands experiment has highlighted the limitation of *laissez-faire* urban development, and London as a whole may prove the principal beneficiary.

The Docklands Light Railway

The LDDC brochure *London Docklands – the Exceptional Place* claimed that amongst the advantages of the area were 'fast, modern and direct transport connections'. The first 8 miles (12 km) of the DLR from the City of London at Tower Gateway were opened in August 1987. A further twelve stations extending the line eastwards via the Royal Docks to Beckton are planned to open by 1993.

The DLR is Britain's first light railway system and employs largely German rolling stock operating between stations designed to a general blueprint formulated by Arup Associates. It was constructed over a three year period by a joint company of GEC and Mowlem at a cost of £77 million, and utilized lengths of redundant railway viaduct. Running mainly at high level, the DLR affords spectacular views of the regenerated landscape of Docklands, and has become as much a part of the tourist circuit as an everyday means of transport for office workers. The driverless trains have proved of inadequate

Figure 3.1

The Docklands Light Railway. Running mainly at high level, the Docklands Light Railway affords splendid views of the regenerated or still unreclaimed landscape of the area. This view shows the DLR extension east of West India Dock with the Reuters building on the left (photo: LDDC)

Figure 3.2

*Island Gardens DLR station.
Designed by Arup Associates,
Island Gardens is the most
successful of the DLR stations.
The rotunda makes reference to
a similar one serving the
pedestrian tunnel under the
Thames which is located
nearby in Island Gardens Park
(photo: LDDC)*

scale to meet peak hour demands, and at present £400 million is being spent upgrading the track and increasing the size and frequency of trains. A system designed to carry 20,000 people per day now regularly transports more than 30,000, and at peak times trains routinely carry three times the projected ridership.

In addition to the extension of the DLR eastwards, the lines have been taken beyond Tower Gateway in the west to Bank station right in the heart of the City of London. Once the resignalling, track realignment and upgrading of stations are complete, the DLR will be amongst the world's most advanced urban transit systems. From a design point of view there are, however, two major shortcomings. First, the connections are poor between the existing rail, bus and underground systems and the DLR. At Tower Gateway station one has a tortuous path to thread from the Tower underground station on the District and Central Lines and at Stratford an equally uncomfortable passage through tunnels. Second, the early stations were hardly distinguished as architectural monuments. Only Island Gardens begins to fulfil civic responsibilities. Elsewhere the stations are windy decks reached by many flights of stairs, and the only advantage of the lack of adequate seating and space on the platforms is in preparing passengers for the trains.

Plans are afoot to improve station design. Ambitious proposals have quickly matured for a grand station concourse designed by I.M. Pei at Canary Wharf. In an effort to avoid repeating earlier mistakes in the second generation of stations along the DLR extension to Beckton, consultants Ahrends, Burton and Koralek have developed a kit of parts based upon three station types. These are viaduct or high level stations; island platform or ground level stations; and intermediate types which integrate road and rail systems. By identifying three station types the architects believe they can provide a framework of stations which relate better to their context than in the first phase of the DLR. The LDDC acting as clients has insisted upon a finely engineered aesthetic employing painted steel, stainless steel, toughened glass and areas of dark blue engineering brick.

Though the DLR is inadequate in terms of scale and provision, it does represent a brave attempt at bringing mainly European ideas of light rail systems into the city. The Docklands rail experiment was the first in the UK and its popularity has led many other cities notably Manchester and Edinburgh to plan similar systems. For a few years the DLR was a symbol of regeneration in the East End of London: the bright blues and reds of its rolling stock and the high technology of driverless trains caught local imagination. By happy accident it also allowed close scrutiny of completed buildings (South Quay Plaza), those still under construction (Canary Wharf) and sites where major redevelopment was planned (Heron Quays). As such, to travel the DLR was perhaps more rewarding than reading about the projects in the architectural press.

To take the DLR was also an adventure in itself. Putting aside the frequent breakdowns, one travelled an almost fairground-like journey through switchbacks and sharp changes of direction. The process of travelling became pleasurable; the sheer kinetic delight of speeding past buildings, 'flying' over water and squeezing through clusters of tower cranes became for many people more important than arriving at their destination. The aim of the journey became not so much travelling from one point to another as being able to sit at the front of the train and gaze upon the spectacle of regeneration.

If the DLR exploits the pleasure of journeying, then the changes of direction and slope merely highlight events upon the way. The journey out of Tower Gateway is first marked by the new flanking buildings of St Katharine Docks, but as the train gathers pace the haunting presence of Hawksmoor's churches provides dramatic railside landmarks. Suddenly the train slows and climbs high above West India Quay, affording good views of Gwilt's sugar warehouses across the water. Soon the train slips between the glass and marble tower blocks of Canary Wharf to emerge again over water before Heron Quay. A near right angle is negotiated with care at South Quay and again the seemingly fragile train slips between massive office blocks to emerge at Coldharbour, and then over the green space of the Mudchute to terminate at high level alongside the Thames at Island Gardens.

The pleasure derives not from speed but from the aesthetics of movement. The juxtaposition of buildings and water, of passing through open and contained views, is the main source of delight. To design public transport is ideally to be aware of these qualities: to temper the prime objective of speed and convenience by a sensitivity towards exploiting the urban spectacle.

Road building in Docklands

In 1986 the LDDC's transport planner and engineer Howard Potter said: 'Any employer will want his staff to have a choice of transport.'[4] A balance had to be struck between public and private transport, yet up to then only £77 million had been set aside for the DLR whilst £500 million was earmarked for new or improved roads feeding into the docks area. Such an imbalance hardly encouraged public transport use, and mirrored well the investment priorities in Britain as a whole under the Thatcher government.

It was argued that the higher level of investment in roads was required in order to move goods around, to provide routes for underground services (especially fibre-optic networks), and to connect Docklands to the national motorway system. Certain areas of Docklands were desperately in need of new road construction – especially the Royal Docks and the north approaches to the Blackwall Tunnel. Other strategic transport matters had to be addressed such as a new East London river crossing near the Thames Barrier, but generally speaking road construction has proved environmentally disruptive and inordinately expensive. It has been claimed that Docklands contains Britain's most costly road, mile for mile – the Limehouse to West Ferry Circus link.

Some of the roads have been necessary to service new development such as the additional routes to Canary Wharf and Heron Quays, but others are required to fulfil the development potential of more peripheral areas. For example, the construction of the Lower Lea river crossing unlocks the potential of the Royal Docks, and at Surrey Docks a new distributor road linking with the A200 allowed the construction of a Tesco supermarket and other commercial developments in the mid 1980s.

Roads are undoubtedly a catalyst for change, but they can become physical barriers isolating areas of the city. Many of the major roads are to be set in cuttings and decked over, and here the wider environment is spared of disruption. But for the motorist and the bus passenger, the dual carriageway tunnel offers little pleasure. Such roads are the very converse of the DLR, but they absorb a great deal of money for only limited benefits. The Limehouse link, which extends from The Highway under Limehouse Basin to the Isle of Dogs (thereby affording a bypass to Narrow Street), has blighted much property during its construction. Planned to be complete towards the end of 1993, this 1.7 km four lane tunnel promises to cost as much as the whole of the first stage of the DLR.

The urban motorway is an antisocial animal. In Holland, France and Germany contemporary thinking is moving away from ambitious segregated roads and towards the more enviornmentally friendly boulevard. Such boulevards can also be four lanes wide but, being lined with trees and edged by shops, cafes and houses, they assume more neighbourly characteristics. The boulevard presupposes two things which are lacking in Docklands: a strategic overview to ensure that warehousing and industry is well located relative to the motorway system; and adequate public subsidy to provide a bus, tram or rail system able to lure commuters out of their cars.

The East London river crossing

If the new road system of Docklands fails to take advantage of the aesthetic possibilities, so too do the proposals for the East London river crossing at the Royal Docks. The Department of Transport has commissioned a design

Figure 3.3

Santiago Calatrava's design for the East London river crossing. This design championed by the developer Stanhope was rejected in October 1991 in favour of a box girder design supported by the Department of Transport. It was designed to act as a gateway to London from the east. Goverment has yet to realize that quality of design in those areas it controls is important in establishing a climate of excellence for others to follow (photo: Heinrich Helfenstein for Stanhope Properties)

from Halcrow Fox which, though cost effective, employs the rather pedestrian system of box girders. The inferiority of the design motivated the Royal Fine Art Commission (RFAC) to give its backing to an alternative design using a bow spring arch prepared for Stanhope Properties by the Spanish architect and engineer Santiago Calatrava. Stanhope's interest in what is principally a matter for the Department stems from the company's ambition to develop a major shopping centre designed by Sir Richard Rogers on land alongside the bridge. Stanhope had earlier refused to sign an agreement with the LDDC to proceed with the shopping centre until there was a clear commitment to construct the Thames crossing.

The East London river crossing raises two issues: first, whether economics should be the sole basis for making infrastructure investment decisions; and second, whether major developers should have the right to shape design policy in areas outside their immediate control. On the first point, Calatrava's design is undoubtedly spectacular and could have provided an emblem for Dockland regeneration. At present the Royal Docks lack a spectacular statement; there are no new towers and there is little in the way of prestige housing.

As Calatrava has shown in his bridge designs in Spain, such structures can be a potent symbol of urban renewal. As for developers shaping aesthetic policy, they are probably only filling the vacuum produced by the retreat of orthodox planning activity from this area. Olympia and York, Stanhope and Rosehaugh have all put pressure on the LDDC to introduce design standards to help protect their own investments. On present evidence the government cannot leave such matters to its own mandarins, especially those in the Department of Transport. This is why the RFAC spoke out so strongly against the Halcrow Fox design, and why it felt that Calatrava should have been appointed without delay 'in order to ensure a bridge which is worthy of our capital city and its great river'.[5] In the event, Calatrava's 'gateway bridge to London'[6] was subsequently rejected by the minister on grounds of cost and the extra time needed to develop the design.

London City Airport

The London City Airport is the third main area where investment has occurred in the provision of a new transportation infrastructure. After plans in the early 1980s for a major city airport in Docklands, the wings of ambition were clipped. Two problems dogged the developer and owner Mowlem: growing concern over the environmental impact of the airport, and the reluctance of the airline companies to use the airport because of poor transportation links.

Early plans for 1.2 million passengers a year to be carried by the short take-off and landing aircraft failed to materialize. The quiet fifty seater Dash 7 aircraft have proved suitable for business travellers but not for the lucrative package holiday market. Plans to allow bigger and noisier aircraft have come up against opposition from community groups and local councils. There is the added danger with more cumbersome aircraft of collision with the high rise buildings on the Isle of Dogs or the pylons of the East London riving crossing.

The London City Airport enjoys an enviable location in the heart of the Royal Docks. The 762 metre runway utilizes the quay between the Royal Albert and King George V Docks, but the insubstantial two storey terminal building testifies to the limited commercial appeal of the airport. After an investment of £18 million by Mowlem, the future of the airport now depends upon permitting noisier aircraft to utilize its facilities, plus a speedy implementation of the second phase of the DLR. Again the lack of an integrated approach to infrastructure provision has resulted in developers having to foot a substantial bill. The 1991 appeal decision by the Secretary of State to allow the airport to expand highlighted the conflicts which occur when infrastructure decisions are left to market forces.

The planned Jubilee Line extension

The limitations of the DLR and the road system have finally persuaded government to invest in a major addition to London's underground network. An extended Jubilee Line is now planned at a cost of about £1 billion to link Green Park (and thence via the Piccadilly Line to Heathrow) to Stratford via London Bridge and Canary Wharf. Nicknamed the 'developers' line' because of the planned contribution from the Reichmann brothers and others, it promises to provide a capacity of 18,000 people per hour during the rush hour. As such it makes a major contribution towards the demand made upon public transport provision by the existence of the Isle of Dogs enterprise zone.

As with the DLR, the approach to design is to employ an architect to prepare a kit of parts and a recipe of details which are then translated to meet the needs of specific stations by further appointed designers. Sir

Figure 3.4

Major transport investment

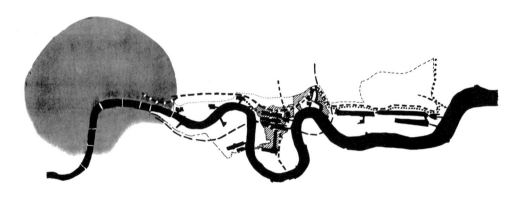

MAJOR INFRASTRUCTURE INVESTMENT
- - - - - Docklands Light Railway
- - - Jubilee Line Extension
.... Major Road Investment
//// Enterprise zone

0   ½   1 MILE

Figure 3.5

DLR and Harbour Exchange

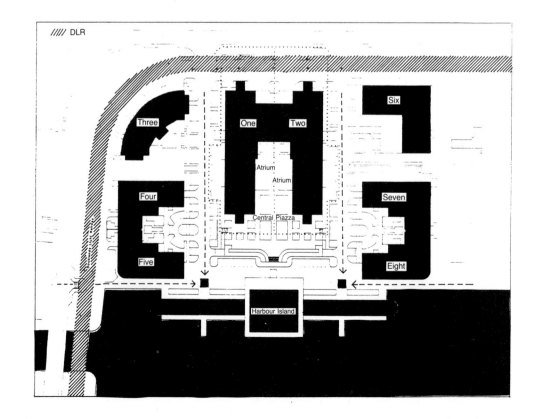

Norman Foster will design the Canary Wharf Jubilee Line Station, Michael Hopkins the new Westminster station and Nicholas Grimshaw that at Waterloo. Such stations may raise the currency of design in London and show that public investment can prove a good source of patronage. One only hopes that the limited perceptions of those at the Department of Transport dealing with the East London river crossing do not dampen design talent on the underground.

The balance between private development and public services

What is most remarkable about Docklands is the reversal of the normal process of urban development. One generally finds public investment in infrastructure preceding private investment in buildings, but in Docklands the buildings have on the whole appeared first. The effect of the enterprise zone and environmental deregulation, coupled with the outflowing of capital from the City (itself the result of financial deregulation), produced a tidal wave of buildings. The necessary roads and railway lines found themselves either underscaled or lagging a few years behind the construction of buildings. The Thatcher revolution placed regeneration before social well-being and enterprise before planning. The ideological high ground was enjoyed by the LDDC and government ministers alike until the arrival of the superjam in 1990. The prospect of prestige developments such as Harbour Exchange and Canary Wharf sitting unlet through want of physical access finally concentrated minds, and in the process the limits to development freedom were exposed. The high ground was lost and more balanced thinking began to prevail. Just as private developers have been instrumental in reminding government of the benefits of some aspects of town planning, so too with transportation planning. With 50 per cent of the floor space unlet in the early nineties, Docklands illustrated why arguments for a metropolitan planning authority for London are now unassailable.

Notes

1 Reg Ward, 'The Years Ahead', *The Complete Business World*, no. 3, February–April 1987, p. 6.
2 Statement by Cecil Parkinson MP, Secretary of State for Transport, May 1990.
3 See for instance *The Planner*, vol. 76, no. 40, where London's commercial competitiveness is compared unfavourably with Paris and Frankfurt, largely in terms of quality of life.
4 Richard Evans, 'London Docklands', *The Financial Times*, 1 October 1986, p. 30.
5 Calatrava backing; *Building Design*, 6 July 1990, p. 1.
6 This is how Stanhope's director John Fairclough, described Calatrava's Landmark lost to London *Building Design*, 4 October 1991, p. 5.

4 The LDDC's Approach to Urban Design

The initial response

As a result of the political and administrative changes introduced by the 1980 Act, the LDDC was under great pressure to obtain quick results. The need to start speedily upon urban reconstruction meant that buildings became the visible emblems of change – not plans or development frameworks. The LDDC wanted buildings on the ground to signal future changes, and it engaged in heavy promotion even before planning guidelines had been prepared. The two years after 1981 (when the LDDC was finally established) saw buildings proceeding in parallel with the first attempts at prescribing what should be happening in the area. Without statutory planning powers and with confidence in the LDDC a prime consideration, the corporation's early urban design and environmental objectives in 1982 can be summarized as follows:[1]

- There was to be no more filling in of the water areas of the docks.
- The isolation of the area was to be attacked.
- New public transport links were to be formed between Docklands and central London.
- Two thousand homes a year were to be built, mostly involving investment by private house builders.
- The major historic buildings of the area (particularly the Hawksmoor churches) were to be restored, and new conservation areas established.
- Dock walls and river banks were to be repaired or reconstructed and polluted land reclaimed.
- New infrastructure of water, gas, electricity and drainage was to be provided at the Isle of Dogs.
- New roads were to have high visual quality.
- Landscape improvement schemes were to be formulated as soon as sites could be cleared.
- The arts – particularly sculpture, history and archaeology – were to play an important part.

What these guidelines conspicuously lack is any visionary framework for the urban reconstruction. The policies are commendable in themselves but do not create a sense of place; they merely repair a disjointed landscape. As initial guiding principles they were clearly inadequate, as later developments have proved. What the guidelines did achieve by default, however, was the impression that development could proceed unregulated. Hence the best sites along the Thames or around the docks were quickly acquired, with property speculation remaining always a step or two ahead of urban design guidelines. And with the declared aim of attracting prestigious private house building to the area, it was rightly assumed that new service industries would quickly replace the old manufacturing jobs. Unfortunately, the implications for urban design were not then explored; political pressure demanded a wave of new building even if the resulting environment appeared suburban or like a business-park.

The approach was piecemeal and *ad hoc.* Development frameworks were established for certain of the pressure points such as Tooley Street, Greenland Dock and the Royal Docks. The framework for the Isle of Dogs, conceived in the first instance by David Gosling and Gordon Cullen, proved too prescriptive and far-reaching for the LDDC in 1982. It sought to bring a measure of order to bear where political will and commercial pressure had tended rather to pull in the opposite direction. Master planning has always

Figure 4.1

First generation development on the Isle of Dogs. Without a masterplan or development framework the initial wave of building on the Isle of Dogs looked not unlike a suburban business park. Until 1985 the urban possibilities were not exploited by the business community. This view along Millharbour shows the tree planting and brick paving of the enterprise zone (photo: LDDC)

demanded a central controlling body; in the LDDC, design freedom not central planning has been the spirit of the boardroom. Hence the plans and guidelines prepared have quickly and quietly been set aside as new developers have demanded bigger buildings and more of the water area.

The ten guidelines for urban design summarized above were soon discarded when G. Ware Travelstead and his First Boston Consortium appeared on the scene in 1985. Their proposals for Canary Wharf expanded across the water area of West India Dock and made a nonsense of the retention of the Gwilt Sugar Warehouses nearby. The scale of Docklands changed overnight: a townscape of small scale fragmentation became one of super-large blocks and new skyline patterns. For these changes the urban design policies of the LDDC proved both inadequate and expendable, and led to the resignation of the corporation's chief architect planner Ted Hollamby in 1985.[2]

Figure 4.2

Contrast between first and second generation development. Without a spatial or land use framework to coordinate different scales and types of development, the Isle of Dogs has become a townscape of ambiguity and contrast (photo: Brian Edwards)

Masterplan or development framework: the Docklands experience

The urban regeneration of Docklands has generally been structured through development frameworks as against masterplans. With a few notable exceptions (such as the plan by Skidmore, Owings and Merrill (SOM) for Canary Wharf) the formal masterplan has been studiously avoided. This is because many in the LDDC believe it to be associated with municipal planning and hence politically suspect. Instead flexible urban design frameworks have been employed to provide the necessary bridge between the broad planning aims of the corporation and the design ambitions of those providing the buildings. The difference between the masterplan and an urban design framework is more, however, than one of semantics. The masterplan has traditionally structured not just spaces and buildings, but land uses, aesthetics and transport systems. By way of contrast the urban design or development framework deals with images and environmental targets. Whilst the masterplan is prescriptive, the urban design framework tends to suggest ways of carrying out development and speaks of principles, visions and guidelines. Not surprisingly the words 'development framework' tend to figure more largely in LDDC documents than 'masterplan' – and in development honeypots such as the Isle of Dogs, any framework tends to be rather loosely drawn.

Both urban design frameworks and masterplans are much concerned with 'parcelization'. This clumsy word refers to the subdivision of large areas into discrete parts capable of separate development but within constraints designed to promote a unified whole. With masterplans such parcels are

Figure 4.3

The Olympia and York proposals for Canary Wharf. The masterplan by Skidmore, Owings and Merrill for Canary Wharf contained several lavishly presented perspective views of the intended development. The objective was to persuade the LDDC of the desirability of the proposals and to interest potential tenants in the attractiveness of the scheme (photo: Olympia and York)

normally meticulously defined with marketing conditions covering details of construction, bulk, height and building edge. For example, at Canary Wharf, Olympia and York's private masterplan requires developers to build arcades along certain streets and insists upon stone or marble being employed on façades facing the major squares.

Urban design or development frameworks are altogether more flexible vehicles. At the Royal Docks future land uses are by no means clear, yet an urban structuring plan prepared by the Richard Rogers Partnership in 1985 was required in order to enable the infrastructure investments to proceed. The development parcels here are mere diagrams, but they are linked to public facilities and provide a structure of urban spaces around which buildings can be accommodated.[3] The size of parcels normally reflects the likely urban function: big parcels for offices, small parcels for housing. Hence, the subsequent development framework prepared by Tibbalds, Colbourne, Karski, Williams for the Royal Albert Dock contains a mixture of large, medium and small urban parcels, with a legible system of streets, squares and footpaths along docksides linking the whole plan together.

If parcelization is one of the key objectives in preparing either masterplans or development frameworks, then marketing is another. In Docklands urban plans have become vehicles to assist marketing. At a broad level the various LDDC area teams have produced and regularly revised their colourful broadsheets listing developments and sites available – all drawn with pastel blue water and margin sketches. The more specific development plans have contained perspective sketches showing what the finished environment will look and feel like. That for Canary Wharf, with a dozen or so splendid perspectives, is as much a marketing document as an attempt to parcel up land and organize the spaces. These plans raise expectations and in the process inflate the value of land and encourage developers to invest in higher quality buildings.[4] The masterplan, like any property portfolio, is talking the language of investment as much as urban space planning.

Filling the void in traditional planning

For these reasons several areas of Docklands have enjoyed the benefit either of precise masterplans to guide development or, more likely, of more flexible development frameworks. Both, however, represent a departure from contemporary planning practice. Planning in Britain has become negative and bureaucratic as the government has produced ever more statutory guidelines. The scope for vision has been eroded, and much staff time in planning departments is spend on trivial details or matters of procedure. The LDDC (as with all eleven UDCs) has sought to cut through the red tape and concentrate upon the development process on the one hand and upon cultivating a creative vision on the other. The development framework or site masterplan encourages this approach, and the LDDC has been at the forefront of adopting such plans at the expense of more embracing city-wide plans. That these new plans have been full of value judgements not validated by the usual political processes has worried few of the developers or corporation staff. Hence, the development framework and private masterplan have filled a void left by the retreat of traditional planning from orthodox urban design.

This new generation of plans has been prepared not by LDDC staff but by private architects and planners. A new skill base called urban design emerged in the 1980s, partly as a response to the opportunities generated in such areas as London Docklands. The authors of these plans are quite unlike their counterparts in County Hall, and the market for their skills resides in big development companies such as Stanhope and Rosehaugh. Since the developers do not control the whole area (unlike, in theory at least, traditional council planners), the tendency has been for these masterplans to concern themselves with relatively small areas of Docklands.

Table 4.1 London Docklands: development strategies, key projects and design approaches

LDDC area	Urban design framework for overall area	Development framework for specific areas	Formal master plan for specific area	Approach to regeneration	Key projects — Name	Developer	Designer	Style
Isle of Dogs	No	Yes, Heron Quays by Gosling, Proctor and Ferguson	Yes, Canary Wharf by Skidmore, Owings and Merrill	Market-led; Design freedom; Enterprise zone; Tax incentives; Commercial core with riverside housing; Mainly single use development	Canary Wharf	Olympia and York	SOM, Cesar Pelli etc.	Beaux arts/modern
					Heron Quays	Tarmac	N. Lacey	Modern Venetian
					South Quay Plaza	Marples Ltd	Seifert Ltd	Modern classicism
					Great Eastern	Standard Com.	HKP&A	1930s modern
					Financial Times printing works	Financial Times	N. Grimshaw	High tech modern
					Reuters	Reuters	R.Rogers Part.	Modern
					Telehouse	Telehouse Int.	YRM	Modern
					Pumping station	LDDC/Thames Water	John Outram	Pop classicism
					Cascades	Kentish Homes	CZWG	Nautical modern
					Compass point	LDDC/Costain	J. Dixon	Vernacular
Royal Docks	Yes, by Richard Rogers Partnership	Yes, Royal Albert Dock by Richard Rogers Partnership; Yes, Royal Victoria Dock by Tibbalds, Colbourne Williams	Yes, Albert Basin by Richard Rogers Partnership	Infrastructure-led; Mixed housing, industry and retail around development nodes	London City Airport	Mowlem	Seifert Ltd	Modern
					Cyprus, Beckton	Various	Volume house builders	Mainly vernacular
					Pumping station	LDDC	R.Rogers Partnership	Modern
					Albert Basin shopping centre	Rosenhaugh/Stanhope	R.Rogers Partnership	Modern baroque

Area	Conservation area	Design briefs / guidance	Further design briefs	Approach	Development	Developer	Architect	Style
Surrey Docks	No	Yes, Greenland Dock by Conran Roche; Yes, London Bridge City phase 1 by Twigg Brown Associates; Yes, Southwark Site by Clouston, Arup etc.	Yes, London Bridge City phase 2 by John Simpson	Heritage-led; Design-led; Offices at Pool of London, housing further east	London Bridge City: phase 1	St Martins Property Co.	Twigg Brown Associates	Modern
					phase 2	"	John Simpson	Post-modern
					Design Museum	Butlers Wharf Ltd	Conran Roche	Bauhaus modern
					Horselydown Square	Berkley House	Wickham Associates	Post-modern
					China Wharf	Jacobs Island Company	CZWG	Eclectic
					Vogan's Mill	Rosehaugh	Michael Squire Associates	Modern
					Finland Quay	Lovell R.Malcolm	Richard Reid	Rationalist
					Swedish Quays		Price and Cullen	Arts and crafts
					Baltic Quays	Skillion PLC	Lister, Drew, Haines, Barrow	High tech modern
					Lawrence Wharf	Islef Ltd	Kjaer and Richter	Rationalist
Wapping	No	No	No	Heritage-led; Mixed use up-market riverside housing; Offices near St Katharine's, housing elsewhere	Shadwell Basin	Sanctuary Land Co.	Richard McCormack	Vernacular
					Narrow Street	Roy Properties	Ian Ritchie	Rationalist
					Tobacco Dock	Tobacco Dock Dev.	T.Farrell Partnership	Rehabilitation; Disney repro.
					Thomas More Court	Heron Homes	Boyer Design	Vernacular
					Commodity Quay	St Katharine's by the Tower Ltd	Watkins Gray	Period revival

Abbreviations: SOM Skidmore Owings and Merrill; HKP&A Howell Killick Partridge and Amis; CZWG Campbell Zogolovitch Wilkinson and Gough; YRM Yorke Rosenberg and Mardall.

In place of a Docklands-wide masterplan, the LDDC has created an environment where developers come up with ideas, design skills and imagination (Table 4.1). The task for the corporation is simple: to make its selection from what is offered. It is an ideology which derives from the practices of the boardroom as against the town hall. Design tendering is more important to the LDDC than design structuring; the system raises the importance of design amongst developers. However, in the process of eliminating of the urban framework, other matters find themselves overlooked. Transportation is no longer integrated into the development process, and social provision and environmental safeguards are often squeezed. The approach of the LDCC led to speedy regeneration and some exciting new buildings, but wider issues were often overlooked.

Urban design lessons from Docklands

The 1980s has seen the emergence of a debate about how to construct a framework for urban design within the development process. Between the extremes of a rigid masterplan (SOM's plan for Canary Wharf is a good example) and open-ended urban design guidelines (such as those given in Chapter 5 for the Isle of Dogs) a number of alternative approaches have been suggested. Agencies anxious to proceed with development are naturally loath to adopt urban design plans which are too prescriptive, but the pragmatic approach need not entail the total disregard of matters of urban design. Conventional land use plans do not establish urban design guidelines to any meaningful degree; in fact, land use plans are part of the tendency towards urban chaos. Recent thinking is towards abandoning land use planning and adopting urban design frameworks to ensure that whatever is built creates a coherent whole. The question these days is what form such plans should take. Since London Docklands has attempted to apply the full spectrum of urban design approaches from almost total permissiveness to strict frameworks, the area is a good place to search for answers.

Gosling and Cullen's urban design study for the Isle of Dogs sought to establish a range of development options within a strong spatial and physical framework. Their approach was essentially that of producing different urban design strategies in an attempt to stimulate ideas for development. Gosling has subsequently stated that urban design frameworks are the best way to weld together existing communities instead of allowing their destruction, and believes this to be the 'primary goal in the reconstruction of declining inner cities in the post-industrial age'.[5]

It appears to be a nonsense to abandon urban structuring in the drive for free enterprise. The outcome is simply to encourage private developers to prepare such plans, with obvious limitations in terms of political accountability and the pursuit of the common good.

The want of a grand landscape design in Docklands

After a decade of investment, the general impression in London Docklands is one of lack of greenery, both as a backcloth to buildings and as a concept permeating the area. There are, of course, pockets of well landscaped developments and attractive green corridors, but there is little feeling that landscape in Docklands is part of a grand design. There are few signs that the LDDC sought the greening of Docklands as a design strategy; in fact, early thinking was towards a hard landscape character which it was thought suited the industrial qualities of the area. Hence there has been much paving in brick or setts and placing of cast iron bollards and seats around the water's edge. The creation of a hard and robust urban landscape in places like the Isle of Dogs or London Bridge City has been at the expense of serious thought about green corridors and a planted landscape. Where vegetation has been generously provided (as in parts of Beckton or near

Russian Dock at Southwark) these are not part of a strategic plan for Docklands; neither do they adequately link into other open space systems such as the Victorian parks sprinkled through Docklands.

The failure to incorporate landscape design in any grand strategy for the renewal of Docklands is, like the failure of urban design, the result of a reluctance to employ comprehensive plans at all. Had the masterplan approach been adopted then the framework for landscape would necessarily have been required. As it is, landscape design exists either within fairly well defined sub-areas of Docklands such as Greenland Dock, or as a by-product of infrastructure development as in Royal Docks. Any knowledge of the history of landscape design would quickly lead one to appreciate the limitations of this approach.

Figure 4.4

View from Stave Hill, Surrey Quays. The axis which focuses upon the City of London is lined with plane trees and finished in stone and gravel (photo: B. Clouston and Partners)

Figure 4.5

Landscape detailing at Canada Water, Surrey Quays. Designed by the LDDC's own landscape team, the details and materials are admirably robust and designed within the traditions of the area (photo: Brian Edwards)

Whether greenness is judged by a green philosophy or the existence of extensive tree planted areas, the reality is that in spite of some delightfully landscaped corners and ecological parks, Docklands is a markedly ungreen place. Within the 5500 acres of the LDDC's area, only 308 acres of open space exist and some of this is not green space. Except for the Newham Council planned Beckton District Park, the regeneration of Docklands has not produced a single new public park; instead, officials argue that the water is the area's open space.[6] Admittedly there are some 430 acres of water, 23 miles of dock walls and 17 miles of riverfront, but water to look at is hardly as valuable as parks to use.

By modern planning standards the 70,000 people now living in Docklands require about 500 acres of open space, and the projected population of 115,000 by the year 2000 would need about 800 acres. Provision is thereby well below usual standards, but it is difficult to see where sites may become available to meet the shortfall. With land fetching £2 or £3 million per acre, the incentive is to build, not make parks. What has been provided is often, however, of a high standard. Stave Hill by Brian Clouston's office, infrastructure planting in the Royal Docks by Gillespies and the treatment of Canada Water and surrounding canals by the LDDC's own staff are commendable. There is nothing wrong with the details; the fault lies in lack of strategic landscape planning.

Two models may prove useful even at this late stage. When John Nash prepared his plan for civic routes and parks from Marylebone to Pall Mall in 1811 (under the title of 'Metropolitan improvements') he incorporated some of the most attractive areas of London into his proposals. By linking Portland Place (formed in 1774) into the street building plans, and through the careful use of landscape design, Nash successfully created a corridor of amenity through the centre of London which had its northern end a planned new park (Regent's Park) and at its southern an existing one (St James's Park). When Daniel Burnham prepared the plan for Cleveland in 1903 he established a framework of public spaces and civic buildings which not only brought a measured monumentality to bear upon this steel making town, but attempted to integrate railway stations and speculative building into a wider park system. Though only partly realized, Burnham's plan, like Nash's, sought a partnership between building and landscape design, and between public

Figure 4.6

Aerial view of St Katharine Docks. An urbanism reminiscent of the US has grown up due east of St Katharine Docks. Here tall office blocks with much car parking nearby give obvious expression to the lack of a masterplan or landscape framework (photo: Sheppard Robson)

monuments and private development. Similarly, the renewal of Berlin under the IBA programme of 1982–5 used landscape design to integrate developments from one side of the city to another. Admittedly Berlin's Friedrichstadt had an inherited urban consistency quite unlike the vast wasteland of Docklands, but the cultural need to incorporate civic and landscape elements reflects poorly upon unplanned London.

The sense of mystery which the old walls and long blocks of warehouses once gave the area has been replaced by Manhattan-like blocks with much car parking at their base. Landscape design could have mediated between these conflicting visions, but too often the design of surfaces is overhard and the planting mean in scale. The ungreenness of it all may be moderated by future planning, but the impression to date is that landscape design has been a way of creating private amenity in the form of the occasional green oasis in a desert of concrete and curtain walling. Where the LDDC has sought to intervene, it has tried to diversify the visual structure through landscape design, arguing that trees are a contrasting natural element in the urban scene.[7] Such trees, however, lack the scale of the buildings and appear too often as merely cosmetic elements.

Quality in the landscape details

If there is a want of a grand landscape design for the area as a whole, certain individual projects are worthy in themselves and in the benefits they bring to local communities. The decision to form the roads and pavements on the Isle of Dogs in yellow and red brick (or at least coloured concrete paviors) was well founded and no doubt inspired by similar action within certain British new towns. The pavior finish unifies a disparate collection of buildings, at least in terms of the pedestrians' experience, and has added much colour and sense of optimism to early Dockland projects. The paviors have proved flexible, allowing the relaying of countless underground services, as well as the planting of trees along the roadsides. Their domestic scale is sometimes disarming, but being laid in large areas the effect is normally more urban than suburban. However, the planting of roses and thorny shrubs around office car parks and along footpaths has tended to undermine what scale existed and weaken the crucial relationship between urban and landscape design. The argument employed to justify these garden-centre-like landscapes has been one of ecological richness, but in reality one suspects that lack of imagination and fear of high maintenance costs has tended to result in mean and prickly planting.

Only with large scale developments do the surfaces around buildings transcend the mundane. At South Quay Plaza much is finished in marble and has a geometry which reflects that of the buildings. Moreover, here the shops and restaurants which spill around the base of the towers establish routes and patterns which become the primary order into which planting design, dwarf walls and steps are accommodated with ease. Similarly Canary Wharf seeks to structure the surrounding space in a fashion which is decidedly urban, contained and monumental in character. The aesthetic adviser here, Sir Roy Strong, is anxious that the street furniture should have a strength and quality matching the details of the buildings, just as Georgian London spread its influence across not just the buildings but the railings, paving and gates as well.

On the Isle of Dogs the major space between buildings is either the road surface itself or the water areas of the Docklands. Generally the well detailed streets represent the back entrance to buildings; their fronts face the water and hence address the principal amenity of the area. The streets are, therefore, largely service channels (as against civic routes) and inevitably lead to car parks before they provide access to the entrance to buildings. Hence car parks are the major environmental feature of much of the enterprise zone and usually provide the foreground to the architecture. This, of course, reverses the pattern of the traditional city where car parks are tucked into rear gardens or beneath ground, and where building fronts are placed hard against the street. The landscape designers' task in such areas has been how to screen the car parks and use landscape planting to direct people towards the building entrance. Some attempt has been made by the LDDC to create an urban impression by treating the major routes of the Isle of Dogs as boulevards, complete with axial tree planting in London planes and parallel road edges. But the fundamental fact of buildings facing not the street but the water (or at least a courtyard formed between the two) has weakened attempts at urbanity. Only in the bigger projects such as Harbour Exchange Square is the relationship between street, entrance and external landscape satisfactorily resolved.

Landscape design at the water's edge

Where the buildings face the water, architecture and landscape design are often happily accommodated. Dockside walkways are linked to raised balconies which spill out from the buildings and often give access to ships moored at the water's edge. On this side too, restaurants, bars and shops are often located, creating a pleasant environment for those who can afford their wares. The richness of forms and details on the dock side of buildings is often in marked contrast to that facing the street.

It has been argued that long waterside pathways would have been monotonous and alien to the character of Docklands where privacy, contrast and variety were the traditional qualities. This argument presupposes that

Figure 4.7

Waterside activity at Millwall Dock. The water basins of the former dock system are often surrounded by buildings of interest and activity. Here alongside Harbour Exchange, a bank, shops and restaurants are built as islands projecting into the water (photo: Brian Edwards)

openness and access should be limited and that monotony of route cannot be relieved by variety of detail, planting and building forms. Without some unifying element at the water's edge the landscape of Docklands threatens to lose any sense of order, since the private developers are each pursuing a different and largely incremental approach to place making. Just as the streets generally fail to provide a unifying urban structure to the area (in spite of their brick finish), so too the loss of connecting waterside walkways weakens the sense of whole. Where waterside routes are extensive, as in parts of Wapping near Tobacco Dock and around Canada Water in Surrey Docks, the quality of finish is admirable, but these walkways lead to nowhere of substance. They are mere internal routes, not perceptual frameworks.

Do the dock basins compensate for the lack of civic squares?

Taking a broad view, the urban landscapes which have tended to attract attention in the last few years have mostly been enclosed spaces. They have consisted, for instance, of Philip Johnson's Thanksgiving Square in Dallas (1975) which, though triangular, is surrounded by buildings of substance and is given a focus of attention by way of a central feature. Within Europe a spate of formal treatments has emerged to give place and dignity to eroded city spaces, such as Miguel Angel Roca's Plaza España in Córdoba (1978), and more recently Oriole Bohigas has carried out some spectacular reconstructions of civic spaces in Barcelona. All of these schemes have one thing in common: the establishment of greater visual clarity through physical reordering. Civic squares have often been cleared of traffic and fussy street furniture, and repaved in bold geometric patterns which both relate to the surrounding buildings and provide a framework for new lamp standards, seats and tree planting. Enclosed spaces provide this opportunity, but the layout of Docklands contains few such areas. The nearest Docklands has to public enclosed spaces are rectangular water basins such as Greenland Dock. These have the potential to perform as true civic squares with the Dock itself, providing both a point of interest and the rectangular geometrics required for formal treatment. The masterplan prepared by Conran Roche in 1984 for Greenland Dock seeks this very treatment with its strict lines of

Figure 4.8

Model of Conran Roche masterplan for Greenland Dock. Unusually for Docklands the LDDC appointed consultants to prepare a masterplan for Greenland Dock. Its European precedents are obvious, though the lack of height in the proposed buildings enclosing the dock weakens an admirable attempt at regulating development (photo: Conran Roche)

perimeter tree planting, formal paving and hard edging of the dock by buildings. Though the buildings constructed are fairly formal (particularly Richard Reid's Finland Quay development) they lack the necessary height to contain the space, but the intentions are evident.

Elsewhere formal spaces exist mostly within the semi-private world of office developments such as Canary Wharf. Here civic landscaping reflects the style and monumentality of the buildings, but as a general rule landscape designers in Docklands have preferred picturesque English style planting to the monumental paved and planted squares of European inspiration. This is partly because the landscape architect is left with pockets of land after the road engineer and building designer have had their say, and partly as a result of a failure to appreciate the traditional qualities of urban landscape. The idea that landscape design can help in place making and aid the stitching together of largely incremental developments has found little currency in Docklands. In a way the new landscape of Docklands is like that of the architecture: all is colourful, varied and strangely incoherent. There are places such as West Dock in Wapping and London Bridge City where the design of paving and public walkways has real quality, but landscape design does not adequately ennoble the public realm or integrate development across the broad and open horizons of Docklands.

The belated recognition of these problems has encouraged the staff of the LDDC to formulate more strategic landscape design proposals in a fashion which closely parallels the rediscovery of urban design. The corporation has recently adopted more ambitious landscape policies. There are now specific objectives related to view enhancement, exploitation of river vistas and green corridors.[8] Except for the Isle of Dogs such a renaissance is not too late, but there has been nearly a decade of lost opportunity.

Notes

1 Ted Hollamby, *Docklands: London's Backyard into Frontyard* (Docklands Forum 1990), pp. 10–11.

2 *Ibid.*, p. 4.

3 *A Draft Development Framework for the Royal Docks Area* (Richard Rogers Partnership 1985), p. 24.

4 *Greenland Dock: A Framework for development* (Conran Roche in conjunction with the LDDC 1984), p. 4.
5 Gosling is quoted in Arnold Linden, 'Development issues', *Urban Design Quarterly*, June 1989, p. 38.
6 Amanda Atha, 'Blue is not green', *The Observer*, 18 November 1990.
7 Tony Aldous, 'Soft centres', *Building Design*, 22 March 1991, p. 23.
8 *Ibid.*, p. 26.

Part Two
The Area Studies

The Isle of Dogs

5

Development background

If the docks of London were deliberately designed to be inaccessible in order to discourage theft and smuggling, this was nowhere more evident than on the Isle of Dogs. The great warehouses of Millwall Docks and West India Docks sat within commercial enclaves protected by high brick walls and guarded entrances. Roads ran around the circumference of the 'island' and cut across its neck at Poplar High Street. The area was relatively inaccessible, a cul-de-sac of warehousing, shipping and isolated housing estates contained within a loop of the Thames about a mile across. Of all the areas of Docklands, none was as closed and impenetrable as the Isle of Dogs, and yet in 1981 none offered quite the potential for waterside development.

The Isle of Dogs as defined by the LDDC extends from West India Road to the River Lea and from East India Dock Road to the Thames immediately opposite Greenwich. It contains well defined townships such as Cubitt Town in the south and Poplar in the north, but the main character of the area derives from the linear dock basins contained within the centre of the island. By way of contrast a number of smaller, more irregular docks are dotted through the area, of which Blackwall Basin and East India Dock Basin are typical.

Cubitt Town is a rare animal in Docklands: it was a company town developed by the great Victorian builder Sir William Cubitt in 1843. The lease obtained from the Countess of Glengall contained a mile of waterfront and extensive lands behind. Along the Thamesside Cubitt established timber wharves, cement works and potteries to service the construction firm then busy laying out terraces of houses in the West End. On the land behind, the company built modest terraced housing for its workers and provided two amenities for more general use: the church of Christ and St John, built to designs furnished by F. Johnstone in 1857; and the park known as Island Gardens, formed on land leased from the Commissioners of Greenwich Hospital.[1]

Cubitt was, however, a relative latecomer to the Island. Shipbuilding and warehousing were already well established, with Millwall providing the economic focus. In 1858 Brunel's ship the *Great Eastern* was launched from

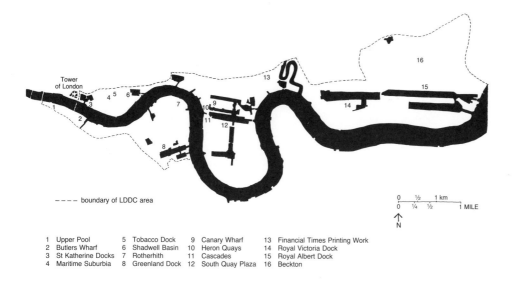

- - - - boundary of LDDC area

Tower of London

1	Upper Pool	5	Tobacco Dock	9	Canary Wharf	13	Financial Times Printing Work
2	Butlers Wharf	6	Shadwell Basin	10	Heron Quays	14	Royal Victoria Dock
3	St Katherine Docks	7	Rotherhith	11	Cascades	15	Royal Albert Dock
4	Maritime Suburbia	8	Greenland Dock	12	South Quay Plaza	16	Beckton

Figure 5.1

Area studies location plan

Figure 5.2

Plan of the Isle of Dogs: (A) high tech enclave (B) main office area (C) middle class housing along Thames

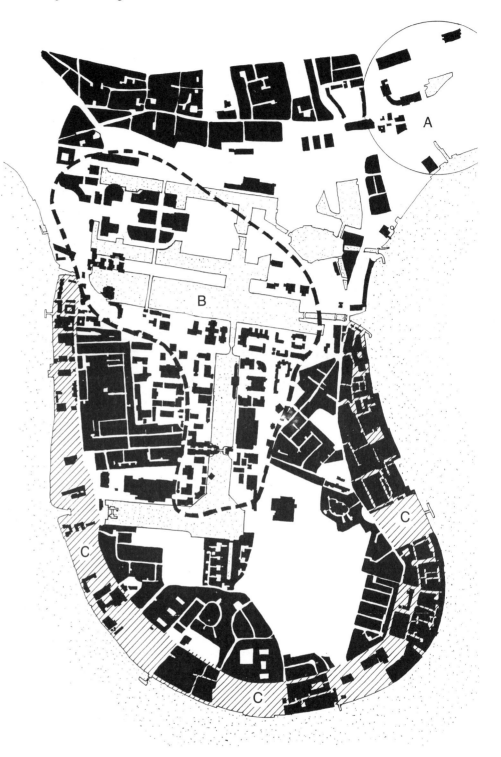

Millwall Dock, and was at the time the largest steamship in the world. The dock system was modified and enlarged in 1867 to plans first proposed in 1829, and by the late nineteenth century handled mostly bulk cargoes such as grain, timber and fruit. Canary Wharf specialized in handling bananas from the Canary Islands, and the northern part of West India Dock dealt in sugar. The arrival of the railways into the dock system, completed by 1896, encouraged even more industrialization, with housing (and this mostly for the working classes) pushed to the hinterland or near to the boundaries of the area.

Figure 5.3

West India Dock in 1985. This view, taken just before Canary Wharf transformed the scene, shows the character of Docklands as it had existed for most of the century (photo: Brian Edwards)

Views and character

The perimeter roads of West Ferry Road, Manchester Road and Preston Road provide rare slot-like views on the Thames as the river sweeps around the island. These views are often between factories and older warehouses, or increasingly between modern apartment blocks which hug the water's edge. At Island Gardens the views are across a Victorian park to the handsome buildings by Inigo Jones and Sir Christopher Wren at Greenwich. A similar park, Sir John McDougal Gardens, on the west side of the island provides views across the Thames to Greenland Dock in Southwark. These two parks are the only relief to a Thamesside often industrial in character and hence by no means beautiful. The LDDC has, however, carved viewing slots out of the dereliction on the riverside, of which Johnson's Drawdock which affords pleasant views of the *Cutty Sark* is the most notable.

The inner basins provide a more attractive scene: long fingers of water enclosed by docksides of finely crafted engineering detail and lined by cranes of great presence but no great antiquity. The areas of enclosed water provide a handsome backcloth to both Victorian brick warehouses and modern glass and marble offices.

Attempts at a development framework

In September 1981 David Gosling and Gordon Cullen were appointed to assist Edward Hollamby in the preparation of 'a guide to design and development opportunities' on the Isle of Dogs. The guide had two main objectives: to define the existing character of the area, and to demonstrate the potential of the area through a number of sketch proposals. The brief issued to the authors by the LDDC emphasized the need for flexibility in order for the corporation to secure 'the island's lasting economic revival'.[2] Edward Hollamby, the corporation's chief architect and planner, who was responsible for the appointment of these two influential urban designers, had earlier employed Gosling alone on more strategic issues. His report had given the

LDDC four options for the development of the area: high technology, water based, urban structure, and marketing strategy. The later report with the inclusion of Cullen in the team was largely to test the urban design reality of the options.

The timing of the study was significant. The LDDC had only been established five months earlier and was anxious to push ahead with the infrastructure needed to regenerate the Isle of Dogs, and particularly that part within the enterprise zone. It was important for the corporation to ensure that the investment in roads, transport and underground services (water, gas and electricity all had to be upgraded) was compatible with physical development. Hollamby was also keen to ensure that conceptual planning and architectural ideas were ambitious enough to fulfil the potential of the area, and that service provision was of an adequate scale to meet urban design opportunities.

Consequently, the Gosling, Cullen and Hollamby study concentrated upon those areas under the LDDC's greatest control – the 'public realm' of streets, squares, parks, water, quayside and riverside. The authors' proposals sought to integrate these civic elements with utility services such as transport on the one hand, and aesthetic matters such as style, materials, vistas and conservation on the other. Central to their approach was the concept of 'visual structure' which was employed as a means of interlocking the various components of the plan. The visual structure was based upon a community circuit following the old perimeter road network, and subdivided into nodes of activity. To link the sides of the circuit together the authors proposed a new central node formed at Glengall Bridge, an existing crossing on the northern arm of Millwall Dock. These nodes and linking routes which were to form the basic perceptual structure were then related to the water areas in a fashion which sought to maximize their townscape drama. The intention was to build up what the authors called 'compression and atmospheric release' based upon contained and open vista views across the water. Weaving through this broad development framework, Gosling, Cullen and Hollamby proposed a scenic and tourist route which again was more perceptual than real and which sought to link the Greenwich axis to the Dock Gate entry on West Ferry Road via Glengall Bridge.

As a result, certain sites carried more prestige than others and placed a civic responsibility (too great in the end to bear) upon developers and the LDDC. Though the authors recognized that the corporation's commitment to 'an unusually flexible planning policy' made any suggestion of a rigid design guide self-defeating, they did sketch out a number of possibilities showing how they felt the area should develop. One should remember that at the time of the report (1982) nobody harboured development ambitions nearly as substantial as those subsequently entertained. The report raised the currency of urban design by indicating an urban rather than suburban scale and a dense network of spaces as against openness. What is most attractive about their proposals is the way ideas are presented as a combination of Cullen's characteristically lucid thumbnail perspectives and a variety of plans, all supported by a terse text.

The report was not adopted by the LDDC. As a guide to design and development opportunities on the Isle of Dogs, it was felt too prescriptive for a corporation perhaps over anxious to appear flexible in its response to proposals. A close reading of the report does, however, suggest that certain ideas which have become common currency in Docklands have their origin in the proposed guide. First, the guide advocated formal treatment of the rectangular dock basins. The idea of picturesque groupings was discarded in favour of strict geometries and deliberate symmetry. Cullen's earlier work, especially the analysis in his book *The Concise Townscape*,[3] suggests a certain Englishness of urban design, yet on the Isle of Dogs all is formal and in the European manner. Second, the guide employs much arcading around the base of buildings – arcades which are related (as in the proposals for the Millwall Arcade) to shops, restaurants and galleries. Though the scale is quite different, Canary Wharf adopts a similar arcade as does Swedish Quays at Greenland Dock. Third, the report emphasizes the value of conservation even to the point of suggesting that the scarcity of worthwhile historic buildings confers on them an important role in defining and sustaining the integrity of the Isle of Dogs.[4] As we have seen, conservation has been an important aspect of Docklands regeneration even if the scale of protection has been meanly defined. The guide introduced the idea of conservation being a matter of maintaining the integrity of places, and providing an element in future spatial restructuring.

Putting aside the free market climate of development which marked the years 1981–5, subsequent policy initiatives emanating from within the corporation have tended to move closer to the Gosling, Cullen and Hollamby proposals. Ironically, it has been the developers themselves who have adopted elements of the design framework of this abandoned report. The proposals for Canary Wharf for instance by G. Ware Travelstead in 1985 had a pattern of enclosed and open waterside spaces, and the masterplan by the Richard Rogers Partnership for the Royal Victoria Docks employs well defined nodes and a linking circuit.

There is, however, one noticable weakness in the study. By concentrating upon 'visual appraisal' and 'townscape structure' the emphasis was on visual aspects of urban design at the expense of practical issues such as transportation, land use and parcelization. Although the earlier study by Gosling (with the assistance of Edward Hollamby) had tackled such issues in general terms, the subsequent report was noticeably reluctant to engage in major strategic issues. Neither did it address questions of social or cultural building provision; the Isle of Dogs apparently was to have no schools, libraries, hospitals or theatres.

Development without a framework

The broad urban design policies outlined in Chapter 4 became the basis for development control on the Isle of Dogs. In reality even these guidelines were often ignored, especially within the enterprise zone which makes up the core of the area. Free market aesthetics led naturally to free market urban design with a corresponding diminution of the public realm. The principal elements of continuity were not urban elements but landscape details such as red brick roads and areas of planting. In spite of the efforts of Gosling and Cullen, urban design as a means of coordinating development and establishing standards of quality was unable to push its way to the forefront of the political agenda. This highlights the then prevailing sanctity of private enterprise and the appropriation of the public domain for corporate expression.

Other commentators have noted the weakness of the LDDC's argument regarding the need for almost total flexibility when matters of urban design were under consideration.[5] The primary concern of the LDDC in the period up to Canary Wharf was what type of development could be attracted to the Isle of Dogs and how much. In the meantime commentators began suggesting a number of urban design strategies which could be adopted for the area. That by Peter Davey attracted much attention.[6] Davey's argument drew upon the term 'capital web' as devised by David Crane at the University of Pennsylvania, which was concerned with using public investment in infrastructure (roads, public transport, civic buildings etc.) to order private development. The capital web covers all public investment (above and below ground) and seeks to structure parks, buildings, streets and spaces according to the rational needs of infrastructure provision. The weakness of the argument concerns the lack or underprovision of public investment on the Isle of Dogs; a capital web here would not have enough substance to order such a diverse area. As a result the bigger developments on the island have become the capital web investment by default.

The arrival of the ambitious proposals for Canary Wharf in 1985 led to a change of attitude within the corporation. Such development could no longer ignore issues of urban design and social impact, and the developers themselves wished urban design guidelines to be prepared for adjoining areas. As a result in 1988 David Gosling, Stephen Proctor and John Ferguson were appointed by the LDDC to prepare a masterplan for the redevelopment of Heron Quays immediately to the south of Canary Wharf. Heron Quays was then only five years old and contained a colourful collection of low rise commercial buildings whose economic viability had been undermined by the arrival of new neighbours.

Gosling, Proctor and Ferguson adopted the basic rules of beaux arts site planning as introduced by SOM at Canary Wharf. Their plans deal with massing, shape and sun angles, not with questions of land use or functional details such as parking and pedestrian access.[7] The general grouping of buildings and the stepped rooflines respond to the development at Canary Wharf just across the water, and the introduction of towers provides a necessary backcloth to that by Cesar Pelli. In fact, the proposed massing is so close in spirit to Olympia and York's proposals that one could be forgiven for thinking SOM were again the master planners. Revised proposals a few months later by Gosling Associates and Paul Hyett Architects for the LDDC introduced welcome stylistic departures. Now circular drums are placed at critical corners, and the art deco ziggurat effect is watered down to make a break with Canary Wharf. However, as with Canary Wharf a deep floor plate (900 m² in the tower elements) made elegant high rise architecture difficult, judging by the published proposals.[8]

As a result of these mini masterplans the Isle of Dogs has been redeveloped on the basis of fragments. The various major projects at Canary Wharf, Heron Quays, South Quay and Harbour Exchange have become like well structured islands in a sea of permissiveness. The resulting environment in the early nineties had what the book *Collage City* calls a 'predicament of texture'.[9] The urban joins are by no means smooth; each of the large developments appears as an island without the benefit of a connecting causeway. As separate building projects each is fine in itself, but the intents and meanings are essentially private and inward looking.

Prince Charles has said of the Isle of Dogs that it represents the triumph of commercial expediency over civic values,[10] but this is largely what the 1980 Act sought. The prime task of regeneration has been achieved; in fact, Prime Minister John Major said in 1991 that the 'results far exceeded our original expectations'.[11] Urbanism on the Isle of Dogs is not coherent or articulate; the lack of a single unifying principle means that buildings are pursuing many ends, with the bigger developments generally unrelated and sometimes contradictory to each other. Deregulation has produced a landscape of happy if competing pluralism. Though this may be a universal trend in contemporary architecture, within the enterprise zone the lack of a unifying grid of streets or civic spaces has resulted in an urbanism where the disparate elements are no longer legible and do not contribute towards a satisfactory urban whole. The lesson is that large development transplants, individually conceived, lack coherence within the wider currency of the city and undermine its welfare.

Hellman's cartoon 'Doglands' shows the popular perception of the Isle of Dogs.[12] It is a city of post-modern skyscrapers with the ground filled by security guards and fighting dogs. The enterprise zone is called an enterprise zoo, and much is clearly unsavoury. Since this cartoon appeared in 1989 official attitudes have begun to change; there has been some recognition that urban design is an essential bridge between government policy for the inner cities and the design objectives of those providing the buildings. In fact, we may have to thank Docklands for providing an unassailable case for the necessity of urban design guidelines and – dare I say it – urban design vision in the regeneration of the inner cities.

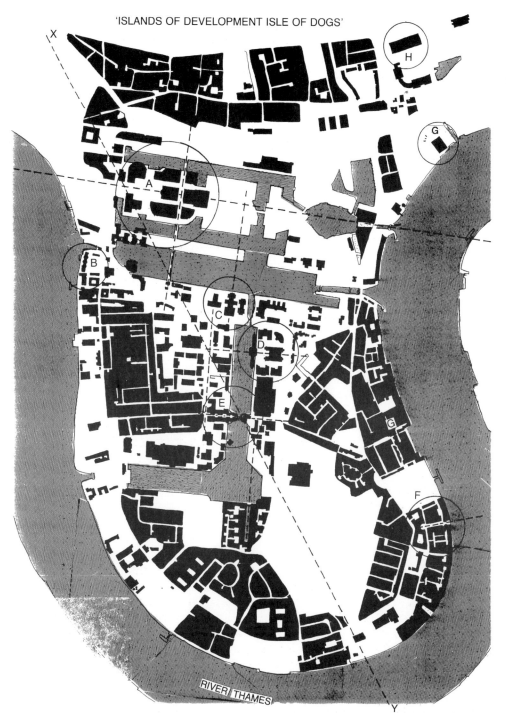

'ISLANDS OF DEVELOPMENT ISLE OF DOGS'

RIVER THAMES

Figure 5.4

Islands of development on the Isle of Dogs. This figure ground plan shows the main islands of distinctive character built since 1981. Each island has its own meaning, intent and development axis, but collectively they fail to aggregate into a satisfactory whole. (A) Canary Wharf (B) Cascades (C) South Quay Plaza (D) Harbour Exchange (E) Glengale Bridge (F) Compass Point (G) Reuters (H) Financial Times

The Isle of Dogs is a pertinent lesson in the key factors which undermined urbanism in the Thatcher years: the dominance of the car, the moral imperative of corporate interests over public ones, and the trend towards large scale, single land use development. With no civic vision other than to regenerate, the LDDC has produced a new office city for London where in the early nineties 50 per cent of the property lay empty, only 10 per cent of the jobs created had gone to local people, and investment in roads had exceeded that in housing and environment put together.

Figure 5.5

Doglands' (Louis Hellman)

Canary Wharf

Canary Wharf represents the single greatest development achievement by the LDDC, and stands today as an emblem of regeneration in the heart of the Isle of Dogs. The agreement by Olympia and York in 1987 to build a 12 million ft² scheme of office towers and lower blocks of mixed retail and commercial use changed the perception of Docklands almost overnight. Until then the Isle of Dogs was seen as a rather suburban collection of light industrial buildings and somewhat Los Angeles-like glass office blocks. Canary Wharf made the area at once urban and desirable, in spite of the inadequate means of getting there. Canary Wharf is the most conspicuous of several recent developments which have allowed the LDDC to promote Docklands as an emerging 'Wall Street on the water'. It also, critics have suggested, personifies the New Right approach to urban regeneration which places development enterprise well above the imperative of planning.

Canary Wharf sits astride the old water basins of West India Dock and extends on a roughly east/west axis to the Thames at West Ferry Circus. It takes full advantage of the enterprise zone established here in 1982. This gave Olympia and York a capital allowance of 100 per cent of the construction costs to be set against UK tax liabilities for a ten year period, plus exemption from property rates for the same period. It has been estimated that the cost to the public purse of these subsidies is about £1.33 billion, assuming construction costs of £4 billion and corporation tax at 33 per cent.[13] Putting aside these fiscal considerations, the fifty storey Canary Wharf scheme is seen as a major vindication of government policy for the inner cities. There are, however, massive consequences in terms of social, environmental and transport provision which have yet to be addressed and may yet stretch government enthusiasm for the approach. Judging urban renewal by city landmarks, the Isle of Dogs can hardly be bettered, even if the principal achievement of Canary Wharf is rather more corporate citadel than part of the public realm. It is no coincidence that the Minister for the

Figure 5.6

Canary Wharf. This huge development by the Canadian developers Olympia and York is well handled in terms of the management of external space, but it is a commercial citadel within the open landscape of the Isle of Dogs rather than part of the public realm (photo: LDDC)

Inner Cities, Michael Portillo, was present at the topping-out ceremony of the tower.

Olympia and York were not the first to see the development opportunity of the West India Docks. An earlier developer, G. Ware Travelstead with the First Boston Consortium, had presented ambitious plans in 1985 for a commercial megastructure on the site, but unlike the Reichmann brothers he had failed to persuade the business community to back the plans.

What Olympia and York achieved when they acquired Travelstead's interests, including the master plan and most of the architectural imagery, was to form a link in public perception between their Canary Wharf scheme and the success of London Docklands as a whole. The tower should be judged as evidence of this link – a kind of physical manifestation of the regeneration of London Docklands. Before Canary Wharf the expectation was for some 8 million ft² of office space on the Isle of Dogs. After Canary Wharf the figure leapt to 25 million ft² as a result of this particular scheme and the encouragement given to other developers. The effect has been to increase the office supply in London by about 20 per cent.[14]

As a single development Canary Wharf promises to create some 50,000 jobs which will eventually diversify land uses on the Isle of Dogs and help break down the reliance upon council housing within this part of London. Both are cornerstones of LDDC policy and desirable objectives in terms of enriching the local environment. All major single land uses create a supporting pattern of more diversified activity around their edge, which generally leads to a more varied and interesting architecture at the periphery. To some extent Canary Wharf recognizes this tendency and seeks to provide 750,000 ft² within the site for a mixture of shops, theatres and restaurants needed to support an office development of 12 million ft². What the Canary Wharf development conspicuously lacks, however, is any serious attempt to integrate such land uses vertically (the diversification is concentrated on the lower two or three floors) and to provide housing within the scheme. Hence the 50,000 workers will need to travel daily from their homes, with all the consequent traffic jams, crowded trains and unnecessary energy use typical of modern London.

In order to provide a measure of land use diversity, Olympia and York acquired the eastern half of Heron Quays immediately to the south in 1989. The initial intention was to build a hotel and about 1000 houses, but revised proposals in 1991 consisted almost entirely of office space. Designed by the Boston-based architects Koetter Kim, the current plan is to build three towers linking across the increasingly scarce water areas of West India Dock. Although housing is now proposed at Port East (to the north) and facing the Thames, the loss of residential areas near the core of Canary Wharf may lead to the central spaces becoming dull and dangerous outside office hours.

The idea of an integrated development with varied activities and different built forms was apparently never seriously entertained by Olympia and York or the LDDC. In this regard Canary Wharf is an example of the late modern city block as against the new 'green' integrated development philosophy of the emerging post-industrial age. Canary Wharf may prove the last throw of a typically twentieth century building type rather than the opening of a debate into the urbanism of the twenty-first century.

The Canary Wharf masterplan

For all the problems of poor access and disconnected townscape it is difficult to find a finer site in Europe for a major development. West India Dock consists of a peninsula of land sandwiched between two large stretches of water just south of a range of Victorian listed warehouses by George Gwilt which provide a welcome barrier to the disjointed district of Poplar. The site now extends to the Thames to the east (earlier proposals were limited by not establishing formal contact with the river) just where the river bends to focus upon Tower Bridge and the City of London behind. The site is flat and surrounded by water, and has a character determined by a mixture of brooding cranes and warehouses, distant housing blocks and the haunting presence of the Hawksmoor churches. As a backcloth for urban redevelopment, few sites in London offer such potential for architectural display.

Canary Wharf is vast by any measure: the site extends to 71 acres, which is larger than London's Green Park. The 12 million ft² of office space is divided into twenty-four separate buildings, each designed by a different architect within the constraint of a master plan and elevational proposals prepared principally by Skidmore Owings and Merrill of Chicago. As formal planning permission was not required for the development no impact appraisal was carried out, but to their credit Olympia and York (and Travelstead before them) issued a comprehensive set of plans and views

Figure 5.7

Canary Wharf perspective sketch. The Canary Wharf proposals of 1986 were accompanied by views of breathtaking beauty. This view from across the Thames shows how the development was intended to look on completion (photo: Olympia and York)

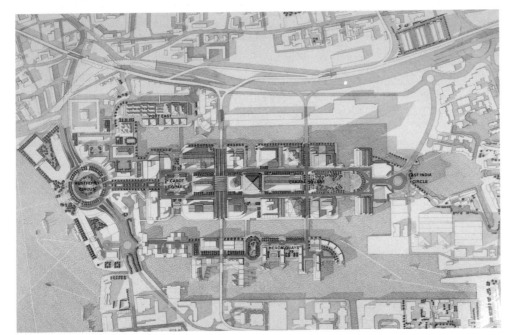

Figure 5.8

Canary Wharf masterplan. The masterplan by the American designers Skidmore Owings and Merrill has a well orchestrated play of solids and voids, but notice how the water areas are now encroached, and how poor the connections are with the wider landscape of the Isle of Dogs (photo: Olympia and York)

Figure 5.9

Figure ground comparisons at Canary Wharf. The relationship between buildings, land and water changed markedly after international developers found the site attractive (A) 1981 (largely unaltered since 1900) (B) G. Ware Travelstead plan 1985 (C) Olympia and York plan 1987 (D) Olympia and York plan 1991 (plan: author)

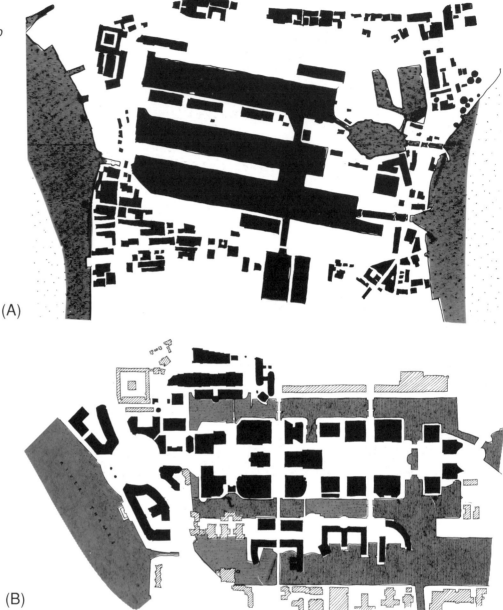

(A)

(B)

outlining the nature of the development. As is the case in Docklands, these are of breathtaking beauty and aimed at winning support for the development from potential tenants.

To ensure development conforms to the plan, design guidelines have been prepared which prescribe colonnades, arcades, courtyards of certain dimensions, setbacks, materials and street wall articulation. In effect Olympia and York have become the planning authority in an attempt to protect their own investment and generate a measure of public amenity. For these Canadian developers beaux arts urbanism provides an image of corporate well-being which draws upon Daniel Burnham's vision of the 'great good city' as outlined in the Chicago Exposition of 1883.[15]

Limits to the masterplan approach

That the layout has the indelible stamp of the beaux arts revival is hardly surprising given SOM's work elsewhere, but the degree to which the spatial components and the aesthetic ones are strictly regulated marks a new direction in British urbanism. Under the plan an avenue of Haussmann-like proportions links together a circle, a square and a double square and ends finally

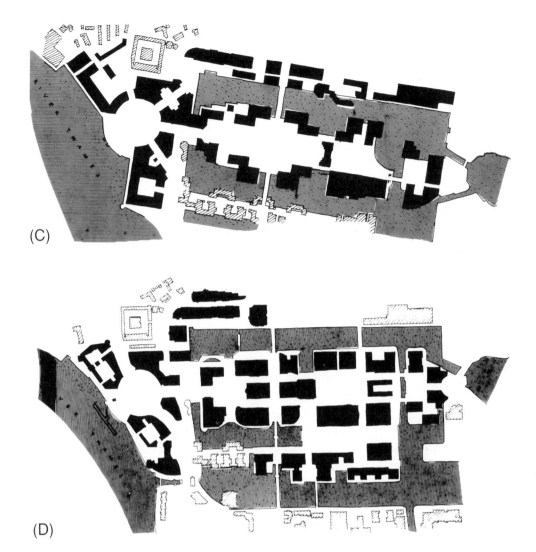

(C)

(D)

in a semicircle. Known respectively as West Ferry Circus, Cabot Square, Canada Square and Churchill Place, the geometries are as strict as in the most highly planned of Georgian developments. More interesting perhaps is the way space is squeezed between the different blocks just to open again on another square. Containment is the primary objective, achieved through an almost baroque composition, but at right angles there are framed views of the water. These mainly focus upon the old Gwilt warehouse to the north and Heron Quays to the south. These are, however, practically the only points where openness asserts itself; generally Canary Wharf is contained and inward looking and hence in the European urban tradition.

Though the central tower asserts itself through sheer bulk, Canary Wharf is almost two developments. There is the skyscraper world and the figure ground – the play of solids and voids experienced by the pedestrian. For all the benefits of its central, almost pivotal positioning, the tower is not well integrated. Sheer size makes the successful incorporation of this element almost impossible and the dominating presence of the tower spoils some of the delightful corners created, particularly in the Fisherman's Walk area.

If the spatial complexity is a tribute to SOM's ability to parcel up a big development into interesting smaller parts, then one is hard pressed to say

Figure 5.10

Tower of Canary Wharf. Though centrally placed the tower is too bulky to be adequately absorbed into the network of squares, crescents and streets created. It shows the incompatibility of the skyscrapers and the square as complementary urban units (photo: Brian Edwards)

the same of the aesthetics of the elevations of the buildings. There is a disappointing sameness in the treatment of façades in spite of a marked difference in materials. Marble, limestone, brick, steel and glass make up the bulk of the building materials, yet a similarity manages to permeate the development. This is the result mainly of repeating elements – round corner towers at the entrance to some squares, pedimented façades facing the Thames, window grid framing, and attic storey setbacks. The tendency towards variety which the use of different materials would suggest has not been adequately counterbalanced by a relaxation in Olympia and York's development codes. As a result Canary Wharf has a corporateness almost as marked as that at South Quay Plaza, and arguably at variance with the spatial complexity of the master plan.

Canary Wharf and the image of skyline

The intention of the Canary Wharf masterplan (as developed for both G. Ware Travelstead and the present owners) was to produce an integrated skyscraper centre as against an isolated tower. Though economic conditions may yet lead to Olympia and York abandoning the secondary towers, the long term success of the scheme demands a collection of towers to stand alongside the fifty storey, 800 feet central skyscraper by Cesar Pelli. This building is not interesting enough to stand as an isolated icon of Docklands regeneration; its profile is rather pedestrian and the use of colour is surprisingly drab, especially after the removal of the blue protective wrapping which adorned the tower in 1990. Compared with other recent skyscrapers, such as Philip Johnson's AT&T building in New York which is a mere thirty-two storeys, and the glass Gothic tower for the same site by Kohn Pederson Fox, the Canary Wharf tower hardly breaks new ground. The lack of a dramatic top and of any manipulation of the profile of the shaft of the tower suggests another bland glass and marble container of late modernism as against a full blown skyscraper of post-modern intentions.

Secondary towers when they occur will diversify the scene and bring a healthy measure of skyline competition to bear. From a distance the Pelli tower dominates the whole of east London and can be seen from the M25, 15 miles away. It stands as an independent monument in a flat and watery landscape. In an age when urban complexity and architectural variety are again valued, Canary Wharf seems a big missed opportunity. The architecture of technological advance and of the telecommunications revolution has produced a collection of buildings at Canary Wharf as undistinguished as the glass gridded boxes of corporate wealth the world over. If Docklands has pioneered a design revolution in the denser parts of Shad Thames, it appears relatively untouched by contemporary thinking further down the river. As a symbolic gesture towards a new skyline signature, Canary Wharf is undoubtedly disappointing and questions the assumption that design freedom produces monuments of distinction.

The proportions of the tower derive from a logical process of tenant need assessment and constructional dictates. The aim is to attract a major banking, insurance or government department to a building where the whole activity can be consolidated under one roof. The floors offer efficient and productive workspace with maximum flexibility to meet future changes in staff and technology. Relatively column-free floor plans, high performance service cores with raised floors and suspended ceilings throughout, and access to fibre-optic cabling make Canary Wharf one of the most expensive modern buildings in London. The commercial dictates of deep plan, high ceilings and great internal volume inevitably lead to an architecture of bulky proportions. Only height, rooftop profile and colour offer the designer much opportunity to make such architecture elegant.

As Canary Wharf is seeking primarily to provide London with high technology floor space for the new medium of electronic trading, the architecture

Figure 5.11

Domination of the enterprise zone by Canary Wharf. Unlike the perspective views of the full proposals, what has been built to date falls far short of the original intentions. With no other tall buildings to act as foil to the Pelli tower, the skyline of east London is dominated by its dull shaft. Skyline competition here would greatly enhance the scene. The view also shows the ignored Greenwich axis (photo: LDDC)

will naturally assume the appearance of office buildings in the other two world financial centres of New York and Tokyo. Hence Canary Wharf has assumed the skyscraper proportions of the international market place, not the less demanding requirements of a typical office block in the West End of London. Comparisons must be drawn with developments such as the World Trade Centre in New York, rather than local schemes such as Broadgate or London Wall. Architectural critics quick to condemn Canary Wharf fail to set the project into an appropriate context.

The masterplan and the public domain

If the tower of Canary Wharf appears to lack the necessary panache for such an important development, the remainder of the development carries a greater sense of responsibility towards the expression of a public purpose. The spaces created and the perimeter block arcades enrich the Isle of Dogs environment. Though there is a tendency towards the citadel approach, the feeling of a semi-private fortressed world of massive commercial blocks is relieved by handsome circuses, squares and tree lined avenues. Individuality exists to a degree: the employment of different architects for the separate blocks has allowed the development of measured variety within the straight-jacket of the beaux arts inspired masterplan.

The scale and complexity of Canary Wharf are unprecedented in British urbanism. Two strategic decisions were taken at the outset to maintain control of the development. First, the masterplan approach was adopted since this helped coordinate the spatial, aesthetic and infrastructural needs. Second, Olympia and York acted in a joint capacity as developer, project manager and subsequent building owner. Hence the developer had an interest in quality, not because of the short term benefit of profit on sale, but because of a long term need to ensure that the project attracts tenants. In a sense both parts of the package were dependent; the masterplan created confidence at the outset, allowing Olympia and York to fund the scheme, and established a datum for subsequent phased developments whose timing can reflect the whims of the market. It also provided a measure of environmental consistency between the parts.

Current urbanism is concerned with questions of quality and variety. There are elements of diversity within the fairly rigid parameters of the Canary Wharf masterplan. The finishes of the blocks vary from brick to stone and glass to steel with a corresponding difference in transparency or monumentality. But Canary Wharf is not the kind of place which appears to have grown up over generations; it looks like an instant city built out of permanent, timeless and universal materials. Hence we have a contradiction: the urban form employs the eternal truths of streets and squares, and the buildings have the tripartite subdivisions of classicism. Yet this is not Georgian or Edwardian London, but the new London of the telecommunications revolution. Purists may argue that modern functions such as trading floors and banking services require an appropriate architecture (such as the Lloyd's Building by Sir Richard Rogers, which freely expresses contemporary technology in the heart of the City) as against the conservative image of Canary Wharf. The architectural taste of the scheme is no doubt aimed at potential tenants, the very people who find the Lloyd's building difficult to come to terms with. Yet architecture can be monumental but employ a classicism of rather greater wit and inventiveness, as Philip Johnson and Robert Stern have demonstrated in recent American projects.

Around the edge of the scheme, walkways provide public access to West India Dock past places named after English architects (Nash Court, Wren Landing etc.). Here the buildings are constructed directly out of the dock and hence there is a Venetian proximity to the water. Though the water area has been squeezed by an expanding Canary Wharf, the move towards an irregular profile around the edge of the development has benefited urban design. Instead of parallel edges, the dock now contains 'rooms' of space, promontories of buildings and slots of water. This brings a complexity to bear in plan, and has encouraged variety and richness to appear in elevation. Though the master plan dictates an overall order, local richness is still possible, especially when architects such as Allies and Morrison, Troughton McAslan and Aldo Rossi are involved. These three firms, all noted for their urban interventions, are each developing a different water's edge building at Canary Wharf. It may yet be possible for diversity to develop within the spatial and elevational controls of the SOM master plan. Olympia and York's development director Tony Coombs, the Australian architect and former planning officer for Toronto, feels that the success of Canary Wharf depends upon the creation of an urban whole which is well structured but offers detailed variety.[16]

The need to diversify or further enrich the master plan led to the appointment by Olympia and York of Fred Koetter in 1990. As we saw earlier in this chapter, his book *Collage City*, written with Colin Rowe, argues for urban complexity based upon informal, accidental and abstract relationships. Normally the processes of history lead to visual diversity, but when a major development proceeds from scratch the tendency is towards repetition and monotony. Koetter will no doubt seek greater land use variety, the establishment of diagonals to break the rigid geometries of the master plan, and more elevational richness, particularly near ground level. One element which could be exploited concerns moving historic fragments of Docklands buildings or large industrial artefacts into the squares of Canary Wharf, thereby breaking down the overwhelming scale and providing a foil to the gridded elevations. Happy collisions and rich layerings which are the basis for collage cannot, however, easily be imposed upon a predetermined plan.

The development process at Canary Wharf

The structuring of Canary Wharf depends upon concise and firm prescriptions which are embodied in the master plan and the development agreement between Olympia and York and the LDDC. The development is parcelled into twenty-four units; each parcel has a set of design guidelines that regulate use, height, massing, relationship of walls to public space etc. Development which conforms to the guidelines does not require LDDC consent, but departures and adjustments must involve specific LDDC approval. Architects working within these prescriptions enjoy only limited freedom to innovate.

Olympia and York see the Canary Wharf development as a district plan, a kind of privately generated framework for creating a new district in the sense of Lynch's *The Image of the City*.[17] The various buildings create the public (or semi-public) network of streets and squares which are then developed to a high standard in parallel with the construction of the buildings. Coombs likens the process to the making of eighteenth century London where the squares were built first, thereby establishing the quality and credibility of the estate.[18] At Canary Wharf the key elements of skyscraper, central spine street, squares and riverside crescent are to be the flagships of the scheme. These will, it is hoped, create a critical mass of commercial viability, and lead to the completion of the project.

The appearance of Canary Wharf reflects fairly accurately the process of construction. Olympia and York have applied their own form of 'fast track' construction developed initially in the company's First Canadian Place project in Toronto (which included a seventy-two storey tower) and perfected at their World Financial Centre in New York. It consists of a concise erection process which rigidly segregates the lifting tasks of cranes and hoists. Under this method of construction one crane is only allowed to lift steelwork, with the result that the steel erectors are never short of material and left idle. In parallel, toilets and canteens are moved up the building as construction proceeds, thereby saving delays as workers wait around for lifts.

Construction proceeds logically: the steelwork goes up first; only three floors below the concrete floors are being poured; three floors below that the ducts are being formed; and again three floors lower the walls are being erected. Hence one team of erectors or constructors cannot slow down without jeopardizing the whole project, and this apparently concentrates minds wonderfully. It depends upon three important factors: first, the employment of a compliant workforce; second, a guarantee that materials will always be available on time; and third, weather that will permit safe working at such height. The last has proved one of the stumbling blocks to early completion; steel erectors are not permitted to work when wind speeds exceed 45 m.p.h., and in the winter of 1989–90 such days nearly outnumbered those worked.

Many of those employed on building Canary Wharf are drawn from the international labour force. The constructional managers are American, some of the technical staff German, and many of the labourers Irish, Scots or East Enders. The project is claimed to be the largest single business development in the world, and the tower alone contains 27,500 tonnes of steel – nearly all provided by British Steel. Construction posed considerable problems. As the ground is a former dock, major piling was required, and the bolts needed to hold the tower to the base are 16 feet long and 3 inches in diameter.[19] Wind loading allows for a sway factor of up to 9 inches, and as the tower is constructed of steel such movement is more easily accommodated than with a concrete frame.

At the height of construction the site team numbered about 4000, with some of the workforce having been specifically trained by Olympia and York. As such, Canary Wharf is both a building and an education in the skills required for modern construction. Not surprisingly such a building exeeds the capacity of local suppliers to provide the components. Over a hundred countries have provided the materials, with marble from Italy, stone from Canada, toilet pods from Holland and cladding panels from Belgium and the USA. The internationalism of the design team (Canadian developers, American, Italian and British architects and engineers) is more than matched by the cosmopolitan nature of the building supply manufacturers and workforce. One day when construction definitely does not take place, even when work is behind schedule, is the Jewish Sabbath from sunset on Friday till sunset on Saturday. In a way this reflects the spirit of Canary Wharf – a modern fusion of high technology and traditional values by a company which is one of the largest owners of commercial property in the world.[20]

Canary Wharf does, however, highlight the conflict between two approaches to urban design. The sequence of streets and squares is in the formal European tradition of town planning, whilst the buildings, and particularly the central skyscraper, are American in spirit. French urban classicism is not happily infilled with Manhattan styled office blocks. The two great traditions of Western architecture – the square and the skyscraper – are apparently seeking a marriage at Canary Wharf. The results suggest the inherent incompatibility of the two approaches: the square contains space by urban mass, whilst the skyscraper is an object in space.

There is a further problem with regard to urban design. The natural tendency towards land use and spatial control exercised by Olympia and York has meant that civic interests are protected by private developers not public ones. Small scale private control poses few problems, but when projects take on the grandiose proportions of Canary Wharf, conflicts of interest can occur. As Kevin Lynch has pointed out, 'behind the concept of big architecture is a wish for big control'.[21] The propensity for control extends across the large estate of Canary Wharf and increasingly beyond. Olympia and York, like the Butlers Wharf Company across the river, have assumed quasi-planning powers. One could argue that this is to fill the vacuum left by the demise of the local authorities under the 1980 Act, but the consequence for urban design is to encourage corporate ambitions to dominate civic ones.

Heron Quays

The conflict of scale between the first and second waves of regeneration in London Docklands is nowhere more marked than at Heron Quays. The familiar red pitched steel and glass office sheds designed in 1982 by Nicholas Lacey now face demolition after a mere decade of life. The presence of Canary Wharf just across the water has elevated land values and architectural expectations to the point where Lacey's buildings look absurdly underscaled. Pleasant and skilfully detailed as they are, these buildings may soon be replaced by dramatic curved towers designed for Tarmac Brookglade by Scott Brownrigg and Turner (SBT).

These towers would make a welcome change from the rather staid skyline, evolved more through corporate economics than design skill, that has marked the regeneration of the Isle of Dogs to date. The twin sail-like towers are linked at dock level by a five storey podium of offices, shops and restaurants which reach out across the water of West India Dock. The design of the towers was developed by Ove Arup and Partners and tested by Oxford

Figure 5.12

Heron Quays. Built in 1985 by Nicholas Lacey, Jobst and Partners, Heron Quays are underscaled when seen alongside their massive new neighbours and face redevelopment after less than ten years of life (photo: Brian Edwards)

University's Wind Engineering Group. Their unusual profile has ruffled some feathers amongst architectural critics (especially the Royal Fine Art Commission), who appear as worried about the loss of Lacey's red sheds as about the impact of the new buildings on the skyline of London.

Since the design of the towers demands aerofoil booms at their bases to shelter pedestrians from updraughts, the requirement has been used as justification to pull the buildings daringly across the water. This has allowed SBT to exploit the water's edge for sailing and other purposes, and gives the scheme a welcome nautical air. In fact, the goosewing shapes are made more sail-like by the inclusion of much steel cabling near the ground. Like the shell shaped roofs at Sydney Opera House (also developed by Arup's London office), this building could become a more appropriate symbol of a regenerated Docklands than the other towers nearby.

Slightly lower than the Pelli tower at Canary Wharf, the SBT scheme rises to 180 metres. It too exploits the design freedoms of the Isle of Dogs enterprise zone but in a more daring fashion. The structural complexity of the proposal is not hidden from view, and neither are the opportunities for interesting vertical movement left unexploited. Cable cars are planned to climb the edge of the sails, providing dramatic means of access to the restaurant at the top of the tower.

The project, which at the time of writing remains a controversial proposal, will provide nearly a quarter of a million square metres of accommodation within two towers – one of forty-six storeys and the other of thirty-six storeys – and a podium. Though considerably smaller in volume than Canary Wharf, the project can only add to the congestion at West Ferry Road. But for all the extra strain placed on an inadequate infrastructure, the new sail-like towers will prove a welcome foil to the dull pillar shaped skyscraper at Canary Wharf.

Figure 5.13

The Tarmac Brookglade plans for Heron Quays. These dramatic sail-like towers designed by Scott Brownrigg and Turner and engineered by Ove Arup's office offered the opportunity of diversifying the skyline of the Isle of Dogs. The LDDC apparently has reservations about the viability of the design (photo: Scott Brownrigg and Turner)

South Quay Plaza

The offices for *The Daily Telegraph* at South Quay Plaza represent the first major development in Docklands in the style of modern classicism. The style was popularized by American architects such as Robert Stern and has found increasing favour on this side of the Atlantic with corporate clients. For them it represents the right blend of sharp, crisp, progressive architecture and traditional values. Modern classicism offers some escape from the glass gridded façades of anonymous corporate architecture; it suggests the re-emergence of individuality even if, as at South Quay Plaza, the classicism is rather more token than real.

Perhaps this is unkind; the classicism here developed by Seifert Ltd Architects deals in an abstract language, not in obvious classical elements such as entablatures and cornices. A site layout based upon geometric formality, well articulated building entrances and a pronounced *piano noble* makes for a classicism easy on the eye. Where pediments are employed they tend to terminate long street axes such as that placed at the north end of Millharbour, or establish a civic scale by facing across the water. If the figure ground layout is symmetrical, the use of pediments placed slightly off centre adds variety and wit to buildings which are of necessity repeating bays of blue tinted glass, polished marble and steel.

South Quay Plaza was the first building on the Isle of Dogs to accept its urban, as against suburban, responsibilities. The jump from two storey business units to the eighteen storeys employed here in 1985 was almost as marked as Canary Wharf's escalation of the skyline to fifty storeys in 1990. What began as an independent building for *The Daily Telegraph* had by 1991 developed into an ensemble of towers of similar style. As they share a common vocabulary, the sense of corporate neighbourhood is pronounced; and as each building reflects the one opposite, the townscape has a surreal quality.

Figure 5.14

South Quay Plaza. This group of related office buildings designed by Seifert Ltd changed the Isle of Dogs from a landscape of low rise business units to one with urban aspirations (photo: Seifert Ltd)

The employment of a pronounced distinction between base, middle and top is the starting point for most designs in the modern classical style. Though the language of classicism is broadly handled, the syntax remains strong. The wide stone base provides accommodation for restaurants, bars and shops; the office floors above are of a repetitive grid of glass and steel; and the attic storey sits behind a deep band of polished granite which establishes the cornice. Taken as a whole the buildings read as a group with framing elements of stone providing visual support for the pediments. With imagination one could view the group as the Isle of Dogs *agora*, each tower masquerading as a temple with the squares between providing space in theory at least for public gatherings. And as the squares are open to the dock and linked via steps to a water's edge footpath, the feeling is one of civic rather than purely private values.

Parking is predominantly below ground or within the plinth behind the perimeter envelope of cafés and restaurants. As elsewhere in Docklands, arcading at the base of the building provides some interest for the pedestrian, but at present insufficient activity is generated to bring the arcades truly to life. The finishes are admirably sturdy: blue engineering brick paving, granite edges and tinted glazing make for a pleasant contrast to those areas under municipal control.

The Docklands Light Railway snakes by the development at high level. At this point the DLR negotiates a near right-angle turn between West India Dock and Millwall Docks, thereby affording close and varied views of the building's glazing. From the deck of South Quay station, some ten metres up, the spectator has a fine view of the surrounding architecture which at this point is dominated by the Seifert building. Unlike the *Financial Times* printing works, South Quay Plaza does not allow penetrating views through the glazing. The reflective glass repeats the pattern of the sky rather than reveals the workings of newspaper publishing.

For all the strengths of a broadly composed classicism, South Quay Plaza lacks sufficient variety to sustain lengthy examination. The competency of the scheme is its underlying virtue – competency in detailing, massing and site organization. The three towers have become part of the skyline of east London and for a couple of years, before the arrival of Canary Wharf, dominated this area of Docklands. In a way South Quay Plaza raised the stakes of the Isle of Dogs; it made an urban architecture both possible and subsequently inevitable.

Cascades: the rediscovery of the tower block

Cascades is a building which does two unusual things for Docklands: it celebrates through quirky architectural form a fine site on the edge of the Thames, and it transcends the usual aesthetic limitation of the tower block. The design of Cascades was prepared for Kentish Homes (who have subsequently gone into liquidation) by CZWG. The building is an attempt to rediscover the tower block after it fell out of favour during the 1970s. Critics quick to condemn high rise living on inner city sites (as against city centre) may well ponder on the social as well as aesthetic success of this project.

Figure 5.15

Cascades. The nautical connotations are obvious in this high rise apartment block facing the Thames by architects CZWG for Kentish Homes (photo: Jo Reid and John Peck)

The site is practically surrounded by water and, from the water buses which now ply the Thames, Cascades looks rather like the prow of some misshapen ocean liner. The south elevation of the block sweeps down at 45 degrees between penthouse apartments on the rooftop and sports facilities on the ground floor. By sloping the south elevation, CZWG open the building to sunlight, not just in plan but in section. The apartments facing directly on to the slope have long, thin cabin-like rooms which end in terraces slotted between angled walls. Here and elsewhere in the block, nautical references abound – not just in the use of porthole windows and funnel vents, but more fundamentally in the way the building is composed. By stepping the section and grading the accommodation almost between first, second and third class passengers, Cascades looks more akin to the QE2 than a block of flats.

Architecture by this practice is as much about expression as about function. Cascades takes the idea of outwardly expressing interior activity to the point where the building begins to fragment. The walls twist and bend as if the ship was being battered by a storm. A sense of angularity reinforces the feeling of fragmentation, and a quirky disregard for order is expressed in the joyful change of building materials and colours. Where most designers treat the balcony as a repeating element, CZWG allow it to grow as it rises through the rooftop.

Cascades is a framed building, though it looks superficially to be built of load bearing London stock brick. There is, however, no denying the frame some expression; it breaks through the brick façades periodically to give the merest hint of modernist orthodoxy. Like much of the architecture of this practice, the language of forms and details derives its inspiration from both contextual references and the buildings of the thirties. Cascades has been described as a B movie, an object to fill time before the main film is shown. But if the principal movie is Canary Wharf then, as in many trips to the cinema, the supporting film outdoes the big picture.

Cascades is quintessentially the architecture of the yuppie years. As a building it does not aspire to be a great work, simply an entertaining place to live and an easy piece of scenery. Rather effortlessly, the building slots 164 one, two and three bedroomed flats into a yellow and white blend of ziggurat, silo and ocean liner.

By angling the external walls Cascades has become a multifaceted building of shallow bays. These do not all rise to the rooftop but stop at various heights, thereby forming balconies at different points on the façade. The plan of the block is therefore full of zigzags, with the walls dividing the rooms placed at different angles. Such invention makes for interesting and individually distinctive apartments. Even the fire escape has a characteristic quirkiness: it is placed on the diagonal running down the south elevation and ends (at least visually) in the swimming pool.

As an urban building, Cascades exceeds the limitations seen already in certain high rise blocks in Docklands. It addresses the sky and the water in a quite unique fashion. The tendency towards picturesque handling of the various elements suggests an Englishness of approach. One can trace its roots back to the stylish inter-war apartment blocks of certain coastal towns and even to Lutyens a generation earlier.

If Cascades has rediscovered a neglected typology in Britain, the lesson should not be lost upon local authorities. What this building teaches is that as a housing type the high rise block is by no means obsolete. There are lessons here for those building residential tower blocks, and also for those engaged in the refurbishment of existing high rise buildings. For Cascades could be a model, not of a new building, but of a drastically redesigned existing one.

Financial Times printing works

Printing works and newspaper offices are among the most conspicuous new buildings of Docklands. They are not, however, all as distinguished as the

Financial Times printing works on the edge of the Isle of Dogs in East India Dock Road; neither do they display their inner functions with such alacrity. Designed by Nicholas Grimshaw and Partners, this printing works continues a fine tradition in Britain of modernist newspaper offices established by Sir Owen Williams in the 1930s. Williams, more engineer than architect, applied a consistent black glass aesthetic to a number of newspaper buildings – *The Daily Telegraph* (1928), the *Daily Express* (1931) and the *Glasgow Herald* (1936). They all adopted the latest technology in an unassuming fashion, whether in the form of smooth glazed façades or highly serviced interiors. Grimshaw's building should be seen as maintaining this tradition in an age which has reduced the printing works as a building type to the limited ambitions of almost any other modern factory.

As a newspaper the *Financial Times* has long campaigned for higher standards of design in industrial buildings. Through its own award scheme and now via direct patronage, the *FT* has demonstrated that the architecture of the printing works can rival any other in producing factory buildings of high aesthetic appeal. That it has done so on an unassuming site in east London right alongside the approach to the Blackwall Tunnel is fairly remarkable. However, more to the point, the *Financial Times* has demonstrated that freedom from design control within the enterprise zone need not result in nondescript or tasteless buildings.

The *Financial Times* printing works was only possible with the introduction of new printing technology in the late 1970s. As with the movement of the printing presses of *The Times* to Wapping in 1978, and *The Guardian* and *The Daily Telegraph* to other locations on the Isle of Dogs in the early 1980s, new technology has led directly to a new architecture. By separating the editorial staff from the printing workers, the new buildings of the newspaper industry have become less urban building types (in the sense of the Fleet Street offices) and more rather poorly designed factories. This building is an exception to the general rule.

The practice of Nicholas Grimshaw and Partners is noted for structural invention and a certain rigour when designing the assemblies of the various

Figure 5.16

Financial Times printing works. Tucked away near the approach to Blackwall Tunnel, this building employs a contemporary modernism appropriate to the building's function (photo: Jo Reid and John Peck)

components which make up modern architecture. At times inventiveness may appear to overrun more normal concerns for human scale and sensitivity to local context (as witnessed by their Sainsbury's supermarket in Camden Town), but here constructional prowess and elegant detailing make an appropriate response to the task of producing a building for the printing of one of Britain's quality newspapers. There are no issues of scale or townscape to clip the wings of Grimshaw's imagination; this is a building happy in its industrial context and confident enough of its workings to show them off to the world.

The building sits parallel to East India Dock Road (here the A13) just behind an unprepossessing security fence and strip of landscaping. The entrance and car park are behind so that the building appears uncluttered at the front, thereby avoiding any conflict with what John Winters calls the dramatic view of the presses at work.[22] At night the sight is undeniably impressive, a kind of science fiction world of automated parts, bright colour and barely peopled activity. The façade fits the part too; it has the air of a missile hanger complete with aerofoil shaped columns, diagonal wind restraint struts and 2 metre square panels of toughened glass separated by the thinnest black silicone joint. The glass wall detailing has a NASA-like quality, the unrestrained transparency giving views of the three storey printing presses which look almost like spaceships undergoing servicing from the lightweight staircases which criss-cross behind the façade.

Grimshaw made a wise decision to make the long façade mainly transparent where it faces the main road. The images employed may be high tech, in fact almost Archigram inspired, but the use of the street for public display was a brave decision. Elsewhere in Docklands the street is relegated to a mere access channel, but here the building addresses the street and opens its inner activities to public gaze without reservation. One only wishes the entrance too had faced the main road so that public façade, main entrance and architectural display could have been part of a more logical progression.

The building makes play of transparent and solid parts. As a printing works there is much storage of paper, and large areas of the plan are required for service zones. Two approaches have been followed. The main storage areas are placed at either end of the building and are clad in profiled aluminium set behind thin extruded bands which recall the horizontality of the Williams newspaper offices. The detailing here is seamless and refined with no doors or windows allowed to interrupt the elegant lines. The service areas, including stair towers, are detailed quite differently. They project from the face of the building and introduce a verticality to act as a foil to the long low lines elsewhere. Windows are slotted into the towers which are now smoothly clad in aluminium and end in soft gentle curves. The towers are outside the perimeter of the main printing works in order to provide future servicing flexibility, and to act as markers to identify entrances.

By having the glazed central areas within solid end sections (formed by the storage areas), the building departs from other high tech predecessors such as Foster's Sainsbury Centre outside Norwich which has highly glazed gables. The press hall occupies the main south facing glazed area (as offices do on the north side) within an uninterrupted eaves line 16 metres high. The solid ends give the appearance of buttressing the transparent centre which extends for 96 metres. The scale is less large than at *The Times* building at Wapping, but more heroically handled. By employing an 18 metre clear span, subdivided into 6 metre columned bays along the glazed façades, the building has a stature larger than that suggested by its dimensions alone. As in much of Grimshaw's work a modernist rigour has resulted in a building which merely highlights the limitations of the work of other architects producing buildings for similar clients.

Not far away the Richard Rogers Partnership has produced a building of not dissimilar philosophy for the news agency Reuters. Again structural

Figure 5.17

The Reuters building. Designed by the Richard Rogers Partnership, the Reuters building has a robust industrial aesthetic in keeping with the traditions of the area. The building is part of a high tech enclave in the east of the enterprise zone (photo: LDDC)

Figure 5.18

Pumping Station, Isle of Dogs. Not far from the Reuters building, the pumping station by John Outram gives exuberant expression to the design pluralism of the Isle of Dogs (photo: Brian Edwards)

honesty, the external expression of services, and flexibility of operation underpin the approach to design. Again too an uncompromisingly modern aesthetic of industrialized materials faces the derelict landscapes of the Isle of Dogs. Unlike much of London Docklands, the decay and fragmentation of an old industrial area has resulted not in neoclassical business enclaves or bright, colourful and overbrash factories, but restrained and sophisticated buildings for clients who recognize the value of good design.

Notes

1 David Gosling, Gordon Cullen and Edward Hollamby, *Isle of Dogs: A Guide to Design and Development Opportunities* (1982), paragraph 1.4.

2 *Ibid.*, Introduction.

3 Gordon Cullen, *The Concise Townscape* (Architectural Press, 1971).

4 Gosling *et al.*, *Isle of Dogs*. p. 21.

5 Colin Davies, 'Ad hoc in the docks', *Architectural Review*, February 1987, and Brian Edwards, 'Docklands the story so far,' *Building Design*, 19 June 1987.

6 Peter Buchanan, 'What City?', *Architectural Review*, November 1988.

7 The proposals are illustrated in *Architectural Review*, April 1989, p. 40.

8 *Ibid.*

9 Colin Rowe and Fred Koetter, Collage City (MIT Press 1978). p. 50.

10 Erla Zwingle, 'Docklands: London's new frontier; *National Geographic*, vol. 180, no. 1, July 1991, p. 46.

11 *A Decade of Achievement 1981–1991* (LDDC 1991), Foreword by the Prime Minister.

12 *Architectural Review*, April 1989.

13 *The Docklands Experiment* (Docklands Consultative Committee 1990), p. 19.

14 This figure was given by Barry Shaw in his lecture on London Docklands to the Urban Design Group in Liverpool on 20 September 1990.

15 Brian Hatton, 'The development of London's Docklands', *Lotus International*, no. 67, 15 December 1990, p. 57.

16 Tony Coombs, 'City ventures', The Kevin Lynch Memorial Lecture, given to the Urban Design Group, London on 21 June 1990. See *Urban Design Quarterly*, no. 36, October 1990, pp. 19–23.

17 Kevin Lynch, *The Image of the City* (MIT Press 1960), pp. 66–72.

18 Coombs, 'City Ventures'.

19 Rodney Tylor, *Canary Wharf: the Untold Story* (Olympia and York 1990), p. 13.

20 *Ibid.*, p. 23.

21 Kevin Lynch, *Managing the Sense of a Region* (MIT Press 1980), p. 49.

22 John Winters, 'Glass wall in Blackwall', *Architectural Review*, November 1988, pp. 42–50.

Surrey Docks

6

Development background

Of the four development zones in Docklands – Wapping, Isle of Dogs, Royal Docks and Surrey Docks – the last best represents the area's variety and richness. Surrey Docks extends along the south side of the Thames from London Bridge almost in the heart of London to Bermondsey and Rotherhithe. The area is managed on behalf of the LDDC by the Surrey Docks area team based within converted premises off Lower Road well to the east of the prosperous areas around Tower Bridge. As such the main focus of corporation activity has been on the poorer areas, near Surrey Commercial Docks. The strip of land just below London Bridge (usually referred to as the Pool of London) has received relatively little attention from the LDDC; regeneration here has not required much assistance in the form of LDDC grants, or a highly structured master plan to guide developers.

The richness of Surrey Docks is a measure of both the area's social diversity and its townscape variety. Perhaps the most attractive street in the whole of Docklands – Shad Thames – is found here, as is Docklands' best area of Thamesside walkway which extends from London Bridge City to Butlers Wharf and after much interruption to near Greenland Dock. Socially the area contains apartments costing over £1 million near Tower Bridge to council flats of decidedly mean proportions. Commercially too there are great contrasts: London Bridge City near Tooley Street contains much high specification office space, whilst just two miles away local industry is more likely to be a motor bike repair yard.

The diversity of the area has discouraged any attempt at structuring the regeneration. As elsewhere in Docklands there is no urban design framework but there are masterplans to guide the redevelopment of specific areas. The regeneration of the area between London Bridge and Tower Bridge has progressed according to a footprint plan prepared in 1982 by Twigg Brown and John S. Bonnington Architects, and Greenland Dock by way of a more highly structured masterplan drafted in 1984 by Conran Roche. Generally speaking, however, masterplans have been eschewed and regeneration has been market-led and rather opportunist in nature. As a result the area is one of the great contrasts: suburban styled housing estates stand alongside handsome apartment blocks of contemporary European inspiration, and smoothly clad commercial architecture sits adjacent to converted warehouses and mannered post-modern offices. In terms of landscape design the ecological park near Stave Hill brings an almost Olmstead-like fascination with natural greenery to the heart of the area, and this corridor of naturalness extends to the formally treated Thamesside embankment.

These largely pleasant contrasts overlay great social and cultural diversity. The familiar Cockney dialect is never far away and neither is the resonating beat of local reggae bands. Redevelopment of the Thamesside has brought a crust of wealth to Surrey Docks, but the hinterland remains largely untouched except where the long fingers of redundant docks push their way inland. Of these Greenland dock is the largest and, like most of the former basins (some sadly infilled), is placed at right angles to the Thames. Such orientation has encouraged arms of middle class housing to push their way into neighbourhoods once of solid working class character. Such contrasts are more marked in Surrey Docks than elsewhere in Docklands, and are one of the main reasons for the area's vitality.

If the want of an urban design framework has led to problems, not least in terms of protecting the approaches to Tower Bridge and certain distant views,

Figure 6.1

London Bridge City phase 1 from the air. This aerial view shows the sliver of land between London Bridge (on the right) and railway lines on which was formed one of the earliest commercial developments in London Docklands. Known as the Pool of London, the upper reaches of the Thames never suffered the same level of economic decline as further afield. This view shows the irregular pattern of development which stemmed from the retention of listed buildings, and is the main reason for the areas's attractive character today (photo: Chorley and Handford Ltd)

the opportunities for contrasting strategies to urbanism have been grasped with relish. This is best illustrated by a walk from London Bridge along the embankment to Tower Bridge and then beyond to Shad Thames. The area contains a mixture of new buildings and old, of new buildings seeking to look old, and others daringly new (the contrast between London Bridge City phase 1 and phase 2). Old buildings where they occur have been faithfully restored or refreshingly modernized (for example Hays Galleria). When the new buildings do not look obviously new (even the Design Museum looks like a 1930s *moderne* restoration) and the old buildings not obviously old (besides Hays Galleria one could cite the Courage Brewery), a healthy ambiguity creeps into the urban scene. Hence the new pluralism and ambiguity of the 1980s finds better expression here than elsewhere in Docklands, though one cannot suggest that this is merely the result of having no coordinating aesthetic strategy for Surrey Docks. The contrasts and complexity of the area are the result of a largely different kind of developer, many of whom harbour small scale ambitions, and seek to redevelop confined or difficult sites, employing often younger design practices. Whilst London Bridge City may be an exception to this general rule, even the need here to preserve historic buildings and respect the old curving line of Tooley Street has resulted in better architecture than across the Thames.

The empiricism of Surrey Docks stands in contrasts to the free market philosophy of the Isle of Dogs and the heavily engineered and largely landscape-led regeneration of the Royal Docks. Only Wapping across the river shares a similar pragmaticism in its approach to place making, but here a scarcity of design talent and the more limited opportunities for developers have resulted in a less satisfying environment.

Another price, however, has had to be paid for abandoning any strategic thinking with regard to urban design in Surrey Docks. Older neighbourhoods have not been well integrated into much of the regeneration. Old and new areas often exist apart with only weak connections being established between them. This is most marked in the Surrey Commercial Docks area just south of Rotherhithe Street. Well established neighbourhoods of council and private housing existed well before the arrival of the LDDC but the new road system, shopping centre and walkways established since 1981 fail to connect adequately with those already in existence. For example, at Greenland Dock new housing estates face away from older residential areas to form a middle class enclave. Similarly the shopping centre at Canada Water (which includes a major British Home Stores) fails to link in with the pattern of older shops along Lower Road and New Road. What connection exists has been dictated by borough council highway engineers, not urban designers. Hence, there is only a weakly extended pattern of land uses, building forms and human interactions. Discontinuity is the price paid for such shortcomings and, though it has its own aesthetic charms at times, becomes unsatisfactory when it is the norm.

Where landscape design has been employed to make both the environmental and social connections it is often attractive, at least in detail. The Thames embankment and riverside walk reappears in Surrey Docks with a frequency rare elsewhere in Docklands, and is robustly detailed. Near Hays Galleria the embankment in polished granite and setts provides a popular lunchtime gathering space for nearby offices and both the lamp standards and seats are a real asset to the area. Further afield a tree lined riverside walk links together new housing projects which line the Thames opposite Canary Wharf. Around Greenland Dock and Canada Water a brick paved walkway threads its way around the perimeter of old dock basins and via a canal (known as Albion Channel), and establishes at least an element of civic order within a rapidly reurbanized area. Attractive as these landscape features are, they are only (at present at least) casually connected to the wider and older system of pedestrian routes and parks.

The Upper Pool and London Bridge City

Of the 25,000 new jobs created within Surrey Docks by 1991, the LDDC estimates that about 12,000 are in the London Bridge City and Butlers Wharf area. Employment here is mainly in the financial services, computer and retail fields, and contrasts with the 3000 less skilled jobs in light industry and printing created on the Surrey Docks peninsular.[1] These simple statistics reflect well the various architecture of the area – prestige offices in the west and low cost industrial parks in the east.

The broad development framework

The architectural form of the high specification office building is already becoming familiar in London, and those buildings of this genre in Docklands are by no means exceptional. Compared with say London Wall or Broadgate, London Bridge City hardly breaks new ground, but the blend of old and new buildings tightly packed together on a strip of land facing the Thames makes for an attractive townscape. They key ingredients of this townscape were established in 1981 by a development plan prepared jointly by architects Twigg Brown and John Bonnington Partnership. The general masterplan specified a footprint of building blocks and public spaces, the retention of a number of listed buildings, the establishment of an embankment, and the construction of a gateway building alongside London Bridge at the west entrance to the site. Most interestingly the plan also included the establishment of a public park immediately alongside Tower Bridge on land gifted by the St Martin's Property Corporation to the borough council. The latter was

Figure 6.2

London Bridge City phase 1 from the Thames (photo: St Martins Property Corporation Ltd)

designed by the John Bonnington Partnership and Sasaki of the USA as an extention to the William Curtis Ecological Park.

The geometry of the site – a thin wedge between Tooley Street and the Thames lying between London Bridge and Tower Bridge – encouraged incremental development from west to east. In fact at the time of writing the large site known as London Bridge City phase 2 lying directly opposite the Tower of London remains undeveloped following a protracted planning inquiry. Further west the sites were smaller and less contentious, allowing development to proceed unhindered by concerns of impact upon national heritage sites.

The footprint plan for the area established a fine network of pedestrian routes through the site. A riverside walk follows the Thames in the form of a grand embankment (not unlike that created by Sir Joseph Bazalgette at Westminster in the 1870s) and a low level walkway threads its way through the site parallel to Tooley Street. Between the two a series of access roads and glazed atria provide attractive connections to the various buildings. The area can be likened to a sliced fruit cake with the various portions distributed slightly unevenly on a wedge shaped platter. What is important is that the spaces between the portions are never very large, and the cake itself consists of a rich mixture of ingredients such as St Olaf's House, a fine art deco office block of 1932 by Goodhart-Rendel, Hays Wharf with its robust Victorian warehouses, and a variety of modern offices. Hence spatial complexity is well balanced by historical layerings within the built elements.

London Bridge City Phase 1

The design of the different buildings reflects contemporary concerns for site context and public amenity. The gateway building alongside London Bridge for instance is splayed at the corner to give a view of the Thames from the bridge approach as well as open up a vista of St Paul's from within the office. Pedestrians are taken through this grand archway rather than around the edge of the building, and even if the scale is daunting the intentions are commendable. Rather than employ a single block the building is split into two granite clad prisms, thereby allowing sunlight to penetrate over the roof to the atrium on the Thamesside walk. This also allows the gateway block to balance Adelaide House at the north end of London Bridge. This is an expensive building by Docklands standards, costing (in 1984) £23 million for 25,500 m² of accommodation.

The retention of existing buildings further east, such as the conversion of Chamberlain's Warehouse alongside St Olaf's House to form London Bridge Hospital, has not only broken down the scale of the redevelopment but, more importantly, established reference points for new buildings. Between the hospital and Hays Galleria, Twigg Brown have designed a large office building which subscribes to a general roofline established by the older neighbours (at least on the Thamesside). The building also employs generous glazed entrance halls and these link through to the atriumed spaces of neighbouring buildings. Consequently one can walk through London Bridge City on a rainy day enjoying a succession of generously proportioned glass rooms each providing glimpses across the Thames.

Hays Galleria is a splendid space formed by the roofing over in glass of the former inlet between two brick built warehouses. The gallery is tall and robustly detailed and follows the gentle change of angle between the older buildings. At the Thames edge the paving surface drops down to indicate the watery history of the space, and to reinforce the point a large sculptured ship stands stranded on the public concourse. Shops and bars line the perimeter of the space and stalls prey upon passing tourists. The warehouses themselves have been so totally refurbished that they could easily pass for recent constructions, an impression reinforced by the unsatisfactory rooftop extensions.

London Bridge City phase 2

After a short interruption alongside *HMS Belfast* moored offshore one approaches the site of London Bridge City phase 2. For the Kuwaiti owned St Martin's Development Company, phase 2 has been a far less smooth path to commercial redevelopment than phase 1. The problem has been one of proximity to the Tower of London and the size of the development. Phase 1 of London Bridge City consisted of smallish parcels of development sandwiched between existing buildings many of which were listed as being of special architectural or historic interest. In phase 2 the wedge between Tooley Street and the Thames has widened and nothing stands in the way of blanket redevelopment. This may not in itself have proved a difficulty were it not for the presence of the Tower directly across the Thames.

The role of monuments in the city as physical and historical landmarks requires that their bulk continues to dominate the lesser structures round about. The three principal architectural monuments in London – the Tower, St Paul's Cathedral and the Palace of Westminster – have all struggled to maintain their premier position within London's townscape. The Tower of London, being relatively low, dominates more through breadth and bulk than skyline. Hence buildings nearby, or directly across the water as in this case, should be designed as smallish units within a bigger backcloth of general townscape. The role of commercial buildings is to frame the Tower and not to bully it by overassertiveness. The ground area of the proposed London

Figure 6.3

Shopping mall at Hays Galleria. The glazed arcade spans what for a century had been a dock serving the warehouses on either side of this view. The resulting galleria is one of several glazed routes through this part of Docklands (photo: Brian Edwards)

Figure 6.4

London Bridge City phase 2 proposal. This view from the Tower of London shows the riverside walk and pedestrian routes through the development. Buildings are shown arcaded and with a clear hierarchy reflecting their status (photo: John Simpson)

Bridge City phase 2 was even larger than that of the Tower of London, and without clear height controls the development could have overpowered its older neighbour across the river.

The first design was prepared by the American architects Philip Johnson and John Burgee in a strangely internationalized Jacobean style not unlike a computer abstract of the Houses of Parliament. The scheme was low and broken into separate pavilions linked by squares and promenades. It was, one suspects, an attempt by Johnson and Burgee to appeal to English taste and to respond to the Gothic outlines further up the Thames. The development did not enjoy a great deal of support even amongst those who usually find Johnson's work thought provoking. Aware that Johnson and Burgee's design, which had been 'called in' for determination by the Secretary of State for the environment Nicholas Ridley, was unlikely to win planning permission, the developers asked two further architectural practices to draw up proposals. When the planning inquiry was finally heard the inspector had three designs to choose from – that by Johnson and Burgee, one in the modern style by Twigg Brown and one of Venetian cum Palladian inspiration by John Simpson. The inspector's recommendation, upheld by Chris Patten the new Environment Secretary in 1990, was to favour the Simpson design.

All three designs subscribed to the same footprint plan and broad design guidance issued by the LDDC. Though Simpson's design was lower and denser in character than either Johnson's or Twigg Brown's, the choice was largely one of architectural style. That questions of the design of a Thamesside façade should concern a minister ought to dispel the myth that government leaves such matters to market forces. Even here on this rather privileged bank of Docklands, the hand of government chose a Venetian replica to face a Norman castle – a measure of the retreat of orthodox modernism. Much further upstream Quinlan Terry has classicized the river-front at Richmond, and Simpson again promises to to the same around St Paul's following the rejection of the sweeping geometrics of the modernist plan by Arup Associates. The new pluralism increasingly evident in London's contemporary architecture will have enjoyed a boost by Patten's decision.

Simpson's design at London Bridge City offers the prospect of bringing the craft of building back to London streets. Although a professed classicist, Simpson is also interested in traditional building construction, especially the rather English craft of brickwork and stucco-work. The design flies in the face of the contemporary practice of fast track construction. These buildings will consist not of a steel frame clad with clip-on panels, but of real load bearing brickwork and structural stone columns. One is reminded of Augustus Welby Pugin's book *Contrasts* published in 1836, which set favourable views of London in medieval times alongside unfavourable Victorian ones from the same point.[2] Simpson does almost the same but gives modern Britain not a Gothic cloak but a classic one. One cannot talk of Simpson without mentioning Prince Charles, who shares a similar vision of London and who was instrumental in securing Simpson's services at Paternoster Square adjacent to St Paul's.

The Palladian or even Vitruvian logic of Simpson's elevations should not disguise the likely mismatch between the technology of classical construc-tion and that of high specification offices. As Terry found at Richmond, modern office space is highly serviced and makes demands upon the placing and size of windows. Securing a correspondence between the inside and the outside of such buildings is by no means simple, though one should add that the life of office interiors is generally much shorter than that of the exter-nal fabric of the building. Simpson and other modern classicists such as Leon Krier would argue that the lasting architecture of the building façade is more important than the transient architecture of the interior, and to seek a correspondence is a waste of time.

Simpson's buildings are restricted to six storeys in height, and most sit above an arcade which follows the Thamesside and central square not unlike the Piazza San Marco. An almost free standing campanile rises above the square and acts as a focus to the internal public spaces and a marker for the scheme from afar. Unlike the buildings in phase 1, there are no atria here, simply squares and internal courtyards. Facing the park a market build-ing is employed as a substitute for a shopping centre. Since the office build-ings are generally low and shallow in plan, they offer the prospect of maximum use of daylight and natural ventilation. As such, for all the criti-cism made in architectural circles of Simpson's approach to design,[3] the scheme draw its inspiration from a period of humanist values and low energy consumption. It may yet prove a lasting addition to the Thamesside landscape and another showcase for the design museum that Docklands is fast becoming.

Tower Bridge, Butlers Wharf and Bermondsey

The area immediately below Tower Bridge is amongst the most interesting in Docklands. Here old and new buildings stand side by side in happy communion. The large brick built warehouses establish a scale sympathetic to the modern offices and apartment blocks, and the functional character of the area is in tune with contemporary design aspirations. If London Docklands has created an environment of richness anywhere within its nine square miles, then the neighbourhood around Shad Thames is surely the most successful.

The attractive character is the result of a wide range of land uses squeezed into a tight network of narrow streets and watery creeks. So much

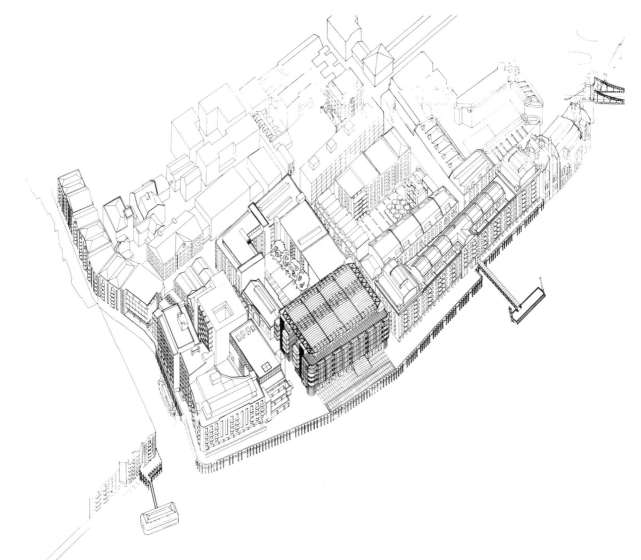

Figure 6.5

Butlers Wharf axonometric view. This drawing by Conran Roche shows the mixture of new and old buildings at Butlers Wharf. St Saviour's Dock is on the left and Tower Bridge is visible on the right. The old buildings establish a clear context for the design of the new (plan: Conran Roche)

survives of the old warehousing days when the area was famed for the storage of tea and spices and the production of beer, that the new buildings have had to fit into the spaces left over. As a result the scale of new buildings has been kept fairly small (unlike at London Bridge City) and the ratio between historic structures and modern construction is attractively balanced. Nowhere do the listed warehouses aggregate into enough fabric to recall a Dickensian reconstruction of old London, and neither do the new buildings swamp all in sight as at St Katharine's across the river. Here the balance is about right, and to walk through the area around the Design Museum is as pleasant a trek through contemporary urbanism as any in Europe.

The reason for such a successful townscape is largely a rigorous approach to adapting and conserving listed buildings. The old brick warehouses are not always beautiful but they have much urban character, and some, though plain on the outside, contain structures of interest within. The retention of these buildings, and the opening of new river views by selective demolition, have established not only a context for much new design, but also relatively small parcels of land for redevelopment. As a result smaller and more enterprising developers have been attracted to the area, such as Andrew Wadsworth who at the age of 23 began acquiring warehouses and sites, and later Sir Terence Conran of Habitat and the cutlery designer David Mellor. Only after the first wave of regeneration had been completed did big companies such as Rosehaugh spot the opportunities. Heritage, therefore, shaped the area and has ensured a pleasant mix of land uses as well as an attractive pattern of buildings.

So strong is the character of the area (much incidentally lies within Tower Bridge and St Saviour's conservation areas) that modern buildings have been able to express themselves in a truly contemporary way. The dominating presence of yellow brick (yellow at least after cleaning) warehouses, and the industrial machinery often mounted on their façades, has provided a robust urban framework for new buildings which have varied from white Bauhaus-like cubes to blue circles and red cut-out gables. It is an approach to urban infill which would not look right in Bath or even Westminster, but here in tough and rugged historic Docklands the resulting environment has great diversity and character.

That so much good townscape has been achieved without a strategic plan is initially worrying. No urban design framework was felt necessary since the area was already well urbanized at the onset of LDDC operations in 1981, and because developers with sympathetic proposals appeared almost out of the blue. Regeneration has proceeded on an *ad hoc* basis with redevelopment or restoration spreading eastwards from Tower Bridge and inwards from the Thames frontage, reaching to Jamaica Road by 1990.

Generally speaking the length of river frontage between Tower Bridge and St Saviour's Dock was regenerated between 1983 and 1989, and east of the dock immediately after. Since so many splendid warehouses were listed and unused, the first action within the area sought to bring these back into mainly residential use. Sir Terence Conran first spotted the potential of the largely unloved and ill-treated buildings immediately below Tower Bridge. Earlier plans had been to demolish the brewery buildings and warehouses facing the Thames in order to carry out comprehensive office redevelopment. Conran was no doubt influenced by Andrew Wadsworth's conversion of New Concordia Wharf facing St Saviour's Dock which in 1983 was the first major warehouse conversion this side of the Thames. In 1984 Conran formed Butlers Wharf Limited in order to acquire 5 hectares of mainly riverside property containing some seventeen different buildings. Conran's approach was unusual for a major developer in Docklands: his revitalization strategy sought to preserve the buildings and maintain the former street pattern. By controlling so much, Conran and his partners Jacob Rothschild and Lord McAlpine imposed their conservation-led approach to regeneration upon a huge area like some latter day Medicis. English Heritage and the LDDC let these enlightened developers proceed largely unhindered by procedural considerations. It was a welcome breath of fresh air for Docklands which was becoming increasingly burdened with ever larger office buildings and cumbersome development agreements.

The philosophy of Conran and his architects was to only demolish when they were confident they could replace the old building by something better.[4] In this sense they took the 'preserve and enhance' aspect of conservation areas more seriously than most, with the emphasis upon the 'enhance' side of the equation. Enhancement was to be achieved by good modern design, and through the creation of new civic spaces such courtyards and riverside walks.

By owning so many of the buildings and by having regard to public amenity, Conran and his company have almost become the planning authority. They have directly or indirectly established standards of design and construction for others to follow, and by disposing of land on leases as against freehold the company has, like a traditional estate developer, kept control of the area. They have also promoted an element of mixed use in the different conversions, and have established quasi-public buildings such as the Design Museum. One could suggest Butlers Wharf Limited had become a small privatized planning authority were it not for the lack of affordable housing in the area.

There is, however, a danger in the approach – a danger increasingly common in British cities. The developer has acquired not only buildings but civic spaces including old streets and passageways. These have gradually

Figure 6.6

Shad Thames. The sublime character of Shad Thames has survived recent redevelopment thanks to the retention of the bulk of the old warehouses and their splendid bridges (photo: Conran Roche)

become private with access restricted at certain times. This is a problem not only around Shad Thames but at Queen Elizabeth Street where The Circle seeks, perceptually at least, to privatize a length of public road. The justification for these actions is one of increased security and enhanced territorial definition, but the resulting environment takes on the quality not of public spaces but of private strongholds. Where Shad Thames has remained open it has been partly roofed over, creating as at the Design Museum a grim tunnel through the centre of a big building. The building due west promises to add further to the urban eradication of this historic thoroughfare. Here Shad Thames will remain open but squeezed and decked over, thereby removing its canyon-like quality. It is a shame that the new buildings here have failed to respond to the sublime nature of Shad Thames which, to quote Edmund Burke in 1757, was the sensation derived from tranquil terror induced by the contemplation of great size, extreme antiquity and decay.[5] In fact not only have the new structures driven sublime character to the winds, but some old buildings have been moved altogether such as the grade 1 listed warehouse at Spice Quay now destined for a new site 100 metres to the south.

Butlers Wharf and restoration along Shad Thames

Shad Thames winds a slot-like path between high brick warehouses just a few metres from the edge of the Thames. It follows the lines of both the river and St Saviour's Dock, turning through a right angle within the heart of Butlers Wharf. The narrowness of this tortuous route reflects its ancient origins. The land here was once owned by the Knights of St John of Jerusalem, who lined the river frontage with mills and employed the meadows behind for grazing (hence the street name Horselydown Lane parallel to Tower Bridge Road). The Dockhead just beyond St Saviour's was the medieval site of Southwark Fair, and these ancient lanes (of which Shad Thames is the main survivor) provided cramped access through the riverside marshes.

The present buildings which form a cliff along the Thameside from Tower Bridge to Jamaica Road were built mainly in the nineteenth century. High, handsome and densely packed, these buildings are quite unlike the sanitized philanthropic housing built at about the same time just a little to the east. With no controls over daylight or the width of access roads these breweries, mills and warehouses grew into a Hong-Kong-like maze of interconnected structures. Goods passed by cart along the gantry bridges which today continue to sail over the streets, or were passed down the face of buildings via projecting hoists. Much of this character survives in the form of restoration or replication. For all the change of use and structural modification, Shad Thames is London's unofficial museum of dockside architecture.

The biggest building is Butlers Wharf itself, constructed in 1874 and converted to ninety-eight apartments most of which enjoy splendid views of Tower Bridge. The front and rear walls have been retained with much careful restoration (mostly on the advice of Donald Insall) but a new concrete frame has been inserted to allow the construction of a rooftop storey and basement car parking. Along Shad Thames the yellow stock brick façade with engineering brick dressings to the roadside openings has been retained, and the attractive cast iron bridges have been repaired, but on the Thameside the building has undergone great change. Viewing balconies have been added to the river frontage where loading doors previously existed, and here as elsewhere the original metal windows have been replaced by timber.

The approach is broadly speaking one of conservation, but the architects Conran Roche have taken a flexible view of the task of restoration. Along Shad Thames new entrance doors have been cut into the brick façade to give access to a number of hallways, felt necessary to avoid employing long internal corridors. These are well detailed, yet they are a far cry from the

original pattern of dark and gloomy windows. The shops and restaurants on the ground floor enliven the scene, but they too are departures from the original arrangement at street level.

Across the street a similar pattern of restoration is being undertaken, though here the original internal structure survives at least in part, and less alteration has been carried out facing Shad Thames. The wonderfully crafted iron bridges which sail across the street reinforce the perception of a united group of buildings. A consistency of approach helps to give the impression that these old warehouses are not separate buildings but a network of inter-connected structures adapted to a variety of new uses. In the process of adaptation one cannot help feeling they have been oversanitized or at least given too liberal a dose of Habitat good taste. Butlers Wharf is not so much the preservation of a group of buildings as their restoration to a rather ideal-ized and convenient version of the original.

Due west the old Courage Brewery presents arguably a happier picture of restoration. The architects Pollard Thomas and Edwards had a building of greater variety and interest than at Butlers Wharf. The approach was to retain the quirks and inconsistencies of the original construction, and to use these to make the restoration memorable. There was no need here to add any heritage bric-à-brac to the façades; the original designers and those who later had a hand in the building, such as Inskip and McKenzie in 1893–5, ensured the building had enough panache to stand alongside Tower Bridge.

Pollard Thomas and Edwards kept even the old Anchor Brewhouse chimney and added to the building's industrial character when ever they

Figure 6.7

Butlers Wharf. This view from across the Thames shows Butlers Wharf converted to flats. The new roof topstorey is unfortunate (photo: LDDC)

could. For example, the timber louvres at the top of the central brewhouse were replaced by smooth industrial glazing, thereby giving the building a decidedly modern appearance. At a cost of over £9 million, the architects have created sixty-two flats as well as offices and a health club in a fashion which has not compromised the spirit of the original.

Along the edge of the Thames individual buildings are well bonded bricks in a city wall. Another fine riverside warehouse is New Concordia Wharf across St Saviour's Dock. This was the earliest of the warehouses in the area to be adapted to residential use and established a standard of taste and technical excellence for later architects to follow. Andrew Wadsworth was the young entrepreneur who realized the potential and set about drawing up plans in 1983 using Pollard Thomas and Edwards. This long and relatively narrow warehouse looks across the green and murky waters of the dock with only a gable enjoying a view over the Thames. Balconies have been freely employed where loading doors once opened out from the riverside face of the building, thereby affording splendid views. The former wall cranes were restored with advice and grant aid from the Historic Buildings Council (now English Heritage) and other industrial features have been carefully repaired or occasionally replicated from evidence of Victorian photographs.

New Concordia Wharf is really a group of industrial monuments crowded around a narrow courtyard. Besides the warehouses there is a mill and water tower all of which have been restored and adapted to new uses. Unlike at Butlers Wharf the original structure proved capable of restoration, and thick timber beams and cast iron columns are a welcome sight in an area where conservation is often only skin deep. Commercial pressure did force Wadsworth to spoil the roofline with some incongruous conservatories, but the care and attention to detail won this project a collection of conservation awards.

The art of blending old and new buildings

The hard edge of Thameside warehouses is only significantly broken by the Design Museum. Contrary to first appearances, the Design Museum too is a restoration though the original structure is exceedingly well disguised. The building is yet another from the stable of Conran Roche and under the patronage of Sir Terence Conran. Some of the flavour of Milton Keynes is evident in this building – hardly surprising bearing in mind that the design directors Stuart Mosscrop and Fred Roche were both at the Milton Keynes Development Corporation before forming Conran Roche in 1981.

The Design Museum establishes a crisp modernist counterpoint to the rustic warehouses of the south Thames. It is both gleaming white and a stepped cube, thereby making direct reference to the international style. Its banded windows and thin balconies with sleek steel handrails all suggest a deliberate attempt to reincarnate the style of Le Corbusier. That so much architectural display has been created out of a 1950s three storey, concrete framed warehouse is itself remarkable, but that it stands amongst a crowded backcloth of listed brick warehouses is doubly so. For this building challenges the usual ethos of contextual design within conservation areas. The Design Museum makes no reference to anything in sight: it ignores the grain of historic Shad Thames, it refuses to be tall at the river edge and it disdains pitched roofs. It is as if the MARS Group (Modern Architectural Research Group) had won the intellectual argument in 1938 and spread the 'new architecture' across the face of London.

The Design Museum is a remarkable building bearing in mind the ugly cocoon from which it grew. Without any virtue or grace the concrete framed warehouse (known simply as Building 14) was transformed with the help of nearly £5 million into a modestly sized but elegantly conceived private museum. The building epitomizes the Thatcher years; this is a privately endowed museum funded on the basis of profits made in the retail field by

Figure 6.8

Design Museum. The White cubist architecture of the Design Museum stands in pleasant contrast to the retained brick warehouses nearby. Stylistic conformity is not always the best solution within conservation areas. The sculpted head is by Eduardo Paolozzi (photo: LDDC)

its principal benefactor. It is also peculiarly Thatcherite in that the objects on display are mainly consumer goods which masquerade as pieces of design rather than the products of consumption that they really are.

The stepped frontage to the Thames and the wide and generous river terraces continue the theme up river of the buildings of the South Bank. Where the Design Museum succeeds and the other examples fail is in the scale of the terraces and the activities which lie along them. At the Design Museum the terraces have become occupied and overlooked: they are truly outdoor high level rooms as the designers of the 1930s intended.

The public activities of the museum are grouped along the Thames edge with the study collection and galleries on the landward side. A central, well lit but hardly spacious stair links the two zones of the building and affords pleasant views across the river. In some ways the Design Museum is itself an exhibit and through juxtaposition with neighbours makes as telling a point about design ideas as the collection of historic Fiat cars inside. Docklands as a whole and especially this particular corner should be seen not as townscape but as an architectural museum where old and new buildings testify to changing tastes, technologies and functions.

The Design Museum and car park nearby make the only significant break to the hard edge of Thamesside warehouses, but behind lies an interesting collection of new buildings constructed on sites carved out from the dense mass of industrial buildings or adapted from their structural remains. One such by architects Allies and Morrison is known as the Clove Building and consists of another white modernist adaptation of a mid century concrete framed warehouse. Conran Roche acted as developer, employing Allies and Morrison to formulate the design philosophy. Borrowing from the Design Museum, their approach is rational, resourceful and mildly Bauhaus-like in the clarity of shapes and forms. The adaptation of the building into studios, offices and shops has opened up the daunting structure and allowed elements of the frame to become exposed to view from the public street. A clear distinction is made between wall, frame and circulation, and the various functions of the building each read with equal clarity.

Figure 6.9

Clove Building in Shad Thames. Another white modernist intervention into Shad Thames, this time by Allies and Morrison. The crispness of the building and its structural clarity makes it a worthy neighbour to the Design Museum (photo: Brian Edwards)

Figure 6.10

Vogan's Mill. The residential conversion of a grain silo by Michael Squire Associates provides a welcome vertical landmark in the area of low buildings (photo: Michael Squire)

Vogan's Mill across the inlet of St Saviour's Dock is another imaginative adaptation. The original building had functioned as a flour mill since 1813, though the bulk of the structure including a dominating concrete silo is of more recent date. Outside the influence of the Conran circle, this development was funded by Rosehaugh but designed in similar spirit by Michael Squire Associates. This is another white building inspired perhaps by Le Corbusier and his fondness for sculpted towers. Less restrained than the earlier examples, Vogan's Mill is another clever conversion of an awkward collection of industrial structures. The tower with cut-away corners and curving roof is a welcome addition to the skyline of this part of London, yet one wonders whether such an intrusion would have been permitted by an orthodox planning authority. These crisp white buildings only make the most tentative references to the brick warehouse character of the area. They stand as fresh and sharp modernist newcomers, admittedly often based upon earlier structures but essentially alien beings. This part of London gives a good foretaste of the type of townscape likely to be generated if the aesthetic aspects of planning control were to be totally removed.

Urban place making near Shad Thames

Another interesting newcomer is Horselydown Square by Julyan Wickham, which makes greater reference to the local context than the white cubes around the Design Museum. Wickham has created two courtyards and surrounded them with a rich mix of land uses (shops, offices and apartments stacked vertically into mainly five storey blocks) and each courtyard has a sequence of well used pedestrian spaces. One could easily be in Copenhagen or Munich, not just because of the variety of uses packed closely together, but also because of the love of colour and the rather idiosyncratic shapes. These buildings frame views and make happy joins with the listed warehouses, but they are not subservient structures trying to build unnoticed within a conservation area. This is assertive, confident, urban architecture which appeals more by bravado than cerebral considerations.

Horselydown Square was one of the first developments in the area to create urban spaces as against urban buildings. The public squares formed relate well to the wider pattern of pedestrian movement through the area and open up attractive glimpses of older buildings through the curved entrances. The square is well used and finely detailed, and makes a pleasant contrast to the squeezed passageways along Shad Thames. Urban

Figure 6.11

St Saviour's Dock. The narrow inlet of St Saviour's Dock is lined by a fine collection of brick warehouses, some gable ended to the water. Many have been converted to flats, others await such treatment. The iron water mounted cranes are an attractive feature and much sought after by the new residents as façade decoration (photo: Brian Edwards) place making requires a good understanding of the potential of the back of buildings; here Wickham Associates have formed squares by utilizing backlands and opening to view the rear of properties.

The willingness with which developers have created urban spaces in this area of Docklands should dispel the myth that planning authorities are the principal means of creating public amenity. Here in this relatively deregulated part of London a mixture of enterprising developers and architects aware of the urban dimension (as against simply the building dimension) has formed some attractive new squares out of a derelict jigsaw of dilapidated warehouses. The chief proponent of the new urbanism is Piers Gough of CZWG working mainly with Andrew Wadsworth. The Circle in Queen Elizabeth Street is their major achievement to date, though the Jacob's Island project further down river did for some time promise to bring an extravagant and expressive urbanism to the docks.

The Circle, is an extraordinary development of apartments, offices and shops grouped around a blue circus carved out of the surrounding townscape. After the confinement of Shad Thames and the busy squares of Horselydown, The Circle has a theatrical unreality. The decision to form a circular aperture in the heart of the city is both brave and unusual, but the choice of bright blue glazed bricks and a severe diagonal grid of metal windows coloured like fool's gold is characteristically outrageous. One

Figure 6.12

Horselydown Square. This development by Julyan Wickham creates urban spaces as much as urban buildings. The spaces are well used, articulated by flowing lines of balconies, and connect together in an intelligible fashion (photo: Brian Edwards)

Figure 6.13

The Circle. The extraordinary blue circus, equestrian statue and diagonally placed balconies are the focus of a development of more sober apartments, shops and offices by CZWG. The Circus has created a node of theatricality along what was once an ordinary London street (photo: Jo Reid and John Peck) cannot entertain the idea of such urbanism easily clearing the hurdle of planning permission elsewhere in London, but here the LDDC had no aesthetic qualms (in any case, the 1980 Act gave it no power of veto).

By forming a circle of space along the street, CZWG have effectively created a zone of territory which no longer feels totally public. With apartment blocks by the same developer on either side of the road, traffic has been restricted and casual parking curtailed. The circular space is now perceived as semi-private territory, though the public has the right to pass through unhindered. At night the area is floodlit, with residents keeping an eye on activities from their encircling balconies. What for a hundred years has been taken for granted as public territory, has become almost an outdoor private lobby to the surrounding apartments.

During the daytime The Circle is a wonderful space: the blue glazed bricks with the merest hint of purple cast a deep and satisfying hue across the surrounding surfaces. Because The Circle is complete, light is forever being reflected off one of the quadrants. In the centre stands a heavy and muscular equestrian statue whose mane and tail seem whipped by the wind. Hence, colour and light make this space immediately memorable and the dray horse gives it a necessary focus. It is perhaps one of the most haunting urban spaces created in Docklands, and in its way as daring an intervention as the much bigger squares and crescents at Canary Wharf.

The Circle is much more than a giant blue vase dropped into east London. The 300 apartments and occasional offices and shops are stacked into five storey blocks which hug the old street lines. By employing similar heights and the same yellow bricks as the old grimy warehouses, the new buildings blend effortlessly into the world of the old. Only the mannerist circus departs from well tried precedents; elsewhere in the development the architects play by the rules of the local context. It is a context explored with characteristic humour. The waving line of the rooftop suggests the presence of nearby water and the balconies are supported (at least visually) by large mast-like diagonal struts. Balconies are arranged diagonally across the façades, thereby giving the blocks a liveliness lacking in some of the housing built nearby. The warehouse vernacular is not slavishly copied, but reinterpreted and distorted.

What The Circle as a whole shows is that a modern addition to the architecture of the area needs to grow out of the building pattern and urban texture of the neighbourhood. In a sense the scheme follows the ten principles outlined by Prince Charles in his broadcasts of 1989. Here the concern for place, hierarchy, scale, harmony etc. are respected, and only the blue circus itself steps out of line. The lesson according to Gough is one of knowing when to break the rules and how extensive to make the modernist interventions.[6] In this development about 80 per cent of the buildings are revivals of the warehouse style; only The Circle is truly a departure, and hence it is absorbed without great effort into the Bermondsey townscape.

Colour and the local scene

Modern buildings in this area have treated colour in different ways. The Design Museum and Vogan's Mill are the most conspicuous of several crisp white buildings slotted into the spaces between yellow and brown warehouses. Their whiteness signifies modernity and makes a pleasant contrast to the burnt clays of London stock bricks. By way of contrast Horselydown Square uses terracotta, blue, pink and cream in an attempt to reflect the colours of earth and sky. Here the terracotta walls form solid almost geological buttresses to the development, whilst the blue trim of the circular windows suggests the chiselling away of the earthen shafts to expose the sky. Colour here is freely disposed and open to wide interpretation, but the use of bright hues is not alien to the industrial or nautical character of the area. The Circle also employs blue but here the colour is sharper and reflective. The source of the idea springs apparently from the indigo and purples dyes found in a nearby dye works and formerly spread across adjoining street surfaces. Such argument may give justification for so bright a colour, but here and at China Quay CZWG employ pure colour as an emblem of regeneration. The cheerful splashes of colour are in their way a symbol of change and a gesture towards a more optimistic future. Unlike the white boxes of Conran Roche, theirs is not a sanitized modernist future but one of fun and theatricality.

Much Dockland colour exists between the extremes of the whiteness of the Design Museum and the primary coloured façades of CZWG's work. The most common colour employed derives from the use of yellow and red bricks. As a result much of rebuilt Docklands is merging quickly into the local street scene. However, the commercial architecture and some of the buildings facing the water apply colour in a more deliberate fashion. Here paint, plastic and epoxy resin surfaces give the Thames edge and the buildings around Millwall Docks a cheerfulness lacking elsewhere in London. But the colours do not always relate to local traditions or even European urban precedents. The blue coated office blocks of the Isle of Dogs make reference not to Turner's paintings of the Thames or to colourful barges which once worked the area, but to the urbanism of Los Angeles. The greyness

Figure 6.14

China Wharf. Designed as a Thamesside landmark, this red apartment block is another by the indefatigible CZWG. Along with Vogan's Mill and the Design Museum, it establishes this length of the Thames as an open air museum of modern architecture (photo: Jo Reid and John Peck)

of the Canary Wharf tower also fails to make local references; this building recalls the silver greys of recent skyscrapers in New York. However, around Tower Bridge colour is employed with greater finesse.

Below St Saviour's Dock

Land prices quickly reduce east of St Saviour's Dock, and here housing of shared ownership and lower rents begins to make an appearance. The river edge continues to contain expensive renovations but further inland social housing diversifies the scene. Much of this dates from the 1960s and has little architectural merit, but environmental improvement by Southwark Council has redeemed some of the utopian qualities it once had. Further west the Dr Alfred Salter conservation area centred on Wilson Grove contains cottage style council houses built on garden city lines in 1928. Hence the student of social housing can experience most of the twentieth century examples in a relatively small area from tenement blocks to cottages and finally tower blocks.

Mention has already been made of New Concordia Wharf because of the influence it had upon Butlers Wharf, but other projects require to be singled out. The most conspicuous if you approach from the Thames is China Wharf, a red template-like building facing the water. China Wharf is a mixed development of seventeen flats and offices immediately alongside New Concordia Wharf and forms a courtyard with it behind. The building makes reference to much around, such as the concrete silos of Vogan's Mill (in the scalloped white rear elevation) and the warehouses (expressed here in brick gable walls with casement windows). But the references are more abstract than in lesser hands. For example, the gable facing Reed's Warehouse employs windows which step in size to make the transformation between the local vernacular and the modern rear elevation, and a giant Alberti-like segmental arch springs from the ground alongside Mill Street not unlike the similar arch employed high up the facade of H.S. Goodhart-Rendel's Most Holy Trinity church just down the street at Dockhead. The references to shapes, building traditions and colours are not blindly copied but applied in an informed way. In the process CZWG have made China Quay another local work of art, a unique development unlike its neighbours and hence both desirable and marketable.

Contemporary urbanism cannot, however, treat every building as if competing in a commercial art gallery. The extent of more neutral buildings and the scale of restoration nearby mean the area is not suffocated by design pretension. Facing the Thames the redness of the cut-out gable and the sweeping circular arches establish this building immediately as a landmark. The expressive central arch provides a focus for the elevation and the large dark blue buttresses an essential support. Between the two, windows and balconies are pushed through the gable like a modernist office block sliding past an old arcaded warehouse. The structural ambiguities are not, however, resolved: one cannot tell if this elevation is finished in sheet steel or concrete. Architecture here is primarily symbol and Thamesside landmark.

The water buses which now ply the Thames have opened to view the old backlands of the riverfront. The perception of London has changed as visitors and tourists have shifted their point of contact from the street to the water. In the past when the Thames was the chief means of cross-city movement the principal monuments faced the river. Hence when Canaletto and Turner painted London they showed the city against a foreground dominated by the river. Today the opening up of the Thames to traffic has refocused attention and given justification to the introduction of new landmarks. These have begun to mark bends in the river and to provide a framework of landmarks along its corridor just as the principal streets (such as the Strand) are given periodic punctuation. China Wharf attempts such punctuation through colour and profile.

Further east a scheme (so far unrealized) promised to give further skyline punctuation to the Thamesside. Known as Jacob's Island, the development was to have extended from the Thames to Bermondsey Wall west to Jacob Street two blocks behind. Again the architects are CZWG working for the indefatigable developer Andrew Wadsworth through the Jacob's Island Company. This particular part of London has many historical associations, from the monks of Bermondsey who had an ancient dock here to Charles Dickens who set much of Oliver Twist in the area. Dickens described Jacob's Island as an area 'surrounded by a muddy ditch six or eight feet deep and fifteen or twenty feet wide . . . the filthiest, the strangest, and the most extraordinary of the many localities that are hidden in London'.[7] Extraordinary also is the only way to describe the current proposals: a number of diagonal streets radiate like a cartwheel from a central crescent known as The Hoop facing the Thames, and an expressionist twenty storey tower rises from the heart of the scheme. To enable vistas to the river the development is placed on a slope which rises fairly steeply from a pair of public spaces formed at the edge of the Thames. Hence the scheme is unusual in plan and equally bizarre in elevation, where exaggerated corbels and curving buttresses recall the architecture of Dutch expressionism of the 1920s.

The modern (or should I say post-modern) city consists of more townscape matter than just estate roads, office blocks and shopping malls. Current urban theory is much concerned with the rediscovery of the street and its integration into a network of other civic spaces such as crescents and squares. The Jacob's Island proposals treat buildings not as objects in free space, but as groups of buildings which channel space into intelligible patterns. Hence, this is urbanism with the prospect of the richness and tensions of the older neighbourhoods along Shad Thames. As in much current urban design the proposals address both the pedestrian's experience and wider civic responsibilities. Rather like Simpson's as yet unrealized scheme for London Bridge City phase 2, these proposals carve out attractive spaces between the various blocks and address the city by punctuating the skyline.

Between Tower Bridge and Bermondsey there are five key lessons for those involved in urban renewal. First, the retention of old property keeps the scale of new development within human dimensions. Second, the adaptation of obsolete buildings for new uses enriches the environment and provides a context for new design. Third, the maintenance of old street lines and pedestrian routes encourages new development to add to the pattern through the creation of new civic spaces. Fourth, new development can and often should add to the richness of colour and skyline definition found in older areas. Finally, attractive and diversified townscape can result from developers having a relatively free hand in deciding how to respond to market needs. It is a freedom not only from municipal planning control but from rigid privately generated masterplans.

Greenland Dock: a study in urban design masterplanning

The well structured spaces around Greenland Dock are the result of Conran Roche's development framework prepared for the LDDC in 1984. The masterplan is European in character; squares, streets and promenades make up the key elements of a plan which places the pedestrian well to the fore. In this respect Greenland Dock is unusual, not just within the context of Docklands but with regard to planning in London as a whole.

The objectives of the masterplan were to create a strong sense of place as a living and working environment. Housing (which is the dominant land use) was to cater for both local residents and incomers, and development was to safeguard public access to the quaysides and Thames frontage. Hence the plan sought broader social and environmental targets than

Figure 6.15

Greenland Dock: development framework of 1984. The master plan for the area devised by Conran Roche sought a regular distribution of rectangular urban blocks. The European rationalist influence is evident in the plan. It is clear also that landscape and building elements were closely integrated (plan: Conran Roche)

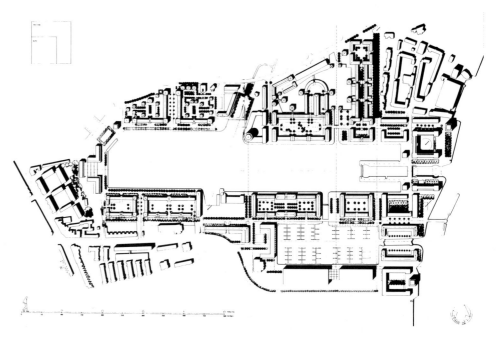

generally in Docklands, and even if subsequent development has failed to fulfil earlier objectives, a sense of purpose is evident in what has been built.

There are, however, two shortcomings which must strike most visitors to the area. Recent development does not relate well to existing communities largely because the new housing faces the water whilst the old faces existing streets. Continuity does not exist – in terms of either land use or urban design. This is evident all the way around Greenland Dock but most particularly on the southern edges of the area, such as along Lower Road and Plough Way. The Conran Roche plan sought the 'integration [of] new development with existing neighbouring communities'[8] but the vehicle by which this could have been achieved, namely the street, has been relegated to a mere servicing route. Hence from the existing road system one sees mainly older housing areas, service yards and light industry, whilst from the water all is new, prosperous and physically isolated.

The second problem is one of scale, or more correctly enclosure. Greenland Dock is 700 metres long and 150 metres wide, making some 12 hectares of water. As a volume to be contained by buildings this represents about ten Bedford Squares (to use Conran Roche's own map of scale comparisons). Bedford Square is about 80 metres across and surrounded by four storey Georgian buildings. By way of contrast Greenland Dock at twice the width is enclosed (if that is the word) by modern three storey houses. As a result there is no real containment of space, no encircling embrace of the large sheet of water. The masterplan did seek to address the issue but it set a maximum limit of four storeys when it should have established a minimum height limit of eight. The copiously illustrated masterplan contains photographs of a site model which suggests the problem was grappled with, but not resolved. In terms of urban design the lack of spatial containment is made worse by the use of pointed gables to the quayside at Brunswick Quay which at a stroke remove any semblance of monumentality.

The two distinct worlds of existing and new community are further held apart by the use of landscape as a buffer zone between the two. A tree planted corridor separates the council housing world of Elgar Street from the largely middle class estate at Norway Dock, and a similar but smaller zone of trees and hedges insulates Greenland Quay from the humble terraces along Plough Way. Landscape design does not here unify; rather it is employed to fill difficult sites around the edge of existing communities, thereby forming green barriers.

Figure 6.16

Baltic Quays at Greenland Dock. The assertive nature of Baltic Quays conflicts with the height limit imposed in the development framework but the tower does enhance the local scene and begins to provide a foil to Canary Wharf across the river (photo: Brian Edwards)

With these reservations the masterplan has many commendable features. Given the distaste for medium or high rise housing in the 1980s, the character is inevitably more village-like than urban. However, the use of square urban blocks has encouraged a move towards a measured monumentality in schemes such as Richard Reid's Finland Quay and the Danish architects' Kjaer and Richter's design of Greenland Passage. These largely rectilinear blocks contain some of the best domestic architecture in Docklands. One only wishes they had been taller and at times more assertive in spirit. An exception to this general rule is Baltic Quay overlooking the South Dock Marina at the edge of the area. This mixed development of flats, studios, offices and shops is contained within a yellow and blue steel framework recalling perhaps the cheerful aesthetic of nearby boats. Boldly detailed and strikingly coloured, this development departs from the masterplan which required buildings here to be no higher than four storeys. The extra height of the barrel vaulted tower does enhance the skyline of the area (especially when Cascades and Canary Wharf are set into the background) but the juxtaposition with Swedish Quays is less than happy.

The philosophy behind the limits placed on the height of buildings in the masterplan was one of forming focal points and entrances into the area. Where Greenland Dock opens at its east end into the Thames, buildings could be up to eight storeys high in order to create a gateway. In the event the developer chose to construct housing only four storeys high. Another high building was to be placed like a hinge on the north side of the dock at the point where a channel once led to Russia Dock. This marker building failed to reach the height planned, with a corresponding lack of punctuation along a dock edge 700 metres long.

Masterplans are after all only guides, and though the lack of containment and the disjointedness are fair criticisms, the plan has achieved much. The square blocks, central courtyards of gardens, corner definitions and fairly generous public spaces are all the result of forethought. Parts of the area almost recall the experiments in urban housing fashioned by the IBA in Berlin in 1982–84, and the use of architects with leanings towards European rationalism (such as Reid) reinforces the impression.

The rectangular blocks established by the master plan not only aid legibility and encourage movement through the area, but also help in marketing the various parcels of land. Land is disposed of by the LDDC on the basis of financial and design tenders received. The latter subscribe to the general rules concerning housing type, tenure mix, density and building height prescribed in the plan. Tenure mix, which was a contentious point with local community groups, was not laid down rigidly; instead the planning briefs aim at about 20 per cent of housing for rent by various means. Whether housing was to be affordable in terms of local residents or more exclusive in character, the planning brief and masterplan diagram became the principal vehicle whereby land was made available to developers. Hence the various parcels of Greenland Dock could be developed in parallel, with each builder having a rough idea of both the social mix and the physical environment he could expect on his doorstep.

If the masterplan process generated confidence, it also set developers in competition with each other in terms of design. The traditional method of disposal of land by public corporation is to seek financial tenders only, but at Greenland Dock developers were set against competitors within both financial and design arenas. This had the advantage of encouraging house builders to employ the services of architects who, generally speaking at least, added a little panache to orthodox design solutions. A good example is at Swedish Quays where the house builder Roger Malcolm employed Price and Cullen. Moreover, as density at Greenland Dock was to average seventy-six dwellings per hectare, most developers had to employ a combination of houses and flats, thereby providing a mix of housing types within the spatial confines of the master plan.

Though 80 per cent of Greenland Dock is residential, with about 1250 new houses constructed in the period 1984–90, there are plans for small scale commercial development. Most of this is to be centred at South Dock where existing brick built warehouses are to be adapted for retail and light industrial

Figure 6.17

Swedish Quays at Greenland Dock. Designed by Price and Cullen, the architectural language is reminiscent of Brighton and the massing bold enough to stand alongside the open dock basin (photo: Price and Cullen)

use (some of this related to the nearby marina). As a result Greenland Dock will become almost entirely residential in character; the European mixed use urban block so popular with contemporary urban theorists will not become a feature of the area. Baltic Quay, already an exception to the height rule, is an exception here too, for this development sits housing above a base of offices and shops.

If the masterplan approach successfully integrates urban design considerations with those of site marketing, the same can be said of infrastructure investment and landscaping. Within the Conran Roche plan a consistent approach can be traced through urban and landscape design, and between parcelization and site servicing. Hence, the same measure of order and symmetry found in the urban elements can also be detected in the provision of trees, footpaths and road surfaces. The approach to hard and soft aspects of the urban environment is much the same with specimen trees marking entrance gateways just as special buildings do. Likewise, the repeating bays of arcading at Brunswick Quay are reflected in avenues of trees which march along the quayside.

As for infrastructural elements such as roads and bridges these too subscribe to a similar language. Civic engineering has not here destroyed the appearance and character of the roads as it has elsewhere in Surrey Docks. If the suburbanization of estate roads has been avoided, so too has the dead hand of municipal asphalt. Surfaces are generally of brick with granite kerbs and solid iron bollards.

Few would doubt that Greenland Dock represents one of the more successful urban reconstructions in Docklands. On balance the place is a success, though the openness of the central water basin will remain a lasting problem. One could suggest islands of development in the dock to break down the scale, or taller buildings behind those constructed to bring the necessary containment. Whatever the limitations, Greenland Dock shows that the benefits of a well structured masterplan outweigh the more familiar free-for-all witnessed elsewhere in Docklands. If the environmental results of masterplanning are encouraging, so too have proved the financial aspects. For an investment in plans and infrastructure of £18 million, the LDDC had by 1990 reaped a reward of £72 million in enhanced land values.[9]

The redefining of Rotherhithe

A thread of regeneration extends along the Thames from London Bridge to Greenland Dock. The loop in the river at Rotherhithe contains the only land under the LDDC's control well away from water. Until the 1960s Rotherhithe was a relatively isolated community surrounded by extensive dockland basins. Most were subsequently infilled, leaving only Greenland Dock as a reminder of the former character. When the LDDC took over the regeneration of the area in 1981 it called a halt to further filling, leaving isolated sheets of water linked for storm drainage purposes by narrow canals. Hence an area which was once about 60 per cent water is now about 8 per cent. What remains is a valuable resource and the LDDC has sought to make the most of it through extensive restoration.

Regeneration in Rotherhithe has followed remarkably closely the planning strategies set out in the 1976 Greater London Development Plan, and the subsequent London Docklands Strategic Plan. These plans called for the rezoning of the area from industry to housing and the filling of the docks to form parks. Difficulties between the corporation and Southwark Council in the early years of the LDDC were not 'because of any great difficulty in development broadly conforming to those plans, but rather the local authority's desire to radically revise them'.[10] What the council sought was greater social housing provision, especially on the key sites facing the water. The LDDC, however, realizing that regeneration could only proceed with the support of the development community, pressed ahead with marketing sites for mainly private housing using local masterplans where necessary. It is worthwhile to reflect that the extent of masterplanning has probably been greater here than elsewhere in Docklands (except perhaps for the Royal Docks), with the result that the LDDC ascribes the financial success of its operations in Rotherhithe partly to masterplanning.[11]

The objectives of the various masterplans or development frameworks have generally been to define spatial patterns, to help link old and new communities, and to prescribe edge conditions where buildings face water. Though the urban frameworks have not always fully succeeded, or been followed, they have established a coherent pattern of development over much of Rotherhithe. The Rotherhithe Street proposals for instance by Price and Cullen (1986) and Nicholas Ash Associates (1989) formed the urban structure for the Islef scheme facing the Thames at Nelson Dock as well as the other gaps along this historic street. The approach has generally been one of introducing an element of formality and classical structuring of space around gateway buildings, the framing of landmarks, and the opening up of vistas to the Thames.

Two developments typify the approach. At Lawrence Wharf the design of riverside housing is arranged about a large and generously landscaped courtyard. The housing is placed in six storey blocks, rising to seven at the southern end of the site, and is cool and restrained in character. Designed by the Danish architects Kjaer and Richter, this development containing 156 units has a scale and quality suitable for the Thameside. The buildings respond to the park planned at the southern end of the site and to the domestic scale of Rotherhithe Street where the scheme stops down to three storeys. Just north and planned to be part of the eventual development stands Nelson House, built in 1740 and presently converted to offices for Islef. Behind stands a pair of seven storey blocks facing the refurbished Nelson Dock; these are not housing as originally planned, but a hotel following the property slump of 1989. They too borrow freely from contemporary Danish classicism and make a pleasant counterpoint to the similarly coloured but more expressive Cascades immediately across the Thames.

Within the heart of Rotherhithe a canal of shallow water known as Albion Channel links Canada Water to Surrey Water. Attractively landscaped in brick, granite and setts, and planted with a formal line of plane trees, this channel is edged mainly by neovernacular housing. One exception is yet another project by CZWG, though now there is a greater mix of social housing types than in the schemes by these architects already examined. This is known as Wolfe Crescent. Here the developer Lovell Urban Renewal has built a cheerful crescent of three storey town houses and placed within its welcoming embrace four octagonal blocks of flats. The crescent and isolated blocks are formally arranged, establishing a pattern of squat landmarks midway between the two larger bodies of water. The raising of the development upon a podium separates the canalside walk from the more private territory within the crescent, and the balconies placed freely around the towers give good views up and down the channel. This is affordable housing but a far cry from much built nearby by more familiar house builders. A particularly clever benefit of the layout is the way the town houses in the crescent still enjoy slot-like views of the water between the octagonal towers. Also, by the nature of the site layout and the extent of overlooking windows, there is easy surveillance of the car parking and small children's play area from within the flats.

The Southwark site proposals

Wolfe Crescent is part of a larger network of sites made available for redevelopment under the *Southwark Site Proposals* prepared by Rendel, Palmer and Tritton, Brian Clouston and Partners, and the LDDC in 1983.[12] The framework established broad land use and urban design standards for an area of some 132 acres (53 hectares) which consisted largely of infilled docks (the Surrey Basin and the Albion, Canada, Stave and Island Docks, plus parts of Russia and Quebec Docks). Earlier proposals such as the Lysander scheme which enjoyed local support had failed to be realized owing to the lack of adequate transport links. The LDDC's objectives were to build upon the Lysander proposals, particularly the large housing component, and to carry out infrastructure and environmental improvements as a necessary starting point for regeneration. The proposals for Southwark Site now known by the more· marketable title of Surrey Quays, structured the area and provided a framework for the integration of three key elements: housing, shopping and industrial development.

The approach was to concentrate housing in the northern and central parts of the area using the Albion Channel as an integrating axis. Community facilities and open space are centred on the northern area of water (known as Surrey Water) with shopping focused upon Canada Water to the south. The latter already had consent for a superstore (at present British Home Stores)

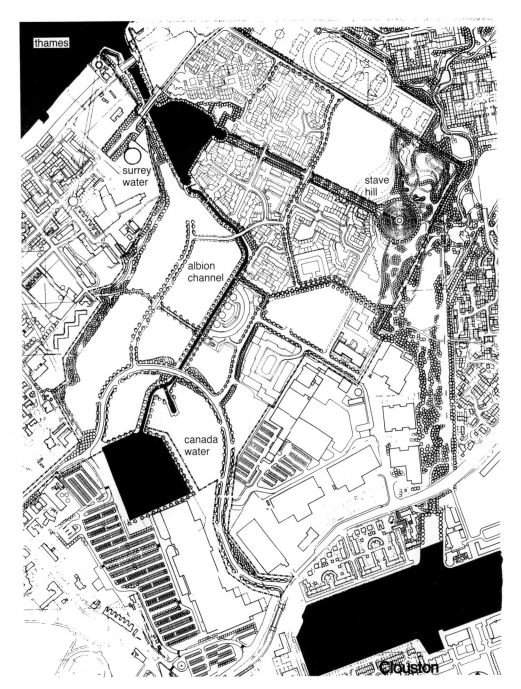

Figure 6.18

The landscape plan for Surrey Quays. Prepared by a team led by landscape designers Brian Clouston and Partners, the Surrey Quays plan links Canada Wharf to Surrey Water via Albion Channel. The Thames is shown top left and Greenland Dock bottom right. The axis from Stave Hill to the City of London is to the top of the plan with the ecological corridor of Russia Dock woodland running southwards to Greenland Dock (plan: B. Clouston)

Figure 6.19

Albion Channel. This attractive route is practically all that remains of the extensive dock system of Surrey Docks. Designed with much attention to colour, texture and durability, Albion Channel has become a coordinating axis for several subsequent housing developments such as Wolfe Crescent on the right (photo: Brian Edwards)

and is a natural focus for further retail development. Recent plans have emerged to build a million square feet of shops and offices overlooking Canada Water in the form of a glazed circus with radiating arms. Designed by Brown Ibbotson Charnley for the Jacob's Island Company with Olympia and York as joint backers, the proposed development strengthens the focusing of community land uses upon Canada Water by linking a sports centre to existing supermarkets. The scheme roofs over a length of Albion Channel which has a pair of taller housing blocks acting as a gateway into Canada Water. Consequently, the broad strategy is to group community buildings around the larger bodies of water with housing facing Albion Channel between.

At the west edge of the site new housing merges into old residential areas, but to the east the presence of the Russia Dock woodland encouraged the allocation of land for additional wildlife space and the siting of schools. Consequently the plan reinforced earlier proposals by Southwark Council for an ecological corridor running through the centre of the Surrey Docks peninsular.

The plan not only parcels up land for development, but also establishes the framework of woods and footpaths. A new distributor road bisects the area roughly north to south, joining Lower Road alongside St George's Field. Whilst some of the developments have sought urban values, the street layout is decidedly surburban in character. The wide viewing splays at intersections and the generous curves mark the road as the product of the highway engineer rather than the urban designer. Finished often in brick or dyed asphalt, the road could easily have migrated from Thamesmead. By way of contrast the canalside footpaths and particularly the axis north-west to the City of London along Dock Hill Avenue beneath Stave Hill have a more urban character. Here axial tree planting and robust granite paving bring a city-like quality to the still thinly developed wastelands.

There is a genuine attempt to mix land uses within the area. The 44 acres of housing are well balanced by 33 acres of shopping and business uses, and 12 acres of industry. Unusually for Docklands, schools, sports facilities and community uses occupy over 10 acres, and 5 acres are given over to woodland. When development values are not excessive, the LDDC seems well able to meet social and environmental needs. The housing itself has a broad social base with a commitment by the LDDC to Southwark Council and the housing associations to make land available for their needs. As development has proceeded, such affordable or state supported housing has tended to be integrated within private developments rather than built in separate estates. A good example is Wolfe Crescent, where 20 per cent of the housing is subsidized by the council.

The success of Surrey Docks

Surrey Docks is not a singular place like the rest of Docklands but a slice of London which relates to a wider community. The Thameside has been reoccupied and urbanized along its length with much improved waterside access. The veneer of middle class housing which faces the Thames is permeable enough to allow views from the public housing estates behind. The texture of London has been well respected in the various redevelopments, especially around Butlers Wharf, and elsewhere urban, building and landscape design are well integrated. If the physical and social connections are sometimes poor (especially between Greenland Dock and Lower Road), the green lung which extends for over a kilometre northwards from the Russian Dock woodland provides a welcome corridor of tranquility. Much of this has been achieved by traditional means – masterplanning, section 52 agreements, and partnerships between public and private developers. Surrey Docks succeeds in the very areas where London Docklands generally fails, but in the process of making a more rounded environment the opportunity has not been missed to create a handful of spectacular new buildings and satisfying urban spaces.

From the viewing platform of Stave Hill one can savour the full prospect of Surrey Docks and much beyond. The typology of Docklands is clearly shown here. At the lower level the brick and tile cottages of the volume builders and housing associations blanket the space not filled by trees, roads and parking areas. Along the riverside and around the dock basins cliffs of tenement-like apartment blocks form generally happy groupings with a few surviving nineteenth century warehouses. Dotted throughout the area stand tower blocks – those of concrete construction being social housing and those of steel and glass being expressions of corporate capital. The cottage, tenement and tower are all typical products of British urbanism, but elsewhere in London they tend to be separated into distinct zones. Here in Docklands they are not grouped into recognizable patterns but intermingle according to market forces. Only at the Isle of Dogs across the river do high rise buildings show any tendency towards aggregation. As so much land has been planted with trees, the impression from Stave Hill is one of pleasant greenery with brick cottages clustered into village-like groups, and silver and white skyscrapers rising picturesquely above the distant rooftops. The lack of deliberate ordering and the love of mixed landscape and urban design are the quintessence of Englishness. Docklands may be the international market place of LDDC perceptions, but from Surrey Docks it remains indelibly English in spirit.

Notes

1 LDDC, 'Surrey Docks fact sheet', January 1990, p. 9.
2 A.W. Pugin, *Contrasts* (1836: Leicester University Press 1969).
3 Hugh Pearman, 'A planning inquiry that missed the boat', *The Sunday Times*, 11 March 1990.
4 Ruth Owens, 'Butlers Wharf: masterplan as model', *Architecture Today*, No. 1, September 1989, p. 30.
5 Edmund Burke, *A philosophical inquiry into the origin of our ideas of the sublime and beautiful* (F and C Rivington 1801).
6 Ruth Owens, 'Blue Circle', *Architects Journal*, 17 October 1990, p. 28.
7 Quoted by Sydney R. Jones in *Thames Triumphant* (The Studio Publications 1945), p. 205.
8 Conran Roche, *Greenland Dock: Framework for Development*, (1984), p. 9.
9 Information from Chris Farrow, Surrey Docks area director at LDDC, 12 September 1990.
10 Letter from Chris Farrow, Surrey Docks area director at LDDC, dated 9 July 1990.
11 *Ibid.*
12 *The Southwark Site Proposals for Redevelopment* (LDDC 1983).

7 Wapping

Development background

The part of the Docklands regeneration known as Wapping and Poplar occupies a corridor of land on the north side of the Thames between the Tower of London and the Isle of Dogs. It is an area of contrasts and some character. At the west it consists of the tourist dominated enclave of St Katharine Docks – an oasis of dubious architectural merit within a bigger landscape of high rise office blocks. The river is generally lined by handsome brick warehouses, mostly now converted to rather expensive housing, though pockets of industry still survive especially around Limehouse. The two most important eighteenth century residential areas in Docklands are to be found here – Wapping Pier Head just below St Katharines, and Narrow Street a mile further east.

Wapping has an extensive hinterland of working class and middle class housing, but it never (unlike Beckton in the Royal Docks) loses contact with its maritime past. This is mainly because of the rather Dutch looking canals which cut through the area, the presence of impressive Dockland buildings such as Tobacco Dock, and a persistent warehouse imagery adopted for many of the new buildings. Of all of Docklands, Wapping is the one area which still retains something of its original character of close grained streets lined by lofty warehouses, with the occasional churchyard and square providing leafy backwaters.

The presence of many listed buildings and fairly extensive conservation areas discouraged the adoption of the masterplan approach to urban renewal. As a consequence the area has that air of *ad hoc* urbanism typical of the inner city and increasingly one of the hallmarks of London Docklands. Here the new office buildings (such as Thomas More House) are not only larger than elsewhere but more expensively detailed, and hence the contrast in scale and wealth is strikingly evident. From within the well protected oases of St Katharine Docks and St Anne's churchyard, the new office blocks of downtown Docklands loom above the old slated roofs with characteristic indifference.

Unregulated urbanism has produced some interesting if uncomfortable townscapes in Wapping. At its most sinister and destructive of civilized values, the News International printing works (where *The Times*, *The Sunday Times*, *The Sun*, *Today* and *News of the World* newspapers are printed) stands as a lumpen structure within a fortified enclosure of barbed wire. Though servicing the media age, this building communicates nothing to the housing areas which line its southern boundary. As urban architecture it is difficult to find a less satisfactory building, especially with its encircling sea of asphalt which provides parking spaces for the workforce. The building marks the migration of newspaper printing from the centre of London, but one wishes it has been dispersed further afield or broken down into smaller parts. The lesson of Canary Wharf is that it is possible to make a big development acceptable by dividing it into separate parts (and making each the responsibility of a different architect) but the News International building spurns such wisdom. It also presents nothing to the street, unlike the *Financial Times* printing works at Blackwall which opens the presses to view.

Nearby stands Thomas More House, a collection of white, cream and pale blue office towers built around three internal courts. The development is not inelegant but it does highlight problems of urban design prevalent elsewhere in Docklands. The sixteen storey buildings dwarf all in sight, especially the one and two storey London Dock House tucked away behind gatepiers

Figure 7.1

East Quay, Wapping. A modernized warehouse style has proved popular with developers especially when facing water basins. Designed by Pinchin and Kellow for Laings, these residential blocks have a scale appropriate for their location opposite Tobacco Dock (photo: Brian Edwards)

Figure 7.2

London Dock House. Built in 1805 and restored by the LDDC, these former dock offices are now dwarfed by Thomas More House. The contrast in scale and urban texture is reminiscent of New York (photo: Brian Edwards)

facing East Smithfield. Believed to be the oldest dock offices in the world and designed by Daniel Alexander around 1805, this gem of Docklands architecture is now bullied beyond reason by its new neighbour. As with the Sugar Warehouses in West India Dock, historic buildings and new commercial architecture seem irreconcilable hereabouts. It is all the more distressing since both lie within conservation areas, a protection which clearly has little influence immediately beyond the designated boundary.

Perhaps a masterplan would have anticipated the problem. As it is the cherished vistas around the Ivory House at St Katharine Docks are terminated by the brooding presence of the new development. Though lightly coloured and hence merging into the sky, the scale of Thomas More House in proximity to the fragile environment of St Katharine's questions again the popular presumption that aesthetic freedom does not damage the wider townscape. In terms of urban space marking the development raises further problems. A high wall (listed as part of the original enclosure of London Dock) separates the scheme from Thomas More Street. Breaks in the wall give access to courts around which the office buildings are grouped. These courts or squares remain private and are patrolled by security guards. They are not part of the public realm, though they look invitingly like civic squares. This is a privatized patch of urban landscape, as private in its way as 'Fortress Wapping'. Because these spaces are private the development has no physical permeability; moreover, the high brick walls permit little visual permeability.

The regeneration of St Katharine Docks

The renewal of St Katharine Docks began over a decade before the formation of the LDDC. The building of the World Trade Centre here in 1969 to designs by Renton Howard Wood Levin established the area as both business and tourist centre. Plans were drawn up by the GLC which sought a comprehensive approach to regeneration based on the restoration of the listed Ivory House built in 1854 and on improved public access to the dockside. Hence by the time the LDDC appeared on the scene the area was already a success and a blueprint of regeneration was well in place. One cannot, however, cast unreserved praise upon St Katharine Docks. Much of the waterside remains inaccessible, the new buildings such as the Tower

Figure 7.3

St Katharine Docks c. 1825. This view shows the relationship between St Katharine Docks and the Tower of London. One is hardly aware of the presence of the capital's premier historic landmark from within the docks. Notice the typological distinction between the Thamesside warehouses and those designed by Hardwick surrounding the dock (photo: Museum of Docklands)

Hotel (built in 1973) pay little regard to wider civic values, and the docks themselves have become filled with ostentatious craft. The height of the new buildings relative to the width of the water means that much of the dock remains in shade, especially in the afternoon. Though there are plans to edge the eastern dock with housing, thereby providing a foil to Thomas More House, the quality of new architecture is poor and the pattern of spaces confusing.

Equally worrying is the lack of a perceptual grasp of major monuments nearby. The Tower of London is only a street away, yet its presence is denied by the World Trade Centre, and the same is true of Tower bridge relative to the Tower Hotel. New buildings hereabouts are bulky – it is largely physical bulk which prevents visual contact. Plans are afoot to redevelop certain buildings constructed in the 1970s and perhaps a correspondence will then be established. The need for such dialogue stems from the difficulty one experiences reaching St Katharine Docks from the Tower of London, and the fact that both lie within the Tower conservation area – a designation intended to preserve character, enhance appearance and by implication establish a meaningful connection.

Ivory House and the Dockmaster's House stand between the west and east docks at St Katharine's. Once the headquarters of the European Ivory Trade, the warehouse was converted in 1973 to retail, office and housing use. Well preserved, Ivory House stands today in an area of larger buildings. Only Commodity Quay makes any reference to the presence of the older neighbours. It does so by building in mellow brown brick and by adopting Ivory House's semicircular arcade for a giant order of arches rising through seven storeys. Commodity Quay is the most advanced technically of all the buildings lining St Katharine Docks, yet it looks the most traditional. Within the hand crafted brick and stone façades are to be found trading floors for the London Commodity Exchange. The building shows the shift in design philosophy from the 1970s to the 1980s. This building responds to its context, thereby generating meaning in terms of the perceptions of the general public. It also accepts a responsibility towards a craft-based building process and appreciates by implication the life cycle concepts of repair and maintenance. The mixing of traditional and high tech elements dates

Figure 7.4

Ivory House, St Katharine Docks. Ivory House (1854), once the European headquarters of the ivory trade, has been converted to shops, apartments and offices (photo: St Katharine by the Tower Ltd)

the building firmly in the mid eighties, and signifies an architecture which respects urban values and supports a more responsive way of life. The building may not be popular with modernist architects but it is typical of the pluralism of the new world order, and hence characteristic of Docklands.

St Katharine Docks is, as Barry Shaw puts it, at the stitching and darning stage of urbanism.[1] The framework of buildings is largely in place, but the spaces between require finishing, and the smaller gaps in the street scene plugging. It is too late now to prepare a masterplan to coordinate an unhappy ensemble of buildings. What needs to be done is to bring detailed order to bear upon public surfaces and to extend the pedestrian routes around the docksides. If one could take a long term view this is the place where a

Figure 7.5

Commodity Quay, St Katharine Docks. Built in 1987 as the offices of the London Futures and Options Exchange, a sophisticated building type is disguised within a traditional shell. Designed by Watkins Gray International, the references to Ivory House are obvious (photo: St Katharine by the Tower Ltd)

Figure 7.6

Site plan of Tobacco Dock. The malls of the shopping area are shown with a diagonal grid, the canal is shaded, and St-George-in-the-East is in black (plan: Terry Farrell and Co.)

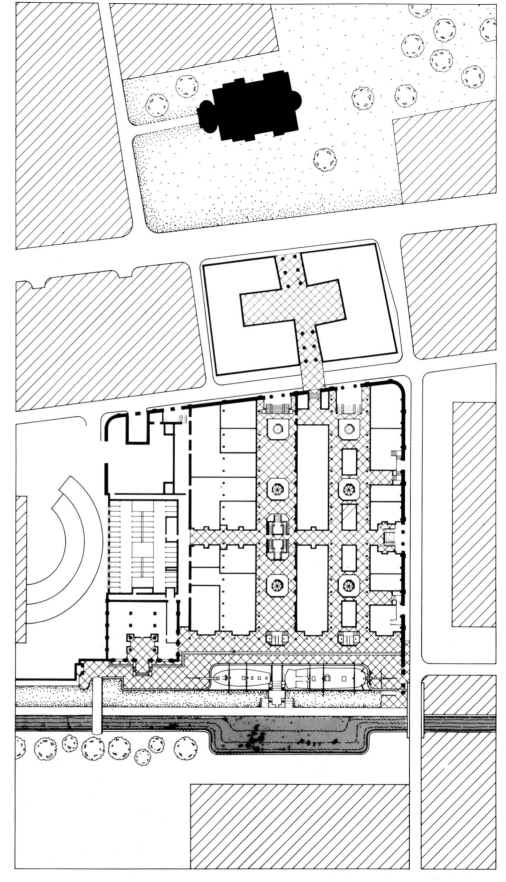

triumphal axis could be driven from the City of London at its west end to Canary Wharf at its east. Then St Katharine's would be truly a gateway to London Docklands, as against a pretty but isolated enclave.

Tobacco Dock

In an area where heritage has become more part of the private than of the public domain, Tobacco Dock presents a pleasant exception. Although converted to speciality shopping by Tobacco Docks Developments and hence technically a private building, the expansiveness of the malls and the long hours of opening make the place feel like a public building. This impression is fostered further by Tobacco Dock's almost axial relationship to Hawkmoor's St-George-in-the-East church, and the presence of two replica clippers moored in the canal on its south side. These civic elements allow Tobacco Dock to sit comfortably within a landscape not yet fully reclaimed by the LDDC.

Tobacco Dock is a building of rare qualities converted to retail use by the Terry Farrell Partnership. Farrell's office has been instrumental in bringing to London a kind of pop classicism much favoured by the development community. A hint of Farrell's post-modernism is to be found in the conversion of this building, but on the whole the integrity of the structure and its atmospheric vaults have been well restored. It is grade 1 listed, and the architect had a particular responsibility to protect its character during the restoration and conversion. Built in 1811 to designs by Daniel Alexander, surveyor to London Docks, the building was constructed as a tobacco warehouse, with wine vaults below. About fifty years later the upper level was used for storing sheepskins and hence became known as the 'skin floor'. The interest of the building derives from its proto-modern structure: a series of parallel roofs topped by long lantern lights above queen-post trusses which are supported by extraordinary tree-like cast iron columns. The internal views, mostly well preserved in the conversion to retail use, are of a forest of steel branches sprouting from iron columns. The lower floor is

Figure 7.7

Tobacco Dock. This view of the vaulted ground floor shows the discreet insertion of shop units into a structure of much beauty and strength (photo: Terry Farrell and Co./R. Cheatle)

equally dramatic, constructed in brick and granite and vaulted into shallow arches. The piers, shaped and much scarred by decades of use, give the lower floors an air of authenticity lacking in some other Dockland restorations.

Farrell's task was to divide the open expanse of warehouse space into shop units with malls between. He also had to connect the two floors and provide markers to the outside world. In the latter regard the replica ships give a Disney-like air to the development and one which is too compromising for this author's taste. Inside, Tobacco Dock is a wonderfully atmospheric place, all the more mysterious for its proximity to the News International printing works.

The plan consists on the lower floor of a double cruciform of aisle-like walkways lined by squat columns and surrounded by rather Dickensian shop units tucked beneath brick arches. The upper level is more open and modern in spirit; the space is filled with light, and tree-like columns which spread almost at eye level like a forest into the distance. Farrell's facility for detailing which combines wit with measured respect is shown well on the upper level. However, the connecting staircases and bric-à-brac of retail development, such as fountains and bandstands, begin to compete with Alexander's work. The visual logic of the original design (columns, arches and wide span trusses) is, however, strong enough to dispel the sometimes aggressive presence of the new functions.

Tobacco Dock sits within a small gated square, not a public promenade. Unlike Covent Garden which the development seeks to emulate, this is a private retail estate dressed in genuine and fascinating historic garb. Security guards patrol the area as they do in nearby office developments. London has so abandoned the public domain that even when grade 1 listed buildings are converted to quasi-social uses such as shopping centres, there is no talk of integrating them into a network of civic spaces.

A maritime suburbia[2]

To the south of Tobacco Dock stands a large area of Dutch inspired housing which extends towards St Katharine Docks for about half a kilometre. The area was once London Dock, an expanse of 40 hectares of enclosed water. All that remains are the present canals such as that alongside Tobacco Dock, formed by partial infilling. Since one side of the original dock structure generally survives, the scale is enormous and the detailing refreshingly rugged. Also, as the docks had parallel sides, the canals have a rectilinear quality which is immediately reminiscent of Amsterdam.

Into this flat watery landscape stand groups of red and yellow brick houses clustered around courts turned away from the canal. Consequently, the houses present a straight and largely formal composition to the public walkways which line the canal. Designed by different architects, the houses have a measured variety within broad similarities of colour, height and layout dictated by the LDDC. Only immediately facing Tobacco Dock does the suburban theme give way to greater height and civic presence. Here five storey gabled flats by architects Pinchin Kellow combine traditional and modern elements. Colour in bold triangular or square panels is applied in almost De Stijl fashion to brick buildings of warehouse shapes. The result is typical of Dockland architecture: complexity and contradiction compete with elements of order or orthodoxy in a way which is both refreshing and disturbing.

What is not immediately evident is the degree to which social housing has been incorporated into these developments. Thomas More Court (by Boyer Design Group for Heron Homes) consists of 25 per cent public housing, though one cannot identify it from the outside. It is typical of Docklands to find social and private housing integrated into developments, rather than treated as separate estates. The process is not without difficulties according to the purchasers, thirty of whom have issued a writ against Heron

Figure 7.8

West Dock, Wapping. The parallel edges to the canal system created by the partial infilling of the docks is reminiscent of Amsterdam, a fact reflected in the design of the houses (photo: Brian Edwards)

Homes claiming they were not told of the partnership.[3] In fact, fifty of the 190 houses and flats are now in use as council housing run by Tower Hamlets Council.

Putting aside the difficulty of social integration within a largely private age, an air of tranquil maritime suburbia survives well in the area. This is the well mannered hinterland of Docklands where old and new communities rub shoulders. Away from the Thamesside and beyond the immediate reach of St Katharine's and Shadwell Basin, this area is fast maturing into one of the successes of inner city regeneration. The LDDC has laid down a structure of buildings and connecting spaces which is leafy, watery and lined by modest but attractive brick terraces.

Shadwell Basin

The transition from suburban to urban housing types in London Docklands has been one of the successes of regeneration during the first ten years of LDDC operations. Early developers were confident only in constructing two or three storey houses, feeling that the market could not support housing with greater urban ambitions. Only along the Thamesside and around some of the finer areas of enclosed water did house builders experiment with greater density and more complex forms. One housing scheme which shows well the growing confidence in Docklands by the development community is Shadwell Basin by architects MacCormac, Jamieson, Prichard and Wright.

The initiative for the scheme derives from the LDDC who appointed the architects to prepare design proposals which were then sold by tender to a

Figure 7.9

Plan for Hermitage Basin. The masterplan prepared by Price and Cullen seeks to link the regenerated areas of West Dock (top right) to St Katharine Docks. Prepared for the developer Regalian, the plan uses towers and rotunda blocks to deflect axes and define routes (plan: Price and Cullen)

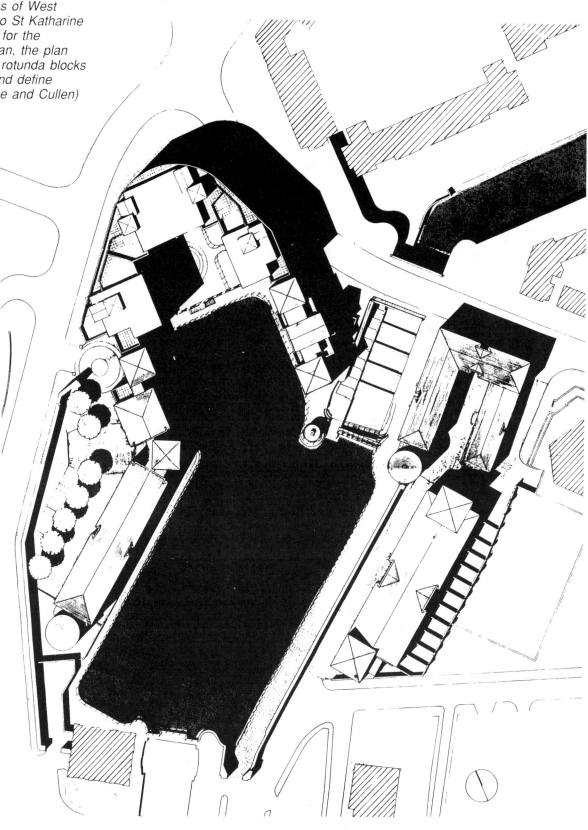

Figure 7.10

Shadwell Basin. Designed by MacCormac, Jamieson, Prichard and Wright, this housing development made the revival of the vernacular warehouse respectable in architectural circles. The variety of house types has, however, stretched the warehouse form to breaking point. (photo: Brian Edwards)

developer. The developer Sanctuary Land and LLewelyn acquired the site and designs in 1985, and after making minor changes completed the scheme in 1987. Unlike Greenland Dock the architects had no urban design framework in which to work, and hence the density, forms and site layout were largely of their making.

With little in the way of examples of contemporary urban housing facing water in England, the designers chose to build upon the far commoner precedent of brick built dockside warehouses. These existed in some number nearby, and their recent conversion to flats had shown the marketability of such housing. Shadwell Basin should be seen therefore as an attempt to re-create the ambience and detailing of a warehouse typology. What is conspicuously lacking, however, is a density which allows this approach to fully succeed. For on the east side of the basin the housing is only three storeys high, and elsewhere the four or five storey blocks appear somewhat underscaled. The problem is not just one of height but of the degree of expression given to the individual units. In warehouse architecture walls are generally plain and relieved only by grids of windows and the occasional hoist or pediment. Housing requires greater individual expression, especially as here if a wide range of house types is employed. Moreover, the modern tendency towards using winter gardens as solar buffer zones further breaks down the wall plane. Hence, a brave attempt at reviving an industrial tradition has been undermined by the practicalities of modern private house building.

If the buildings generally are too low, thereby allowing space to escape freely between gables facing the dock, the detailed richness and ingenious planning of the various house types is commendable. This richness derives mainly from the warehouse tradition, and the arches have the further benefit of defining entrances to the different blocks. At ground level the dockside illusion is sustainable but the excessive use of gables and particularly broken gables recalls the neovernacular of nearby surburban housing schemes. The need for such rooftop display is partly the result of providing residents with high level viewing balconies and partly the complex planning of the blocks. The top floors contain two or three bedroom maisonettes, the second floor one to three bedroom flats, and the ground and first floor a mixture of flats and maisonettes. Within each block of flats there are usually six different house types, each making demands upon the building's elevation.

As each flat has a balcony and most have a glazed room to the view, the facade facing the basin is highly modelled. The complexity of the frontage is given further expression by the use of the bright colours. A strident red and dark blue for the glazed areas and balcony steelwork confront the brown brick and reconstituted stone in a fashion reminiscent of the local industrial tradition. Such colour coordination may not be maintained in future redecoration, though whether this will undermine the scheme is a moot point.

The urban layout maintains a broad viewing slot alongside St Paul's church (1820), a fine classical building facing Commercial Road. This allows the spire of the church to be seen from the dockside and almost all of the building from an attractive paved area on a peninsular at the south-east of the basin. The church is not, however, fully integrated into the development; it remains hidden behind a wall and insulated by its churchyard.

Parking is placed behind and beneath the blocks, providing a distinct front and back to the development. As in much recent dockside housing the back of the blocks face on to well established residential areas round about. The resulting urban environment lacks physical continuity since the service areas form a buffer between old and new. Like much of Docklands, Shadwell Basin is an attractively detailed middle class enclave within the inner city, but it fails to fully exploit the warehouse tradition. Also, by turning itself to the water, the design does not extend the pattern of activities and land uses round about to the quayside.

Notes

1 Interview by author with Barry Shaw on 15 April 1991.
2 The term 'maritime suburban' is borrowed from Catherine Slessor's article 'Tobacco Trader' in *Architects Journal*, 13 December 1989, p. 43.
3 See Robert Cowan, 'The Market Stalls', *Architects Journal*, 8 November 1989, p. 24.

The Royal Docks

8

Development background

For those who advocate a traditional approach to urban planning, the Royal Docks pose a dilemma. A comprehensive masterplan which integrated land use with infrastructure was prepared, and much of the transportation provision and landscaping put in place, but to date developers have been noticeably reluctant to invest in the area. For all the limitations of the unplanned Isle of Dogs, development there has at least proceeded apace. Here, one is struck by the unrealized opportunities, and almost embarrassed by the volume of plans and the precision of the vision. The Royal Docks has a framework for urban renewal in place, and an investment in roads amounting to £150 million, but except for the London City Airport, nothing really is moving.

One needs to ask whether the adoption of a planned approach has acted as a deterrent to development. New Right thinking sought the abolition of municipal town planning and its replacement by a culture of enterprise. The results at the Isle of Dogs are testimony to the wisdom and limitations of the approach. Here, save for the suburban housing areas around Beckton and the new airport, a landscape of stunning opportunity has been spurned by the development community. There are reasons for this, such as the indecision over the East London river crossing, but perhaps the extent of prescription in the adopted urban plans persuaded developers to focus their attentions upon other dockland sites.

The enterprise zone helped Millwall Docks to undergo an exceptionally swift transformation from dereliction, first to low rise industrial sheds and then to high rise office towers. The decade of construction fanned by general governmental policy in the 1980s failed to reach the sleepy backwaters of the Royal Docks. Ten years into the anticipated fifteen year lifespan of the LDDC, the three massive arms of enclosed water formed by Royal Victoria Dock, Royal Albert Dock and King George V Dock stand devoid of significant investment. One cannot blame the presence of plans alone (if at all)

Figure 8.1

View of the Royal Docks. This view looking west along the Royal Victoria Dock shows the desolate character of the area ten years after the founding of the LDDC, but also the wonderful opportunities. The tower of Canary Wharf is visible in the background (photo: Brian Edwards) for this, but questions need to be asked of development frameworks which fail to attract development. Incremental and market-led planning shaped much of Docklands (as it has in other riversides such as in Liverpool or Glasgow), but here the ambitions of the LDDC have not been realized in spite of, or maybe because of, the nature of the plans. With hindsight one could suggest that had the Royal Docks enjoyed an enterprise zone, matters would have been quite different. Then the plans could have been prepared with a reasonable expectation of implementation. With no such designation the Royal Docks have suffered a double blow: the plans have perhaps been too deterministic, and indecision over bigger questions such as access to the motorway system and new bridges over the Thames has acted as an effective deterrent to development.

One can easily see how areas to the west of London have become urbanized as a result of their good communication links. Stockley Park has grown up as an attractive high tech business estate upon derelict land near Heathrow Airport, and places like Hammersmith have blossomed as a result of good road and rail connections. But the poor historic provision to the east of London, exacerbated by the reluctance of government in the eighties to address the transport issue, has been the Royal Docks' downfall. Staff at the LDDC admit that one may have to wait another generation before the Royal Docks realize their potential, and then many of the current master plans and development frameworks will presumably have to be redrafted.

There are clues to the future, however, even in the present desolate landscape of this part of London. The London City Airport offers a host of European connections by way of its so-called 'hush' aircraft. The European cities of the future are to the east of London, thereby in theory at least acting as a magnet of regeneration to the Royal Docks' advantage. Within the area a science-fiction-like collection of huge satellite discs marks the British Telecom Teleport. From here a fibre-optic network extends into London via the new office empires of the Isle of Dogs. If the future British economy is to be based upon information services, then the Royal Docks has a crucial role to play. The airport and teleport are mere skeletons, waiting to be fleshed out by future growth, and the same is true of the Docklands Light Railway extension presently under construction. The stations provide the justification for urban centres planned by various urban design consultants, though the question of relative scale may well prove as difficult as it has elsewhere in Docklands.

These clues to a future order exist today in an open, windy and scarred urban environment. Sections of former dock structures survive amid acres of despoiled land which spread out beneath the gaze of the high rise council housing blocks of North Woolwich. This is Docklands' only truly deconstructivist landscape, a place where fragments of order exist in a disjointed and alienated world. The Royal Docks is a problem not of finding lost space in the sense of reclaiming urban land between buildings for public use, but of regenerating over 200 hectares of derelict land and nearly 96 hectares of redundant water.

The development framework

In 1985 the LDDC published its draft development framework for the Royal Docks, aimed at establishing a vision which responded 'to this magnificent site'. Prepared in collaboration with the Richard Rogers Partnership and environment consultants Gillespies, the plan formulated a largely unrealized strategy for development. The framework establishes a number of general principles which are subsequently developed around specific issues such as land use and transportation. Of the general principles, mention is made of the removal of physical barriers, the retention of the water areas, general environmental upgrading, and the need for 'incremental, progressive and flexible growth'.[1] The development framework speculates upon whether small scale, low key development is preferable to major individual developments, and opts for a combination of both. The subsequent urban framework, published under the title *Royal Docks: the Vision for the Future*, shows how a flexible strategy could be accommodated, with the DLR stations providing high density nodes supporting a suburban hinterland.

The development framework has one interesting component within the cultural or political climate of Docklands. Unlike much effort elsewhere the plan talks of the corporation being 'committed to encouraging the confidence in the area needed to assure existing employers and residents about the future'.[2] This will, the plan accepted, mean providing employment, housing and leisure facilities. In reality little has been constructed alongside the dock basins but, towards the edges of the area, housing, dry ski slopes and shopping centres serve mainly local needs.

These broad principles are translated in the development framework into more specific intentions. Under 'accessibility' a number of proposals are put forward including the need for a new Thames road bridge which is shown in the plan as a suspension bridge (the latter proved unacceptable from the point of view of airport operators at the nearby STOLport). The linear nature of the three main dock basins encouraged the development of a major east/west spine road which was subsequently integrated with a services corridor, and provided the justification for the spatial framework. As a result, the plan has a marked east/west bias which has further discouraged the integration of the Royal Docks into the wider landscape of east London. To the north it is isolated by the suburbs of Beckton and to the south by a wide and by no means beautiful river. The inability to decide upon the design of the new Thames bridge has been another factor in thwarting development to date and reinforcing the sense of isolation.

Three nodes of development are identified in the plan – at the north-west and north-east of the Royal Victoria Dock, and at the east end of the Royal Albert Dock. Each was intended to attract large scale development in the form of either commercial activities or leisure functions. For a short period the area promised to become the focus for London's bid for the Olympics (to emulate Barcelona's use of international sport to regenerate dockland areas) but Britain's entry fell to Manchester. Between the nodes, sites were identified for 'development of a lower key and less concentrated nature'.[3] The development framework therefore established a hierarchy of function and activity across the dockland wastelands, and used an illustrative plan to demonstrate the spatial pattern of what was proposed.

An emphasis of the plan was upon transport and water sports use of the 96 hectares of the enclosed dock. An internal water transit system was proposed for the 3 miles of dock, linked to the Thames and hence to the river bus service. More realistic perhaps were proposals for active recreational use of the docks, either wind surfing or power boat racing. The use of leisure as a generator of urban renewal is well tested, and the development framework sought to keep open the water areas. The LDDC's adopted strategy says that 'the key to the character of the Royal Docks is water'[4] and, in marked contrast to what has happened on the Isle of Dogs, talks of the creation of a great new water city.

A central ambition of the plan has not been realized. In spite of considerable pump priming the LDDC has been unable to establish any large scale developments which would have acted as a catalyst. Six years after the publication of the development framework the area remains idle. Admittedly, the filling in of the detail has occurred in the form of local housing and community recreation facilities, but the focal point developments which are such a feature of the master plan have failed to win the support of the business community.

Proposals for the Royal Albert Dock

The Richard Rogers Partnership was principally responsible for the urban design structure of this area. It consists of a well regulated pattern of development nodes around proposed stations on the DLR extension and the adjoining roundabout intersections of the Albert Dock spine road. Hence commercial development, transportation and urban form are carefully integrated. Between the nodes, buildings are to be lower key and developed in a more incremental fashion. At the extreme east end of the dock, Rogers proposed a major retail and business park for the developer Stanhope. This ambitious and so far unrealized proposal extended the development axis of the Royal Docks to the Thamesside immediately alongside what the LDDC hoped would be a 'spectacular bridge' to form the East London river crossing.[5]

The Stanhope scheme promised much, but its development has been delayed by a dispute over the design of the Thames crossing. Whilst designs were being prepared for the bridge, some involving the Spanish engineer Santiago Calatrava, the London City Airport lodged a planning application to extend the runway in order to introduce a new class of aeroplane. This had the effect of changing the angle of the flight path, thereby making an arched bow spring bridge a potential hazard. At the time of writing matters were unresolved. The affair highlights the connected nature of decision making in urban regeneration, and the difficulties of leaving strategic matters in the hands of private companies.

The masterplan by Rogers for the Albert Basin was based upon a huge semicircle of shopping facing southwards across the water, and divided by glass roofed internal malls. By adopting the crescent-like form the design overcomes the problem of long internal malls evident in other large shopping

Figure 8.2

Royal Docks development framework. This plan shows part of the development framework for the Royal Albert Dock prepared by the Richard Rogers Partnership with environment consultants Gillespies. The structure of developoment nodes around the DLR stations with rectangular parks in between suggests a highly regulated basis for regeneration (plan: Richard Rogers Partnership)

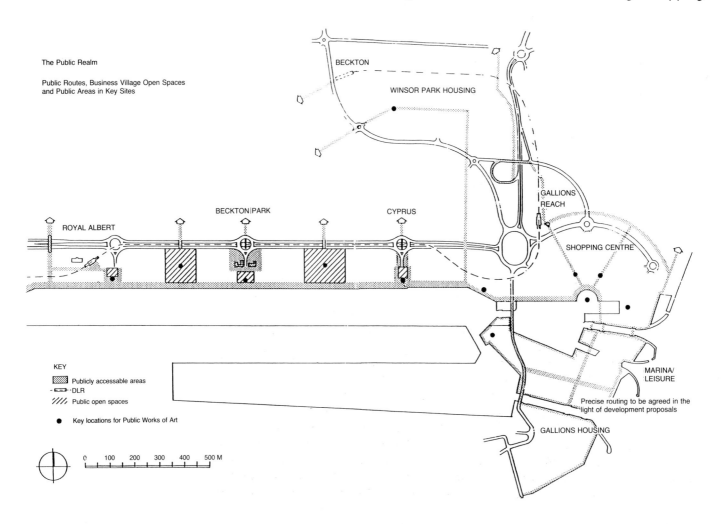

The Public Realm

Public Routes, Business Village Open Spaces and Public Areas in Key Sites

BECKTON

WINSOR PARK HOUSING

GALLIONS REACH

BECKTON PARK

CYPRUS

ROYAL ALBERT

SHOPPING CENTRE

MARINA/LEISURE

Precise routing to be agreed in the light of development proposals

GALLIONS HOUSING

KEY

Publicly accessible areas

DLR

Public open spaces

Key locations for Public Works of Art

0 100 200 300 400 500 M

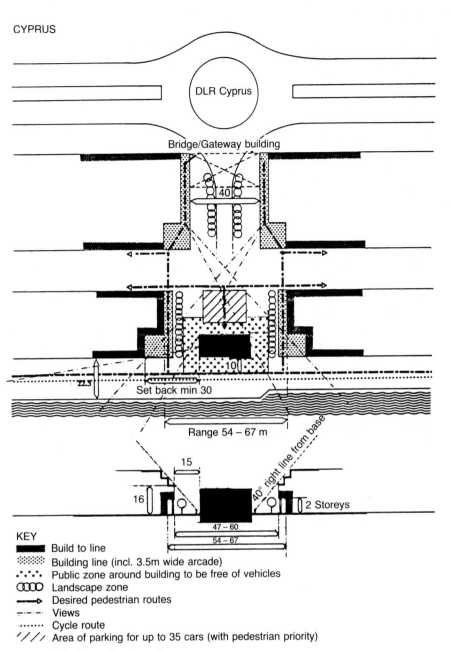

CYPRUS

DLR Cyprus

Bridge/Gateway building

40

10

Set back min 30

Range 54 – 67 m

15

16

40° right line from base

2 Storeys

47 – 60

54 – 67

KEY
▮▮▮ Build to line
▒▒▒ Building line (incl. 3.5m wide arcade)
·ᐧ·ᐧ· Public zone around building to be free of vehicles
ⵁⵁⵁ Landscape zone
➝ Desired pedestrian routes
–·–·– Views
······· Cycle route
//// Area of parking for up to 35 cars (with pedestrian priority)

N.B. Dimensions in metres

Figure 8.3

Detail of development node. The spatial parameters for development are clearly prescribed, as is the structure of urban space and landscape design. Notice how the DLR and road system are integrated (plan: LDDC)

centres such as the Gateshead Metrocentre. Within the concourse formed by the embrace of the circular shape, cafés were to face out across the water. Characteristically of the architect, the structure promised much technical daring with its combination of inflated roofs and umbrella forms. Across the dock a range of mainly circular business and conference buildings were planned, each of modernist simplicity. Stanhope has currently lost its option to carry forward this £800 million development, a victim of the bridge controversy and, one suspects, the downturn in Britain's economy.

An unsolicited and controversial proposal by local architects Spiller Farmer seeks to break with the structured regeneration of the area. Their ideas spring from the concept of Dadaist collage and what they call an 'intravenous injection' of related insertions such as a new bridge to the East London crossing, a racecourse floating in the dock and a helipad.[6] The integration of these elements into a fine art assembly of fractured and spalling forms is

Figure 8.4

Retail and business park at the Albert Dock Basin. Designed by the Richard Rogers Partnership for developer Stanhope, the implementation of the proposal has been delayed by the dispute over the design of the East London river crossing. The masterplan has an almost baroque exuberance suggestive more of a world fair than a retail development (photo: E.O'Mahony/R.Rogers Partnership)

a far cry from Roger's neobaroque master plan. If unrealistic in the present climate, the Spiller Farmer proposals look to a future when (according to these young architects) high and low life are again reconciled. After all, Docklands evolved as a landscape of commerce underpinned by a subculture of crime and gambling. The architects' plan is rather more a conceptual model than an ordering mechanism, yet it recognizes the important tendency of Docklands to grow by fragments and ill-fitting parts.

The Royal Victoria Dock

The broad strategy for the Royal Victoria Docks outlined earlier has been developed (or at times contravened) by subsidiary masterplans prepared by a variety of urban designers employed by different potential developers. To the north of the dock, a plan to build a large rectangular Londondome for sports and exhibition purposes replaces the more elegant circular form shown on the development framework. The proposal from American developers envisages nearly 4000 car or coach parking spaces between the DLR and the dockside. To the south of the dock and extending to the riverside at the Thames Barrier, Tibbalds Colbourne have prepared a formal masterplan based upon European urban squares and development blocks.[7] Inspired no doubt by the IBA in Berlin, this plan of 1989 seeks to establish an ordered implementation framework for a reluctant market.

Figure 8.5

Dadaist proposals for the Royal Docks. The grand Rogers masterplan has yet to be realized. In the meantime unsolicited proposals have been put forward including these ideas based upon the notion of Dadaist collage by local architects Spiller Farmer. They stand in marked contrast to the concept of development by regulation which has been the philosophy to date in the Royal Docks (photo: Spiller Farmer)

The formal elements of the plan consist of a generous crescent of offices and houses facing the Thames, enclosing a semicircular park 600 metres in diameter, with rectangular blocks of housing or mixed used development elsewhere. Many of the squares and courtyards are open to the south, thereby benefitting from solar penetration, and the proximity of different land uses within a finely grained area suggests a concern for energy conservation. A major road bisects the area on an east/west axis and is lined by trees to reduce its impact. Internal estate roads are also tree lined, reinforcing the European thinking behind the master plan. An existing park alongside the Tate and Lyle factory is extended in the plan by way of a street and crescent from the Thames to the waterside of the dock.

The plan is well integrated and finely composed, but to date it has not helped to coordinate actual development. The parcels of land and their supporting design guidance are so far paper exercises. Should a developer be interested the plan states that each 'parcel will have a development brief setting down a preferred mix of uses, and clear design and landscape guidelines of a mandatory and advisory nature'.[8] In marked contrast to the Isle of Dogs and much of Docklands, this plan envisages not market-led development but well controlled and coordinated urban regeneration. Former chief executive Reg Ward warned against prescription, and Michael Heseltine said in 1982 that Docklands was not in the business of creating Haussmann's Paris, yet this plan shows how far attitudes have changed over the ten years. It also shows that the economic climate must be right for the implementation of such formal plans, and perhaps if local employment is important, then a looser framework for development should be put in place.

Figure 8.6

Development framework for the Thames Barrier lands. Another unrealized plan, this time by Tibbalds Colbourne, seeks to impose a European rationalist structure of urban blocks, squares and boulevards upon the wastelands north of the Thames Flood Barrier (plan: Tibbalds Colbourne)

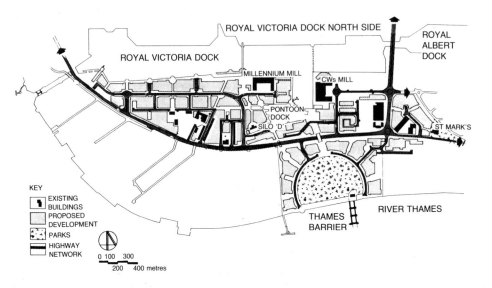

PRIMARY ELEMENTS

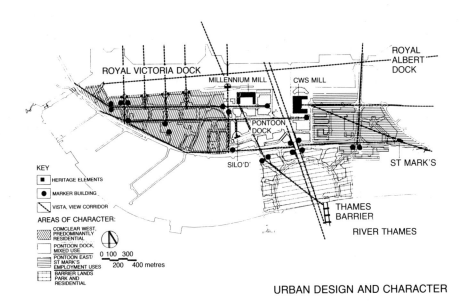

URBAN DESIGN AND CHARACTER

New housing at Beckton

In contrast to the grand plans, what has been built in the Royal Docks since the inception of the regeneration orchestrated by the LDDC are rows of neat English styled cottage houses, plus a district shopping centre. Beckton has none of the qualities of maritime suburbia found in Wapping or of formal housing inspired by the European rationalist movement as at Surrey Docks. Here the layout and style of the houses are indelibly British, right down to the mock Tudor boarding and pretty tile hanging. The estates adopt suburban road patterns, giving the impression of a garden suburb built in the inner city. Here in Beckton three key ingredients of the modern suburb are to be found in abundance: the well wooded park, the retail centre and the private garden. Even the allotment has not been overlooked in the area's regeneration; a strip of allotment gardens extends alongside the A13 right on the northern edge of the Royal Docks.

Beckton looks to be a middle class suburb in the city, but much of the housing is for local people with rents at affordable levels. Winsor Park Estate, for instance, promises to provide 409 homes subsidized in part by the LDDC, and elsewhere the language of the private suburb has been used to disguise social housing. As urban design Beckton aspires to be a model suburb, complete with village greens, graceful crescents and cul-de-sac layouts. The sense of unmitigated suburbia is reinforced by the mildly California styled Beckton District Shopping Centre built around an Asda superstore. Here local buses thread their way through heavily planted car parks. Not far away the retail park provides a collection of lightweight DIY warehouses beneath the dry ski slope at Beckton Alps. Hence land uses are well segregated, with roads and landscaping assuming greater prominence than in more central areas of Docklands. Above the tiled rooftops looms the not graceless tower of Canary Wharf about 4 kilometres away. The almost axial relationship of this landmark to the water basins of the three main docks means that it also often terminates the short vistas down local estates roads. Though Beckton is in the relatively distant and increasingly well established hinterland of Docklands, it remains beneath the gaze of the area's singularly most dominant landmark.

Beckton does not feel part of Docklands; neither does it fit comfortably into the wider landscape of East Ham. The area suffers from a sense of isolation which stems from the scale of road and rail construction on three of its sides. To the south the barrier of the high level DLR segregates Beckton from the Royal Albert Dock and beyond to the Thames. To the north Newham Way (A13) forms a dual carriageway of speeding traffic which separates Beckton from other well established areas, and to the east a similar scaled road is planned to link into the East London river crossing. Just as the old dock walls created island-like townscapes in the area, so too recent road construction has led to landscapes of segregation. To take the no. 101 bus from North Woolwich is to experience a series of physical barriers, each containing a distinct and largely isolated area of east London. Beckton is one such, a district of pleasant houses surrounded by overscaled infrastructure.

Notes

1 *Royal Docks: a Draft Development Framework* (LDDC, 1985), pp. 14–17.
2 *Ibid.*, p. 16.
3 *Ibid.*, p. 20.
4 *Royal Docks: a Vision for the Future* (LDDC undated).
5 *Ibid.*
6 Brian Edwards, 'Art of the possible', *Building Design*, 26 July 1991.
7 The full title of the LDDC published plan is *Royal Victoria Dock (South) and Thames Barrier Lands: Interim Master Plan and Development Framework* (1989). The design team was led by the Tibbalds Colbourne Partnership.
8 *ibid.*, p. 12.

Part Three
Observations and Speculations

Docklands: Success or Failure?

9

Design values in Docklands

Until the economic slump of summer 1990, London Docklands was the fastest growing area of Britain and perhaps the biggest exercise in urban renewal in Western Europe. A nine square mile landscape of desolation, near dereliction and undermaintained council housing estates has, in a mere decade, been transformed to one of glistening office blocks, gaudily coloured business parks and Dutch gabled riverside apartment blocks. The scale and speed of regeneration is impressive even if the stylistic, spatial and technological contrasts between the various developments have led some observers to note that they look like they were not built within the same century, let alone the same decade. But if you examine the various developments closely, you will quickly see a similar range of building elements employed. The tiles and bricks are from the same manufacturer, and the curtain walling, window details and cladding assemblies share a consistency almost as great as in the making of Georgian London. What is different here (and this is important for understanding the architecture of Docklands) is the lack of a concensus amongst participating designers regarding how close a correspondence should exist between form and function on the one hand, and between technology and society on the other. Hence some architects have seen Docklands as a chance to give expression to the sophisticated technologies of building and manufacturing processes which marked the 1990s, whilst others have allowed consumer taste and the surface interests of a service industry economy to shape their buildings. Naturally and inevitably, in the political climate of the Thatcher years there was little attempt by the LDDC to impose an aesthetic consistency within this deregulated environment.

The result has been an architecture of pluralism – a townscape of mixed values, diverse forms and different meanings. Whether 'complexity' is a word to employ in describing the environment built so far is quite another matter, for complexity requires elements of order to moderate the double codings and deliberate manipulation of scale and detail evident in many of the more recent developments. To paraphrase Robert Venturi, complexity and contradiction are infinitely more desirable in city making than simplicity, but they do require both an agreed platform for the perception of the complex codings (i.e. the street or the façade) and a measure of shared values.[1] However, as the redevelopment of Docklands sits (perhaps happily) between the modern and the post-modern age, there is an inevitable architectural battle between the freestyle eclectics as represented by Piers Gough and Jeremy Dixon, and the mainstream purists as represented by Nicholas Grimshaw and Richard Rogers. In some ways, however, Rogers poses a dilemma: his work in London Docklands is more mannered than elsewhere and more influenced by the geometric concerns of the European rationalists. But in an age of change and of unprecedented design interest, London Docklands provides a rare opportunity to see architectural design as more than the mere satisfying of internal programme. Docklands presents a landscape that asks two important questions of our age. First, can cities live by pluralism alone? Second, if every building is designed to reflect a slightly different position or theory, do we end up with a city or just a huge riverside design museum?

In some ways London Docklands was fortunate in the timing of the economic collapse of the traditional industries of shipping and warehousing, and in the rise of the new economy of financial services, design and information technology fostered by the Thatcher government. Dockland decline and regeneration has been a world trend, though few cities have seen its influence quite so sharply as London. A mixture of failed planning policies for the Docklands up to 1981, and a UK economy anxious rather more in the post-war years to hold on to older industries than develop new ones, led to increasing loss of morale. By way of contrast, the new architecture of London Docklands represents the optimism of the eighties, just as Milton Keynes captures the state controlled, aesthetically sanitized seventies. The high minded – such as certain editors of architectural journals – claim that Docklands has driven what integrity architecture once possessed to the wall. But there is a counter-argument, and this borrows from Marshall McLuhan.[2] When the medium becomes the message, architecture assumes the wrapping for more important matters, such as making money or writing newspapers. If you view the new buildings of London Docklands as the commercial envelopes into which evolving service industries are placed, then your approach to design shifts from an expectation of clarity or honesty in the use of materials and technologies to a more open acceptance of the architecture of advertising or private display. With such a changed perspective one can begin to understand that as Docklands is more concerned with constructing private fortunes than public monuments, architecture here is at the mercy of corporate ambitions and hence often balanced on the knife edge of taste.

Is there a place for masterplanning in a deregulated world?

One dilemma faced by the LDDC at the outset was whether London Docklands as a whole, or at least parts of the area, should be developed with the help of a masterplan. Masterplanning has been a recurring feature of British urbanism for at least 300 years. After the Great Fire of London in 1666 Sir Christopher Wren produced a highly regulated plan for rebuilding the city. Wren's unrealized plan placed new public buildings at key road crossings or at the ends of axes, and sought to establish a hierarchy of streets around existing monuments such as the Tower of London and new ones such as the planned cathedral of St Paul's. Likewise when Bath was much expanded in the eighteenth century John Woods, together with Robert Adam, prepared elaborate street plans which established a visual, functional and spatial structure for anticipated growth. Similarly when Edinburgh expanded from the insanitary confines of its old town in 1767, the city council prepared a masterplan for the laying out of a new town. Even in nineteenth century urban renewal, the masterplan was adopted from Glasgow's remodelling of 1866 to Birmingham's of 1875. Both were inspired by Haussmann's reconstruction of central Paris from 1855 to 1870 which achieved a partnership between sanitary, aesthetic and commercial reform.

Well into the twentieth century the masterplan continued to be an essential feature of British urbanism. Raymond Unwin's plan of 1903 for Letchworth inspired action for later state promoted new towns from Harlow to Cumbernauld. Though the organizing function of the street and the layout of town centres varied considerably, the need for a masterplan was rarely disputed. In fact at Milton Keynes the masterplan was given additional weight by linking broad design principles to a traffic engineer's layout of roads on a loose 1 kilometre grid. The plan allowed for both flexibility and order through a marriage of controlling mechanisms which integrated the interests of urban, landscape and building design.

In terms of size and scale of investment London Docklands is greater in extent than most of the British new towns of the twentieth century, yet no overall masterplan was adopted. Several attempts have been made to structure the development of different areas, such as the John Bonnington and Twigg Brown footprint plan for London Bridge City in 1982 and Conran Roche's masterplan for Greenland Dock in 1984, but on the whole development has been free of constraint in terms of land use, spatial organization and external linkage. The result is there to see and should be judged on its merits. However, with masterplanning again in the ascendancy (e.g. Leon Krier's proposals for Poundbury in Dorset for the Prince of Wales) London Docklands may be the best example in Europe of a free enterprise and largely unplanned approach to urbanism. The legacy of Docklands may be to demonstrate the shortcomings of market-led urban design as a solution to the problems of the inner city.

After ten years of a free-for-all, when 'dynamic contextualism' was a phrase employed by Max Hutchinson, the RIBA president, to describe the Isle of Dogs,[3] we are now witnessing the beginnings of a return to traditional master planning even in London Docklands. The meretricious architecture of deregulation is now facing the wind of beaux arts structuring, which has shaped renewal exercises as distant as the IBA in Berlin, Les Halles in Paris and the waterfront in Boston. And with the economic boom collapsing after a decade of unprecedented construction in London Docklands, the combined forces of a financial slump and a return to tradition have clipped the wings of the New Right experiment in urbanism.

The reluctance of the LDDC to invest in masterplanning has led to many problems and may yet undermine the value of the investments made. If master plans guide the aesthetics of development and establish spatial rules, they also have the effect of safeguarding the interests of developers. And here is the rub for the free market urbanists: the buildings constructed to date run the risk of poor connections in terms of both public space and urban transport, and have little protection from unsuitable or unfriendly neighbours.

For all of its size and presence the long term success of Canary Wharf depends upon protecting the hinterland from amenity devaluing development, and ensuring that its workforce can get to the Isle of Dogs without excessive discomfort. If public transport links are inadequate or an apartment block springs up to mar the view of the Thames, then Olympia and York suffer. After ten years of building it is the developers who are now pressing for traditional urban planning to protect their not inconsiderable investments.

But will a masterplan prove feasible after over half the building blocks are in place, and can the pluralism which is the one endearing feature of London Docklands survive the often dead hand of a masterplan? And if the polycentric pattern of Docklands is to be maintained, will not the future structure reflect the infrastructural investments in, say, an extended Jubilee Line rather than the existing pattern of buildings? Moreover, if civil engineering in the form of roads and transport systems is to establish the patterns of activity and urban space in the future, then it could be argued that we need a centralized agency able to coordinate the needs of architecture and municipal engineering. Or put another way, the London Docklands Development Corporation will have to assume the centralized planning powers which it has been so careful to avoid to date, and which were deliberately excluded under the 1980 Act.

What a masterplan can now achieve

Any urban area has two main aesthetic preoccupations: first, how to protect and enhance its inherited collection of monuments which reflect the cultural and social memory of the area; and second, how to create good new buildings and urban spaces which fulfil the needs of contemporary society. The great bulk of buildings between the two timescales of past monuments and future designs can be left to market forces and the day-to-day demands of maintenance and adaptation. The masterplan can address both extremes and bring a sense of continuity to bear in terms of old buildings and new construction. Here the LDDC has been most recalcitrant: because the masterplan has been eschewed, there is little correspondence between the architecture, monuments and engineering of the Docklands up to 1981 and

Figure 9.1

Figure ground comparison of Docklands. It is evident from the figure grounds of the four areas of London Docklands that disjointedness has been the general result of a decade of building. Old and new areas do not relate well to each other, the core areas of the inner docks do not connect well with the Thamesside, and a legible structure of public spaces has yet to emerge. (A) The Isle of Dogs (B) Surrey Docks (C) Wapping (D) The Royal Docks (plan: author)

(A)

(B)

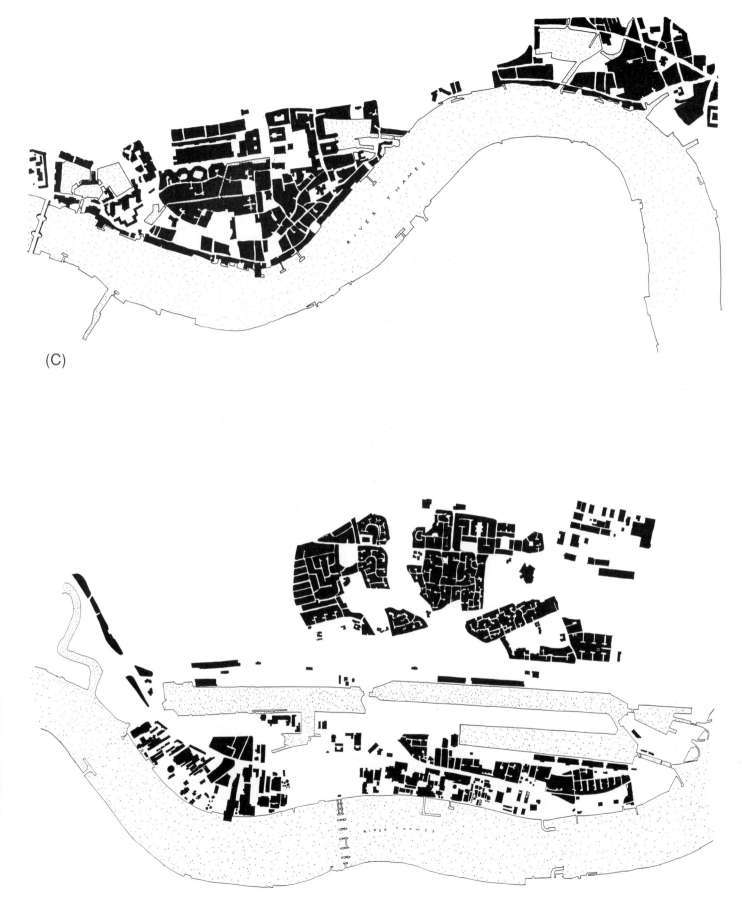

(C)

(D)

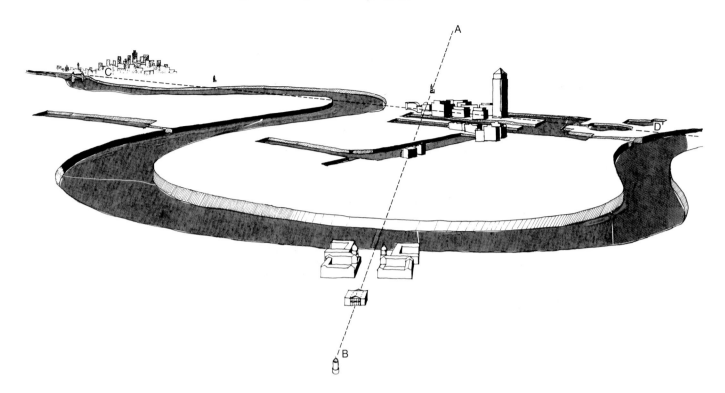

Figure 9.2

The Greenwich axis: a lost opportunity. This drawing shows the relationship of the Greenwich axis (A–B) to Canary Wharf, and the relationship of the Canary Wharf axis (C–D) to the City of London

that of the LDDC years. For example, the splendid Hawksmoor churches are relegated to well preserved backwaters and do not help establish visual corridors across the area. Similarly, Gosling and Cullen in their rejected plan of 1982 sought to extend the Wren-Greenwich axis over the Thames and into the Isle of Dogs so that development could be structured around one of London's principal urban gestures. Such visual corridors employed as development axes could have cut through the run-down architecture of the area, thereby creating a sense of hierarchy between old and new, public and private, and monumental and domestic. As they stand the churches have little real influence in terms of urban design, and though the corridors may not always have been discernible on the ground, their presence would have provided some spiritual uplift to relieve the sense of unmitigated commercialism.

Similarly the River Thames remains an overly private amenity, rarely visible and except for short lengths not given a grand riverside walkway as it is at Westminster. Most European cities treat their principal river as a public event – a place to promenade and to enjoy prospects of the city. Joseph Bazalgette at the Embankment in London and Baron Haussmann in Paris ensured that whilst the riverside provided handy routes for the sewerage systems of the nineteenth century, they could also be turned into public assets through the construction of paved walkways and planted gardens. No such concern for public domain exists in London Docklands and, though the dock basins are generally better treated and more accessible than the Thames, the lack of a masterplan is the single main reason why such issues failed to reach public debate.

With hindsight it was an error of judgement to reject the masterplan or urban design framework approach to urban regeneration. The reason for this rejection was fear of stifling investment and creating urban structures which proved inflexible or unattractive to the development community. But the result is hardly any better, and what we have now in London Docklands are fragments of a language which require tying together. The squares and crescents of Canary Wharf are the beginnings of a pattern language (to use Christopher Alexander's term[4]) as is the Embankment at London Bridge City, but they take us nowhere.

Urban design or urban collage in Docklands?

There is a counter-argument to this rather traditional and essentially European fondness for the masterplan. That is the idea of urban collage put forward by Colin Rowe and Fred Koetter.[5] They argue that the modern city consists of chance encounters with history and that the bizarre relationship of monuments in their altered state suggests that orderly and predictable arrangements are no longer desirable or even possible. Their vision of urban collage has to date been largely theoretical, but maybe London Docklands is the best expression yet of such a city. For *Collage City* deals with the modern urban phenomenon where monuments, gardens, streets and squares are in happy collision, or at least where the 'constructive disillusion' is allowed to exist alongside permanent city references. This alternative urban view has some currency in Docklands since it grows from the complex interactions between order and disorder and between innovation and tradition. Without the foundation of traditional town planning Docklands has grown into an area of *ad hoc* urbanism where the 'predicament of texture' responds to modern circumstances and political expediency more effectively and justifiably than order and regulation.

The argument deals with the values and perceptions of contemporary society. *Collage City* was written in 1978 when modernism was largely unassailed and by two authors who sought to marry the urban traditions of America and Europe. They looked closely at the history of urban design through spectacles coloured by the paradoxes of the pop age. The conclusions drawn are relevant for Docklands since a sense of failed modernist utopia, which was the starting point of Rowe and Koetter's argument, marks too the years up to the inception of the LDDC. In their different ways, the collage city and the Isle of Dogs trace an alternative urban view – a vision if you like where the coordinates of corporate happiness and individual freedom are not hampered by a unifying structure of social value.

As long as individual developers are allowed to masterplan not just the isolated aesthetics of Docklands but also self-contained elements of its

Figure 9.3

The appropriation of history for modern purposes. London Bridge City phase 2 has adapted the cultural icon of St Mark's to give lustre to the proposals. The obscuring of history, of cultural reference points, has been a feature of Docklands regeneration, and adds to the feeling of collage as against reality (photo: John Simpson) spatial structure, the more the area approaches the collage city. For they too recognize the universality of the square and the memorable street, and employ these cultural references to create private wealth within the enclaves of separate developments. They go further too: for by adapting culturally recognized forms, be it Piazza San Marco at London Bridge City or Place de la Concorde at Canary Wharf, to new building programmes they obscure the relationship with historic reality. Our cultural heritage then becomes part of the intellectual abstraction, a situation beloved of pop artists where states are altered and meanings exaggerated by new bizarre relationships. Hence one could argue that the collage city has become a reality in Docklands and, rather than design away the elements, one should accept the inevitable.

Engineering as a basis for planning

If the masterplan approach to urban design has been rejected on the whole by the LDDC or found too cumbersome to implement (as in the Richard Rogers development framework for the Royal Docks), then the means to organize the reconstruction has fallen upon the shoulders of transportation or civil engineers. There is a long and largely honourable tradition of using engineering to structure the spatial development of new areas, from the laying out of gridded towns by colonial engineers in America, to allowing the railways to dictate street layouts in cities such as London, Liverpool and Glasgow. One cannot reject the civil engineering approach to urbanism out of hand and, even in modern day France, investment by public authorities in new bridges and roads has led to some highly attractive urban interventions.

Urban design by transport engineering depends, however, upon a partnership between the participating agents. The developers of buildings need to understand the investment priorities of those providing the infrastructure. If the developers begin to doubt the willingness of the public agencies to keep abreast of their own investment targets (as happened with regard to the Jubilee Line extension to the Isle of Dogs) then the essential marriage between infrastructure design and building design breaks down. The lesson of history is that the infrastructure side (the streets, railways, bridges etc.) must always be a step ahead of the building developers. If positions are reversed, either the developers are forced to pay for the public services or the basic logic between the connectors and the connected is lost. In terms of urban design there is normally a correspondence between the two, with the infrastructure dictating the density of development and its spatial distribution. Except for investment in roads (and here not entirely) London Docklands has failed this litmus test, for whilst the light railway has its virtues, the diminutive scale of its operation makes a nonsense of any serious dialogue between levels of building use and its carrying capacity.

Had infrastructure been the basis for urban design then some benefits would have followed. First, the railway stations would have become nodes of activity, with buildings and supporting activities such as shops and cafés grouped around them. Instead of descending flights of steps or waiting on windy high level platforms, passengers would perhaps have found the station incorporated within a group of buildings which themselves could have acted as an emblem for the station and provided space for circulation. Such buildings could have been arranged as a square or crescent to give some celebration to the existence of the station. One could then have met friends or business colleagues within the sheltered space, stopping perhaps at an outside café to savour the atmosphere. Such stations would also have acted as nodes supporting bigger buildings, thus establishing some visual coherence to the area. Only at Canary Wharf has this pattern emerged, and here because of the initiative of the developer, not of those planning the infrastructure.

Infrastructure engineering could also have given some clarity to the road system. As it is the roads are mere transport channels with no attempt to treat movement as an enjoyable experience. One has no real chance to experience the new architecture of Docklands from the roads. There is little exploitation of view, skyline or serial vision for those travelling by car or bus. The scale of buildings in Docklands, their often brash colour and their apparent random positioning suggest that only in rapid movement are they truly enjoyable. Yet the road system (unlike the Docklands Light Railway) fails to employ switchbacks or changes in direction to exploit the kinetic possibilities.

By way of contrast, a journey down the Thames on a river bus gives the observer a full frontal view of the building operations. Typically CZWG, with their love of display, place the red gabled China Wharf as a riverside spectacle and further down river employ Cascades as a marker to West India Dock. Conran Roche's white cube of a Design Museum addresses the river with more seriousness than its contents, yet it fulfils certain riverside responsibilities, as do most buildings which face the Thames hereabouts. But unlike the Thames, the major roads and the Docklands Light Railway slip between buildings rather than force them to address the transport system as an aesthetic opportunity. Given the sense of display and consumerism prevalent in Docklands, this is one of the most disappointing aspects of a decade of construction.

Both Robert Venturi et al. in *Learning from Las Vegas* and Kevin Lynch in his equally perceptive book *The Image of the City* recognize in their different ways the role of the street or highway strip as a unifying corridor.[6] Though they come to conclusions more applicable to American cities than European ones, the idea of the street as urban regulator and image giver seems not yet to have filtered through to the bulk of architects working on Dockland buildings or to LDDC planners. One only has to look at the relationship between building entrances and the street to see how unsatisfactory are most Dockland buildings. The *Financial Times* building, for instance, places a security fence to the busy East India Docks Road (the A13) and the entrance around the side. If the consumer's view of the city is from the roads or railways, then in the deregulated and increasingly private Docklands the perception is one of security fences, blank walls and guarded cul-de-sacs.

Deregulation and the failure of urban design

The trouble with London Docklands is that there is no urban grid or substantive development framework to tie the architectural pluralism together. The traditional city had its streets and squares as a structure for later stylistic changes, but Docklands treats the streets as inconsequentially as its buildings. In twentieth century British new towns the streets and public squares (in modern guise) remained important elements in the spatial and hierarchical organization of buildings from Letchworth to Milton Keynes. And in other twentieth century new settlements such as Chandigarh and Brasília there was a clear relationship between urban space and urban building. Pluralism of building forms and styles needs an underlying structure – a grid of streets or framework of squares to stitch the various elements into an environment we can understand and appreciate.

Where street arrangements have been inherited in London Docklands, as in parts of Wapping, or where dock basins provide a strong unifying element, there urban design is most successful. The so-called dynamic contextualism here has a strong spatial framework which keeps the competing elements within aesthetic bounds. But devoid of such a framework, the visual competition becomes overwhelming and unsatisfactory. Although elements of a pattern language exist, as at Canary Wharf, the more usual situation is one of conflicting scale, colours, shapes and land uses. There is an undeniable excitement in the competing architectures, a tension which is both arresting and disarming. The problem exists not so much with the aesthetics of architecture, but in the practicalities of urban design.

Figure 9.4

The view from the air. Without a unifying grid of streets, the Dockland landscape has become overbearing. A sense of development competition dominates civic values with buildings of different colours, styles and shapes shouting for attention (photo: Chorley and Handford Ltd)

There are two approaches to this problem. The first is to create the framework which will tie all the different sizes and types of buildings together. This will probably entail re-establishing the traditional dominance of the street (as against the estate road), making greater use of the dock basins and riversides as unifying elements, and forming nodes of activity with some sort of architectural celebration around the new railway stations. These nodes will then require linking by key streets, and the new districts established by all the current building activity will further need to be defined by landscape and urban measures. One cannot expect true urbanism to develop incrementally.

The other approach (and both should be followed) is to reurbanize London Docklands. The spaces between buildings, the lack of height in the business parks, the abrupt transition from high to low buildings, the inability of many buildings to address the street in any meaningful fashion, all lead to a suburban rather than urban character. In fact, it is an American suburban character and not even a British one, for the subcentring of Docklands is at least superficially reminiscent of Los Angeles. How this reurbanization is to take place is discussed elsewhere, but the need for it is doubted by few commentators, and even the key players in the LDDC are now aware of the problem. During the first decade of Docklands redevelopment, urban design as a distinct discipline emerged upon the British scene. London Docklands has been one reason for this reawakening; in fact the failure of urban design in the area has focused minds upon the limits to city making by architecture alone.

There are undoubted limits to design pluralism in terms of making new cities. One could argue that existing cities with a strong sense of character, such as Paris, Barcelona or Boston, can comfortably absorb new and outrageous structures into their built fabric, but new cities or substantial urban transplants such as London Docklands cannot live by pluralism alone. If London Docklands can teach the world anything it is that just as you have to design a building or a new town, so too you must masterplan urban renewal. Design cannot be relegated to market forces or dissipated into the conflicting energies of a multitude of different design firms. There is a need for central control through some form of masterplan and the adoption of design codes.

Critics of this approach will argue that London Docklands represents an urban openness which reflects freedom and opportunity. To restrict the spirit of openness will, they argue, curtail the prospects of pluralism. In his perceptive essay on New York, Christian Norberg-Schulz argues that openness is the key to American cities and that it actually breeds a healthy pluralism by cultivating 'islands of meaning' within the city.[7] Docklands may be Europe's most visible expression of this trend – a mini New York exploiting the eclecticism of the modern experience.

Skyline as private trophy

New York is the image of cityscape which has most influenced the development of Docklands. The sense of scale, proximity to water and willingness to punctuate the skyline are all traits associated more with Manhattan than the City of London. Just as the Empire State Building or more recently the World Financial Centre by Cesar Pelli sought to make its mark upon public perceptions of the city through manipulation of the silhouette of Manhattan, so too Canary Wharf seeks to reprofile the skyline of London. Many argue today that skyline represents the quintessence of civic values and should only be altered by buildings of public intent, but London's silhouette has long signalled private wealth rather than public value. Canaletto's famous views showed the Wren monuments of St Paul's and Greenwich Hospital dominating all else, but by the mid twentieth century high rise office buildings in the City and apartments blocks in the West End had already challenged their supremacy. Not long after, the towers of public housing and private banking squeezed St Paul's into an uncomfortable dip in an otherwise growing skyline. Canary Wharf, Simpson's planned St Mark's inspired

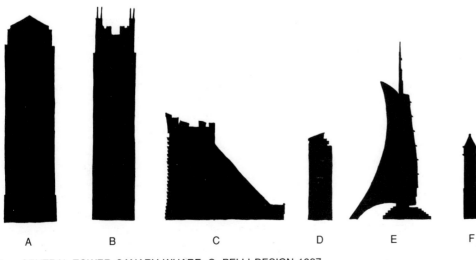

A CENTRAL TOWER CANARY WHARF: C. PELLI DESIGN 1987
B CENTRAL TOWER CANARY WHARF: KOHN PEDERSON FOX (UNREALIZED) 1986
C CASCADES: CZWG 1988
D VOGANS MILL: MICHAEL SQUIRE 1990
E HERON QUAYS: SCOTT BROWNRIGG AND TURNER, 1990 (UNREALIZED)
F LONDON BRIDGE CITY PHASE 2: JOHN SIMPSON (UNREALIZED)

Figure 9.5

Skyline profiles. Deregulation and freedom from planning control has encouraged the development (or merely design) of several new towers in east London. Whilst Canary Wharf dominates the skyline of Dockland through height and bulk, the lower towers have arguably more interesting profiles.

Figure 9.6

Canary Wharf and the dominating tower. The skyscraper commands all in sight and provides a central pivot for the development. The American urban precedents are obvious

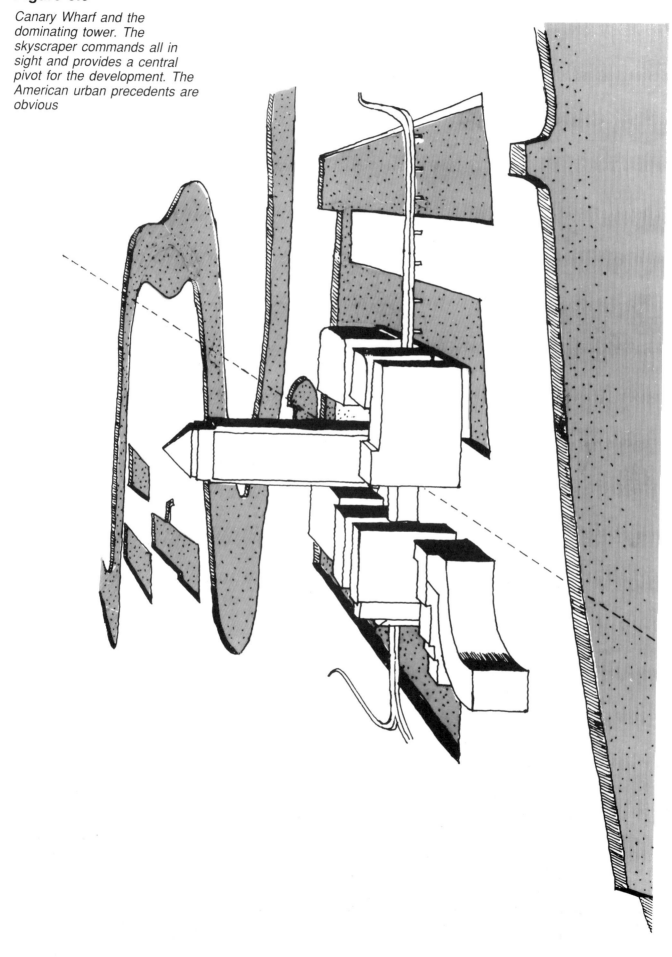

office at London Bridge City phase 2, and Seifert's South Quay Plaza continue, therefore, a fairly honourable tradition.

What is most Manhattan-like about Docklands is the proximity of towers to water. The base course of lower buildings barely exists (except in some absurdly underscaled business park sheds) so the towers generally rise unimpeded from the wharfside or even directly from the water itself. This characteristic makes the buildings look even more North American than their profiled or pedimented tops. The tower blocks and skyscrapers of most European cities grow from a well developed base of six or seven storey buildings. They are seen above old rooftops and strike streets which contain much activity. In Docklands the reverse is true: the towers rise from car parks or estate roads, sail almost over water, and hit the clouds with a certain relish. Between top and bottom may exist forty storeys of near identical, fast track marble and glass curtain wallings, but arguably the eye wanders pleasurably over the way the buildings strike the sky or rise from the ground.

Another Manhattan characteristic is the way the towers are becoming gathered into happily competing groups. The pattern elsewhere in London is to come across nearly isolated towers which bully all in sight and add nothing to the visual currency of the capital. Only in parts of the City and now on the Isle of Dogs do towers begin to form metropolis-like relationships with each other. The more they fight for attention, the greater their richness and use of elaborate profiling. The baroque churches of Rome and even Wren's fifty or so London churches demonstrate the pleasures of competing towers.

Some would argue that Docklands is given its identity by the new skyline of Canary Wharf; if so, the architectural signature is written with a magic marker as against fountain pen. Canary Wharf presages a new era of high rise office building in London; it takes the debate about scale, bulk and rooftop profiling further than most of its predecessors. Unfortunately, it stands at present as an independent monument rising loftily above the waters of Millwall Docks with only CZWG's Cascades near by. When more towers are constructed the townscape of the Isle of Dogs will become richer, since the new towers will form foothills (to use Piers Gough's term) to the mountain of Canary Wharf.[8] And if each competes for a place in the city skyline or amongst the foothills, a true skyscraper centre may yet emerge.

Two things must not be allowed to happen. First, a height limit imposed now would destroy the ensemble effect sought; it would simply leave Canary Wharf as another isolated London high building. Second, tall buildings should be encouraged to rise from the water's edge without interruption. In parts of Docklands low buildings have been allowed to squeeze along the docksides (usually in the form of restaurants); these destroy the urban scale and discourage high buildings from becoming celebratory monuments at the critical water's edge.

In American cities the skyscraper has a special relationship to the street. The typical gridiron street plan forces skyscrapers into parallel configurations. Hence they are not randomly oriented but share the same parallels and street edges. Also the best towers are often placed at intersections of principal streets or even where a diagonal slices through the rigid geometries of the grid. The primary order imposed by the streets arranges the skyscrapers into tidy groupings where the main freedom for expression occurs at the pavement or in rooftop profiling. In Docklands there is no primary order dictated by gridded street layouts; instead there are estate roads and new highways. Without the organizing geometries of streets and urban blocks, the Dockland skyscrapers have become detached from the public arena. This makes them even more objects of private architectural trophy then their counterparts on Fifth Avenue.

Amongst the towers of private wealth in Docklands stand a few relics from the days of high rise social housing. These system built slab blocks are as

Figure 9.7

Harbour Exchange. Because of the building in front of the towers, the crucial relationship between tall building and water's edge is lost (photo: Charter Group)

featureless as any from this nondescript period of British architecture. Undermaintained and rarely cherished by their residents, these tower blocks dominate more recent cottage style private housing and often close the vistas of open Dockland views (especially around Southwark and Blackwall). They stand as fitting reminders of changing high rise fashions and different political aspirations. If the skyline of the city is truly to represent cultural memory, such towers must remain to set the skyscrapers of the nineties into context.

How green is London Docklands?

London Docklands can hardly be called green in any ecological or environmental sense. By 'green' I mean not so much the landscape framework for development, but the holistic approach to environment and particularly the use of land and resources, especially energy resources. Within the LDDC there is no energy strategy for the area; and, save for the notable contribution of one or two buildings, the environments created so far cannot reasonably be described as green within any broad definition of the term.

An ungreen place

Unlike Milton Keynes, which adopted a positive attitude towards energy conservation in the policies which underpinned the development of the town (or city, as they pompously called the place), London Docklands has followed no such path. Instead, we find practically a new city with no serious commitment to public transport (in fact with positive incentives in terms of road layout for private car use); strict land use segregation in most of the major developments; no attempt to create favourable orientation in building development; little structural tree planting to improve microlimate; and no attempt to encourage district heating through combined heat and power schemes. All of this is remarkable bearing in mind the energy problems of the eighties and the growing awareness of the impending crisis of global warming. It is also ironic that if predictions of global warming come true and the sea rises by half a metre over the next four decades, then much of Docklands itself faces periodic flooding. The Thames Barrier nearby should have been warning enough for the LDDC to place energy conservation amongst its initial priorities.

Energy use in the UK is divided between about 50 per cent consumed in heating and lighting buildings, nearly 25 per cent in transportation and the remaining quarter in manufacturing industry, agriculture and various electronic services. Good planning and design, therefore, has the potential to impact upon about three-quarters of the energy used in Britain. Consequently major development, since it remains in place for about fifty years (though perhaps less in Docklands), should seek to use energy wisely because fuel reserves will dwindle. Though building designers have a clear responsibility, so too do those who fund development, and so too does the corporation.

By not requiring an energy audit to be made part of the development assessment process, and by not encouraging energy initiatives generally, the LDDC has allowed a high energy consuming environment to grow up. Had energy conservation been part of the development strategy (as it is in the redevelopment of Swansea Docks and the waterfront in Toronto), then we would have expected to see greater mixed use development (with a clear reduction in car journey requirements), more heavily funded public transport, fewer tall buildings or the use of deep plans, more consistent southerly orientation within housing, and a framework of planting which provides shelter from chilling winds. The environment which would have been created by greater energy awareness would also have benefited other objectives such as urban design. For mixed use development leads to greater richness and more variety of forms than single use; more investment in public transport would have led to nodes of activity developing around well used railway stations; and the abrupt changes in building height which are such a feature of the Isle of Dogs would not have occurred. Energy consciousness could have been the motivating element which gave Docklands its spatial and visual structure. If traditional town planning is abandoned, masterplans are eschewed and social provision and energy awareness are ignored, the result will naturally be a formless, structureless environment. For all the superficial greenery, Docklands is not a green place.

Even in terms of building design, greater energy awareness would have had aesthetic benefits. The bland, gridded, glazed boxes of much of Docklands commercial architecture is symptomatic of indifference to energy. The building façades are not modelled differently between south and north elevations; there are few sunscreens (*brise-soleil*) to shade façades and reduce the need for expensive summer ventilation; and buildings do not usually take advantage of the energy benefits of atria. Most Dockland buildings are constructed as if energy was an infinite resource and as if global warming was the invention of irrational scientists. As a rule Dockland office blocks employ deep plans, sealed environments, wrap-around curtain walling and elaborate lifts and escalators. A green office is an altogether different animal and is generally scarce in Docklands, though Rick Mather's recently completed speculative office block on The Highway in Wapping experiments with green principles such as natural lighting, ventilation and personal control over the working environment. Certain residential developments take advantage of passive solar principles for space heating (e.g. Hythe Point at Surrey

Quays) but most apply standard house plans and orthodox estate layout in spite of well documented disadvantages. One could argue that the extent of residential or office conversion of redundant warehouses represents an energy saving, since the energy costs of demolition and reconstruction are avoided. This is certainly true: however, the motivation was not to utilize a typical Victorian building's high thermal mass but to exploit riverside views and take advantage of the marketing benefits of heritage-led development. Energy conservation, though it tends to favour building conservation, was not the motivation behind any of these schemes.

Possible green initiatives

Timing is perhaps the major reason why energy was not given much priority by the corporation, developers or architects. Most of the development proposals evolved when energy was relatively cheap and when other targets were on the political and design agenda. Now after the Gulf crisis and widespread appreciation of the environmental consequences of indiscriminate energy consumption, a new appreciation is emerging. But any retrofit of Docklands and its buildings to achieve the type of energy initiatives outlined will entail great difficulty since private worlds have been firmly established and the incentive for improvement rests with public rather than private bodies.

However, there are two opportunities which should not be missed. First, much space exists in the form of surface car parks and pockets of landscaping around many of the new buildings. If these areas were built up to create the mix of uses lacking in many parts of Docklands (especially on the Isle of Dogs) then both the energy performance of the area and its urban design would be improved. Such infilling of gaps would gradually lead to an urban block of mixed uses, relatively even height and elevationally varied buildings – a model in fact of energy consciousness with a European precedent, as against the American one now employed. Second, by investing adequately in public transport we would find focuses of pedestrian activity which would in time generate diversity of uses (pubs, shops etc.) around stations, and free some of the road space for civic use. Public transport investment would not only reduce pollution, improve health and save on fossil fuel consumption but also enhance the sense of *civitas*.

The urban pattern to date (which is essentially suburban) suffers not only from an energy point of view, but in terms of poor community identity and lack of environmental quality. One could unlock the problem by using the key of social provision (as is frequently proposed by the surrounding local authorities) but a more appropriate and pressing remedy is to introduce sensible energy policies into the development of the area. This should extend beyond the provision of public transport services to include the design or redesign of buildings, the introduction of climate sheltering planting, the protection of solar aperture, the provision of cycleways and cross-city walkways, and the establishment of an energy office within the LDDC. Developers too could set an example by building prototype energy efficient offices as they have at Stockley Park or housing as at Milton Keynes. If such a path was followed then the environment of disjointedness in Docklands would gradually be replaced by one of greater order and perhaps environmental harmony.

If a pattern is to be sought for a more energy efficient urban structure it lies ironically within nineteenth century precedents which grew up when energy was relatively expensive and when the bones of a national transport system were being established. The urban housing type almost universally employed then was the terraced house and this is a relatively efficient model, especially with favourable orientation. The factory or mill was solidly built, ventilated by windows and accessible on foot to most workers. The office was fairly tall, built cheek by jowl with other uses such as banks, and normally near a railway station. Recreation was provided within parks which took advantage of riversides or central locations to provide green lungs for often polluted cities. Hence the package of work, industry, home and leisure existed within an integrated landscape where the connections were provided on foot or by train or tram. Such inefficiencies as pollution and poor public health are, of course, well known, but the great Victorian towns responded to energy in a fashion which could offer useful models for the future.

At present there is some interest amongst LDDC officials in formulating green policies for Docklands. The issue raises a fundamental problem for the free market planners of the corporation: any environmental strategy will run counter to the development principles employed to date (except, that is, within the small pockets of conservation areas). If green tendencies are to be encouraged it will be through persuasion rather than control, and will require the cooperation of developers. However, the inclination will probably be to leave matters of environment and energy to economic forces, on the assumption that the market is more in tune with public opinion and green concerns than administrators. If London Docklands is ever to become green it will be because that suits market needs, not because the corporation dictates such a policy. The market has only recently moved on this point, but Docklands could be a good place to demonstrate that life in the inner city can be healthy, energy efficient and full of greenery.

The neglect of the Thamesside

The LDDC's area of responsibility focuses upon the Thames, the most potent symbol of change in Docklands, yet the corporation has not adopted guidelines for the treatment of the river corridor. Unlike the GLC which published *Thamesside Guidelines* in order to coordinate development along the river,[9] the LDDC has allowed developers to shape the land use, spatial and aesthetic profile of this important area. As a consequence the Thames has not matured into a civic asset under the LDDC's guardianship; neither have the long term problems of poor cross-river communications been addressed. In 1981 the corporation inherited a private landscape of riverside warehouses, wharves and industry, yet for all the investments in new buildings the Thames remains a private and largely inaccessible world.

By controlling the regeneration of both banks of the river the LDDC had a splendid opportunity to treat the Thames as an area of special character. After decades of neglect, the chance existed in 1981 to create a corridor of amenity slicing through the dereliction of east London. Prime sites could have been made available for new parks, for buildings of distinction and even for new bridges. The lack of connection between Wapping and Surrey Docks and between the Isle of Dogs and Greenwich could have been tackled. One could also have floated the idea of new islands within an ever widening Thames, perhaps as tax-free havens to provide the economic motor of regeneration. The lack of urban design vision which characterizes the early years of the LDDC is nowhere more marked than in the neglect of the riverside.

Without a visionary plan the Thamesside has been redeveloped in an *ad hoc* and incremental fashion. The opportunity was missed to create a place of beauty out of the capital's greatest neglected environmental asset. In 1988 the Royal Fine Art Commission published a report *A New Look for London* which contained a chapter on the opportunities presented along the whole length of the Thames.[10] This report and the subsequent Thames Study Exhibition coordinated by the architect Terry Farrell highlighted the extent of missed opportunity in the first ten years of the LDDC. As in much of the corporation's early measures to promote regeneration, a fear of stifling investment by overprescriptive guidelines resulted in many missed opportunities. The Thames sadly has been the major loser in the ideological battle for development freedom.

Figure 9.8

The Thames: a private world. This view from the approach to Tower Bridge shows a wide but not beautiful river. The warehouses hug the water's edge without a Thamesside walkway, and high buildings sprout uncomfortably above the rooftops of older buildings (photo: Brian Edwards)

Space exists today to form new bridges or to create islands within the muddy estuary, but with 50 per cent of the offices unlet and many apartments unsold, the economy no longer supports grand gestures. After RFAC prompting the will may now exist within the LDDC board to tackle the Thamesside as a special area, but the means to implement the measures have probably passed London by. All that one can expect within the remaining years of the LDDC is the welding together of the various waterside developments or points of interest, perhaps in the form of a riverside walkway, and the making of the Thames more visible to the hinterland of Docklands.

The reincarnation of the riverside warehouse has plagued the Thames from Richmond to the sea, but Docklands has seen a particularly unfortunate flowering of this building type. One can accept the logic of a warehouse revival facing enclosed docks such as Shadwell Basin, but not on the wide and handsome Thames. Here a collection of splendid Victorian bridges, and the palaces of which the Tower of London, Somerset House and Greenwich Naval Hospital are obvious examples, suggest a landscape of greater ambitions. Sadly few Thamesside buildings in Docklands have risen to the occasion; most address the river with as much enthusiasm as they devote to their civic responsibilities when facing a typical London street. Only in plans for London Bridge City phase 2 have architects sought to revive the Thamesside palace, and here in the John Simpson scheme for Venetian dress. This lack of vision is largely the result of the LDDC's reluctance to see the river in anything other than utilitarian terms.

The river buses which now ply the lower Thames open to public view the fronts of countless riverside buildings. The river has become a 'path', to use Kevin Lynch's term,[11] and hence requires subsequent definition in the form of secondary landmarks. Travelling from County Hall, the passenger will find the Thames bridges providing obvious perceptual divisions in a journey of some interest. Between the bridges the façades of several fine buildings such as Billingsgate Market provide important points of interest. Below Tower Bridge the river widens, the landscape suddenly becomes more industrial, and the landmarks begin to disappear. New apartment blocks, offices and the occasional tower front an increasingly derelict hinterland. Few landmarks now occur and there are no bridges to divide the Thames into recognizable parcels. Standing out from the background, China Wharf marks the entrance into St Saviour's Docks, and just below there are viewing slots to the churches of St-George-in-the-East and St James. Further down river Canary Wharf dominates the scene, including Cascades at the Thamesside, and around the bend the square apartment blocks of Burrells Wharf provide a secondary focus. The Thames refuses to be landmarked in any obvious sense, with the colourful Baltic Quays shouting in vain for attention amongst lesser structures.

Had the Thames been made the subject of a design guide (as it is in Wandsworth) then landmarks could have been placed at regular intervals and a widening river faced by buildings of growing height or enlivened by the introduction of islands. A design guide could also have protected the

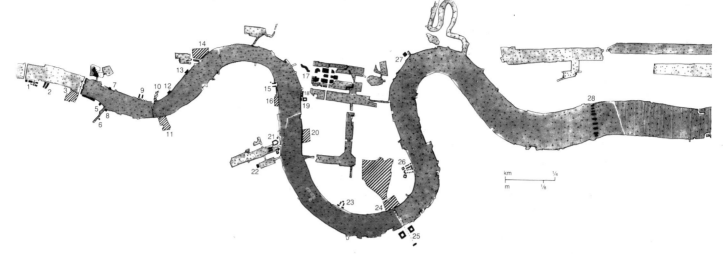

1. LONDON BRIDGE CITY PHASE 1	8. CHINA WHARF	15. LAWRENCE WHARF	22. BALTIC QUAYS
2. HAYS GALLERIA	9. WAPPING PIER HEAD	16. DURAND'S WHARF GARDENS	23. BURRELLS WHARF
3 WILLIAM CURTIS PARK	10. WAPPING GARDENS	17. CANARY WHARF	24. ISLAND GARDENS
4. BUTLERS WHARF	11. KING'S STAIRS GARDENS	18. CASCADES	25. GREENWICH AXIS
5. DESIGN MUSEUM	12. GUN WHARF	19. SUFFRANCE WHARF	26. COMPASS POINT
6. VOGAN'S MILL	13. METROPOLITAN WHARF	20. SIR JOHN McDOUGAL GARDENS	27. REUTERS
7. 84 ST KATHERINE'S WAY	14. KING EDWARD MEMORIAL PARK	21. GREENLAND PASSAGE	28. THAMES FLOOD BARRIER

Figure 9.9

Points of interest along the Thames

vistas of Thamesside churches and ensured that the few listed buildings facing the river such as Wapping Pier Head had a considered relationship with newer neighbours. The guide could also have established a spatial framework for the integration of high rise buildings into the visual currency of the river.

Market-led regeneration has achieved great change along the Thames, but in qualitative terms many opportunities were lost. The LDDC's prime task was to regenerate, but the inability to equate the political will for regeneration with wider civic aspirations highlights again the limitations of what has been achieved.

Housing in Docklands: past, present and future

Speculative house building is a very old way of making money in London. It is also a well established means of giving the capital its urban order of terraced houses and straight streets intermixed with the occasional square. The makers of Georgian and Victorian London from Nicholas Barbon to Thomas Cubitt were the mainspring of the capital's residential expansion, first westwards then northwards and southwards until by about 1850 the City and Westminster were ringed by new solid housing. Only the East End of London remained substantially untouched by the speculative endeavours of these influential builders.

By way of contrast the Docklands were built up not with great terraces of houses designed by architects but with grand blocks of warehouses designed by engineers, and later residential estates built by local councils. As a result Docklands is quite unlike other areas of London, even those of a working class character such as Peckham or Hackney. Docklands conspicuously lacks the rows of neat English houses found elsewhere in London, and as a consequence churches, public baths, schools and libraries are rare. The speculators of the period invested in dock and canal construction, warehouses and pubs. The housing which was built filled not the prime riverside sites (these were needed for warehouses) but the areas on the fringes of Docklands. Hence Docklands has few Thamesside terraces of handsome houses, no public squares to rival those in the West End, and a markedly limited collection of houses for the artisan. Even the rows of working class housing are surprisingly limited in scope and invention, with the notable exceptions of Cubitt Town and the model estates built by Poplar Borough Council in the 1920s.

It is with this landscape that the new housing of Docklands seeks to establish some kind of dialogue. Naturally dialogue tends to be in the direction of the warehouse rather than the domestic tradition. This is hardly surprising since much of the new housing takes the place of the dockside sheds or Thamesside warehouses. Where the warehouses are listed they have been converted rather than demolished, and these survivors provide the contextual justification for much of the new housing.

Britain lacks a strong tradition of riverside housing, and hence Docklands has seen almost the invention of a new residential building type. The warehouse form of generally five or six storeys has been used to house a variety of flat types and social class. At one end of the spectrum, as witnessed in the Broseley Estates scheme at Tower Bridge Wharf, such flats may cost £200,000, whilst nearby in Wapping High Street similar blocks contain modest flats constructed for the East London Housing Association. The tall, brick built warehouse, plain to the street and opening into a galaxy of balconies on the riverside, has been a recurring theme in Docklands. Various interpretations have stemmed from this basic form, some bizarre such as CZWG's China Wharf, and others more orthodox. At its most full blown the residential warehouse provides attractive townscape and gives a firm edge to dock basins and riversides alike.

A variation on the theme is to be found particularly in Surrey Docks. Here the residential block is treated as a square, formal apartment house linked often by lower wings containing parking. Such an arrangement gives greater urbanity than the more picturesquely handled warehouse, and allows a formality to grow which responds well to the rectangular water basins. A good example is Richard Reid's Finland Quay facing Greenland Dock, and the scheme by Danish architects Kjaer and Richter at Lawrence Wharf. The latter example exploits the perimeter block layout popular with the European rationalists and already well developed in Germany and Holland. Docklands gives expression to much new thinking in residential design, at least in terms of British practice.

Away from prime docksides, housing of a more suburban character has been built. At Beckton, rows of essentially English terraces follow the curving road layouts in a fashion which could be anywhere in the south of England. Hints of arts and crafts detailing and Tudor boarding are a far cry from the robust vernacular of other housing projects in Docklands. A good blend of sensitivity to both market needs and the local context is to be found around Western Dock in Wapping. Here volume house builders have adopted their plans and elevations to recall the red brick architecture of Dutch towns. Rows of neat terraced houses facing the dock are given rhythm and sense of place by semicircular arches which extend through to the first floor. A more sophisticated application of the same general theme is to be found in the development around Shadwell Basin by MacCormac, Jamieson, Prichard and Wright.

Compass Point on the Isle of Dogs is one of the few schemes which seek to incorporate the full range of residential types within a single development. Here Jeremy Dixon has combined elements of crescent, terrace, apartment block and semi-detached villa into a scheme of English refinement for the LDDC and Costain. Rather than look to the revival of the warehouse, Dixon exploits the long and varied tradition of domestic building types in Britain. He uses Nash-like detailing mixed with elements of Victorian and Edwardian layout to re-establish qualities associated with the London street. Hence we find riverfront houses which could have migrated from Richmond, a white crescent from Chelsea, rows of mews houses from Fulham and semi-detached houses from Blackheath. Although employing a full and sometimes competing repertoire of house types, Dixon establishes a formality across the site. A main axis is placed at right angles to the Thames (and is terminated by the silos of a cement works across the river) with a pair of squares facing on to Manchester Road behind.

Figure 9.10

Compass Point, Isle of Dogs. Designed by Jeremy Dixon and BDP, this housing scheme facing the Thames (on the right) mixes all the housing types of English domestic design within a single development. Manchester Road is on the left (plan: Jeremy Dixon)

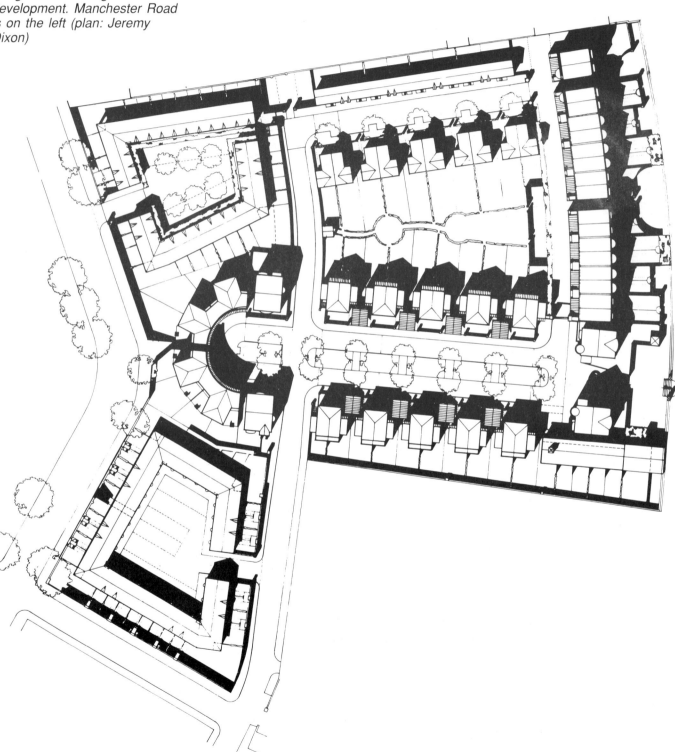

Figure 9.11

Compass Point: mews housing. Whilst the major commercial developers have sought international values, many residential designers have aped English traditions (photo: LDDC)

Of the 17,000 homes built in Docklands in the first ten years, about 50 per cent have been sold to local people. Hence the ambition of the LDDC in 1981 to diversify tenure has been partially successful. The LDDC aimed at moving from 85 per cent of local residents in council housing schemes to 50 per cent by a combination of judicious land sales to developers, financial assistance and design encouragement. Although regeneration through job creation remained the prime target of the LDDC, behind the scenes the corporation has quietly re-established a new social order through housing provision. At the Amos Estate for example the LDDC bought a derelict housing scheme from Southwark Council in order to speed through its refurbishment via a partnership of Barratt Homes and a local housing association. Changed tenure and a new image through housing design have been part of the LDDC's strategy of regeneration. The link between job creation and home ownership has been fostered by the development of residential estates of distinctive form and different social profile.

By diversifying the range of housing types in Docklands the LDDC has encouraged the evolution of new residential neighbourhoods of some architectural interest. A combination of design competition for prime residential sites, the attraction of entrepreneurial developers to the waterside, and a culture of aesthetic freedom has produced some of the best housing of recent times. It is, like the new commercial buildings, an architecture of colour, brashness and vibrancy. Even where these qualities are absent, as in Beckton, the new residential areas offer an environment of responsiveness and greenery. If Barbon and Cubitt left little mark in Docklands, the new builders of the eighties such as Barratt, Lovells and Kentish Homes have continued a tradition of using speculative house building to give the capital its fundamental character.

The un-Englishness of London Docklands

In his book *The Englishness of English Art* Nikolaus Pevsner argues that there has been something fundamentally English about the approach to landscape design and urban planning in England since the eighteenth century.[12] He puts this down to the twin influences of climate and the picturesque movement. The latter owed much to literary argument and to examples of house and garden making set by Alexander Pope and Lord Burlington. At Twickenham and Chiswick respectively the two shaped English taste directly for a hundred years and indirectly for much longer. The key elements of Englishness were surprise, unexpected vistas and changes of level, pleasant contrasts, and the use of unadorned nature in close proximity to buildings. Pevsner traces certain of these elements into the twentieth century via a route which includes the eighteenth century London square, which not only created enclaves of the countryside in the dense fabric of the city, but established the English tradition of urban palace fronts facing not a street but a park. Twentieth century examples in London cited by Pevsner include Sir William Holford's Paternoster Square and Barbican redevelopments (with the LCC Architects' Department) and Sir Leslie Martin's Roehampton Estate of highrise blocks of council flats. What makes these schemes English is apparently their deliberate avoidance of straight axes and artificially symmetrical façades, and the adoption instead of a Nash-like love of variety, surprise and skilful management of urban scale and planting. By these standards little in London Docklands is truly English except perhaps the quirky housing schemes by CZWG (especially those behind Butlers Wharf), Jeremy Dixon's Compass Point on the Isle of Dogs, and the unadorned nature garden around Stave Hill in Rotherhithe.

Elsewhere Englishness, at least by the criteria adopted by Pevsner, appears thin on the ground. One could argue instead that much of Docklands is deliberately un-English; the employment of axial planning, the regimentation of planting and the formal treatment of certain water basins recall European rather than English practice. Moreover, the monumentality of the bigger schemes suggests American heroic urbanism rather than the subtlety of the English picturesque movement or European rationalism.

By appealing to an international audience at the outset of operations in 1981 and by wooing transatlantic finance and urban designers, the LDDC deliberately eschewed Englishness. The examples cited by Pevsner embrace not only English patrons but more importantly English designers building homes and gardens with English money. The internationalism of Docklands has led to a landscape as recognizably un-English as the West End terraces and squares are English.

Canary Wharf is a good case in point but by no means the only example. Developed by the Canadian company Olympia and York, employing mainly American architects of which Cesar Pelli and Skidmore Owings and Merrill are the most prominent, financed by international banks from Tokyo to New York, the massive scheme is naturally placeless in terms of national identity. The beaux arts axial arrangement of squares and crescents is French in spirit, the tower design is reminiscent of Manhattan, the gridded aesthetic of marble and glass curtain walls could be anywhere from Johannesburg to Dallas, and the landscape design recalls the formality of the Italian Renaissance. Added to this the plush new Docklands railway station of Canary Wharf has the opulence of the Moscow metro and is integrated into the development in a fashion which the Italian futurist Sant 'Elia would have approved. Englishness here is not only mildly insulting to the more elevated ambitions of the Reichmann brothers who controlled the £3 billion empire of Olympia and York, but is inappropriate for this scale of activity. The complexity of Canary Wharf exceeds the limited horizons of English variety, surprise and unexpected changes of angle or level. By plundering a bigger repertoire of images and by concentrating upon rationalist as against picturesque organizing principles of site layout, Canary Wharf inevitably looks un-English.

If Docklands is un-English in terms of place making at a bigger scale, one should not ignore the Londonness of much of the new domestic architecture. Mention has been made of CZWG and Dixon's housing, each in its way an attempt to build upon the English domestic tradition back at least as far as the Nash terraces around Marylebone. Piers Gough of CZWG has employed crescents, serpentine curves, Soane-like distortions of scale, blowzy bow windows and equestrian statues to evoke the carefree architecture of Edwardian and earlier times. In similar spirit Jeremy Dixon has continued a tradition which extends back through the Regency and early Victorian villas, terrace and mews cottages of such areas as Hammersmith and Richmond. His Englishness is different from Gough's but both address *genius loci* in a way beyond the reach of the American designers.

The emergence of an urban vernacular based upon certain London precedents is not the preserve of these two firms of architects. Price and Cullen at Swedish Quays and Richard McCormack at Shadwell Basin interpret the Georgian traditions in different ways but still manage to produce housing which sits comfortably in their particular parts of Docklands. Englishness here derives from attention to detail, whether in urban space making, in the employment of mixed stone and brick façades, or in the use of colour.

Taken as a whole Docklands appears one of the most un-English areas of Britain and this is why traditionalists feel unhappy about the scene. The sharp contrast between low rise factories and houses and towering skyscrapers is reminiscent of urban areas without any planning controls. The way in which Docklands has become less a place than a series of subcentres of economic activity evokes not so much the European city but places of recent origin such as Los Angeles. The polycentred subcity of Docklands is a far cry from the urban models of Englishness catalogued by Pevsner. Only on the edges of Docklands where the influence of older urban areas establishes a pretext for contextual reference does the regenerated city continue English traditions, but here it it the details as against the principles of Englishness which are being revived.

Notes

1 Robert Venturi, *Complexity and Construction in Architecture* (Architectural Press, 1977) p. 16.
2 Marshall McLuhan, *Understanding Media: The Extensions of Man* (Routledge and Kegan Paul, 1964) p. 7.
3 Max Hutchinson, (RIBA President) BBC 2 *Three Minute Culture* 1988.
4 Christopher Alexander, *A Pattern Language* (Oxford University Press, 1977) pp. 164–174, Alexander proposes systems of land use and physical patterns which establish connections between different scales of development and community needs.
5 Colin Rowe and Fred Koetter, *Collage City* (MIT Press, 1978) p. 50.
6 Robert Venturi, Denise Scott Brown and Steven Izenour, *Learning from Las Vegas* (MIT Press, 1972) p. 31; Kevin Lynch *The Image of the City* (MIT Press, 1960) p. 47.
7 Christian Norberg-Schulz, 'The prospects of pluralism', in Heinrich Klotz (ed.), *New York Architecture 1970–90* (Prestel 1989).
8 Piers Gough, Personal communication with author 23 Nov 1990.
9 Thamesside Guidelines *Greater London Development Plan (GLC, 1976).*
10 *'The Thames for Pleasure' in* A New Look for London (Royal Fine Art Commission, 1988) pp. 75–86.
11 Kevin Lynch, *The Image of the City* (MIT Press, 1960) p. 47.
12 Nikolaus Pevsner, *The Englishness of English Art* (Penguin, 1964) p. 181.

10 The Future of Docklands

Is Docklands more than a riverside design museum?

In his painting in the Tate Gallery *Still Life with a Beer Mug*, Fernand Léger depicts a scene which captures the vitality and energy of the modern industrial world. All is brightly coloured, strongly patterned and strangely composed. Black and white diamonds and circles are suspended within a room of apparently arbitrary shape, with a yellow table and red beer mug floating in space. The composition is made up of layers of machine shaped forms which defy perspective or orthodox arrangement. Léger's approach to cubism was perhaps more colourful and dynamic than his contemporaries, yet to appreciate the architecture of the Isle of Dogs requires one to have at least experienced the paintings of Léger and to a lesser extent Picasso and Braque. Orthodox perceptions do not stand one in good stead for the abstract and often incoherent urbanism of the area. One should seek beauty in Docklands not in classical or picturesque yardsticks of taste, but within the altered perceptions of space and time which cubism represents.

If the Isle of Dogs (especially the enterprise zone) is really a huge dockside painting, the whole of Docklands is best appreciated as some enormous art gallery or design museum. Each building or element of townscape (such as Canary Wharf) is constructed according to its own whims or technical dictates, so that the landscape gradually evolves into a canvas of diverse intentions and mixed media. Of the many examples of contemporary urbanism in Britain, nowhere begins to approach the *ad hoc*, surreal and carefree disjointedness of the Isle of Dogs. Interestingly, as the area has become more developed the sense of arbitrariness has increased, and so too has the tension and beauty. Like a Léger painting much depends upon built-up layers and superimposed, often skewed, pattern. It is perhaps stretching the point to suggest that the Isle of Dogs is urbanism based upon cubist principles; it is rather an area fortuituously abstract in form, the result of removing the normal mechanisms of regulatory control at a time when few designers subscribed to central canons of taste.

When development projects were relatively small the mismatch between building provision, infrastructure and social welfare was not that marked, but as proposals grew larger the shortcomings of the system became glaringly obvious. In terms of urban design, the physical mismatch bred of competition has led to a measure of spatial almost cubist abstraction which for the reasons already given has its own attractions. But with the vast bulk of development being privately financed, Docklands has evolved into a separate township of London with practically no public buildings; it is a new urban node without town hall, museum, church or civic square. Compared with the City and the West End of London, the Isle of Dogs in particular is noticeably starved of a public domain. One could argue that the dock basins are themselves huge water squares, places where people can promenade at lunchtimes and in the evenings. But without a supporting structure of public buildings, such spaces are meaningless in civic terms. The only semi-public functions which occupy the dock edges are public houses and restaurants, and these hardly compensate, either architecturally or socially, for real public buildings.

So if Docklands is an art gallery or design museum then it is a private gallery, not a public one. Visitors can take the Docklands Light Railway or drive along West Ferry Road and marvel at the architecture, but it is largely an external spectacle, not an environment of genuine participation. Enjoyment of the buildings, which can be beautiful in the right light and with

Figure 10.1

Still Life with a Beer Mug (1921–2) by Fernard Léger. The collisions of shape, line, texture and colour in this painting are superficially reminiscent of Docklands. A cubist collage of buildings has grown up not only as a result of development freedom but as an expression of the new space/time concepts of the post-industrial age (photo: the Tate Gallery. © DACS 1992)

Figure 10.2

An incoherent townscape. Only in the altered perceptions of cubism can one fully appreciate the dynamic, if disjointed, townscape of Docklands (photo: Brian Edwards)

correct juxtaposition, is however a matter of surface appreciation like the Léger in the Tate. The Isle of Dogs is not a place in civic terms because making a sense of place was relegated to market forces. Some developers, recognizing the problem, have sought to form squares and circuses to ape the traditional city, but want of public architecture makes such spaces largely meaningless. Other cities such as Paris with its grand projects and Barcelona with a programme of public square enhancement have used civic

Figure 10.3

Isle of Dogs: a landscape of diverse intentions. The diverse intentions of the different developers are manifest in the contrasts of scale, materials, angle and style in their various buildings (photo: Brian Edwards)

architecture to regenerate older areas, but this has not to date been the Docklands approach. Docklands has been regenerated through the vehicle of private architecture, with each building superficially at least a mere exhibit within an open air museum along the Thames. In parts it is a museum of consumer paradise where architecture is displayed as street fashion and urban space reduced to circulating room in a gallery. Docklands is not yet a place; rather it is an experiment in market-led urban regeneration, a confirmation of Mumford's assertion that one of the greatest values of the city is to serve as a museum.[1] Docklands is a museum of its age – the urbanism of the market place, with all the strengths and weaknesses that such a concept entails.

Does design pluralism have aesthetic limits in city making?

Lessons for Hadrian's Villa

The sense of urban place making by isolated fragments, so evident today on a visit to the Isle of Dogs, has an honourable pedigree in the form of the virtual new town outside Rome built by the Emperor Hadrian between AD 117 and 138. Known as Hadrian's Villa, the development consists of a number of temples, baths, villas and gymnasia constructed as separate inward looking geometric forms. It was only towards the end of the development that Hadrian introduced elements such as canals, terraces and grand walkways in an attempt to bring a measure of order to the separate and largely isolated parts built to date.

There is one important lesson in Hadrian's Villa: crisis is not inevitable when development precedes infrastructure planning. As long as space exists to insinuate the connecting parts (roads, railways and parks) there is no reason why buildings cannot proceed unhindered by conventional planning. In fact, there may be two distinct advantages in reversing conventional practice. First, developers do not have to wait for public facilities and the broad framework of environmental services to be in place, and thereby avoid the risk of missing the market. Second, the want of a townscape overview may enrich the resulting environment since diversity will be encouraged by the various developers not knowing what is expected of them, and their designers will be unhindered by concerns of neighbourliness or smooth connection. Just as Hadrian's Villa grew without a masterplan and on the basis of separate, self-contained, architecturally distinctive structures, so too much of Docklands has developed a character of happy fragmentation.

Civic ordering or market-led disjointedness?

There comes a point, however, when the scale of disjointedness begins to demand some introduction of ordering. At the Isle of Dogs the disbenefits of excessive fragmentation of built forms and ill-considered physical connection have begun to outweigh the sheer delight in the Los Angeles style chaos produced to date. One should pause to compare the Isle of Dogs with the Royal Docks which has developed in a more British fashion. The Royals have been rigidly planned, mostly in response to infrastructure proposals prepared by the Richard Rogers Partnership. Hence the Royal Docks have a clear ordering framework made up of new roads, bridges and extensive planting. The buildings at the Royals have yet to appear, but the urban structure is in this sense already in place. The Isle of Dogs has reversed the practice; the buildings have been put in place before the infrastructure (except for the inadequate Docklands Light Railway). Now the roads, railways and public parks have to respond to the dictates of size and capacity imposed by the buildings, not vice versa. As long as space exists to create an acceptable public presence of transportation and amenity, there is nothing injurious in the process, except for a great deal of inconvenience and upheaval.

If the first decade of development at the Isle of Dogs has exceeded expectations in terms of scale of building and investment, this simply clarifies the priorities for the next decade. Activity now must concentrate upon creating civilized values within the urban chaos of central Docklands. The happy fragmentation cannot now be eroded except by demolition since the size of the principal buildings and the abrupt changes in scale are fixed by the economics of the area for at least a generation. This is fortunate in the way that parts of Hadrian's Villa were not demolished when the ordering system of terraces and canals was imposed upon a wild and uncivilized Tivoli landscape; they simply made happy collisions with existing structures.

The Los Angeles model?

Parallels with Los Angeles have already been drawn, and here much debate amongst urban designers concerns how to address the balance between city buildings and city freeways. The urban freeways of Los Angeles are now being greened and treated almost as corridors in an art gallery – routes, if you like, for viewing the architecture of the city. The freeways of US cities expose to public gaze the buildings of corporate America and the abrupt changes in scale or wealth evident in unplanned places. Docklands has no road equivalent to a US style urban motorway, but the light railway exposes Wapping and the Isle of Dogs to similar critical examination. From the admittedly underscaled and overcrowded trains, Docklands too can be enjoyed as an urban art gallery. The new buildings are crisp and clean, framed in open space and lit by the seemingly endless sunshine of east London. The wealth of Canary Wharf and Harbour Exchange Square stand in contrast to the squalor of the council estates of Hackney passed soon after leaving Tower Gateway Station. The view from the train is part art gallery, part museum of mankind and part lesson in contemporary dilemmas of urban design. The railway does not pass real places in the way that freeway 101 through Los Angeles passes the themed worlds of modern America. But whatever is seen in Docklands is viewed from the embryonic road system, the Docklands Light Railway or the Thames river bus. The next decade will consist of making some sense of these impressions and hopefully highlighting the pleasures and convenience of moving through the area.

Has urban collage led to design pluralism?

But the Isle of Dogs has more fundamental questions to face. Discontinuity, disjointedness, fragmentation and urban collage are all the results of a hands-off approach to development control and a reluctance to invest intellectual effort in masterplanning. The lack of enthusiasm for infrastructural provision undermined any argument which could have been constructed in support of aesthetic or spatial planning. Now a case is being made for addressing the infrastructural limitations, especially transportation, and with it voices are being raised in support of a masterplan to solve the visual chaos of what has already been built. The question now for urban design is whether chaos and a masterplan can happily coexist.

The Isle of Dogs is the one place in London, and maybe Europe, where large scale chaos produces a truly dynamic and exciting landscape. The largely happy chaos of the place is clearly un-English (in the Pevsner sense) and often inconvenient to those who read the visual clues of environment in European terms. But if the Isle of Dogs has a sense of misplaced 'place', it is certainly not a placeless part of London. The Isle of Dogs has a distinct feeling of place, albeit disjointed and alien to British traditions. The masterplan normally seeks to establish connections between parts employing streets, squares, boulevards, monuments and parks to stitch together the components of a town to form a distinctive neighbourhood. Traditional masterplanning combines these elements with an appreciation of the impact of transport systems and land values. Hence the configuration of buildings, the spatial structure of streets and squares and their relationship to bus and railway stations all interact within the masterplan.

Put this way, a traditional masterplan for the Isle of Dogs would be destructive to the cheerful character of the place as it exists: it would simply bring forced legibility where ambiguity presently reigns. An old style masterplan which seeks recognizable relationships would be counter-productive on the Isle of Dogs, but a new kind of masterplan which seeks to develop the idea of collage and fragmentation may be useful. Its use would be primarily that of ensuring that the transportation framework currently on the drawing board did not impose too much order upon this undisciplined place. The elements of order within a city of many layers like Rome tend to be casually disposed over time with many consequential collisions of geometry. A masterplan which seeks such a quality for the Isle of Dogs may yet be useful since it would allow the new axes of such developments as Canary Wharf to extend outwards and collide with each other and those of the water basins and Thamesside, as well as planned new routes through the area in the form of roads or extended tube lines. The more the geometries are connected by superimposition or slight shifts in angle, the greater the richness and the denser the collage.

Towards greater urban complexity

Docklands as a whole is more like an open tentative collage by Braque or Léger than a full blooded one by Picasso. Collage in Docklands is a matter of disjointed developments rather than the detailed complexity of individual places. Fragments of heritage, new squares and skyscrapers are superimposed like some fantastic painting. It is an open sketchy canvas with lines of development drawn across a landscape which seems ever to be suspended between order and disorder.

Where the parts collide the townscape is the most dynamic, as in the sliver of land between Tooley Street and the Thames or between West India Dock and Island Gardens. The key elements of collage are the archetypal ingredients of town making – square, street, garden, tower, axis – arranged in complex and contradictory patterns (to paraphrase Rowe and Koetter, and Venturi). What makes Docklands extraordinary, at least in parts, is the

Figure 10.4

Townscape of collisions. The central areas of the enterprise zone where controls are most relaxed have grown into a townscape of colliding geometries, deconstruction and superimposed architectural mass (photo: Brian Edwards)

presence of two additional features: the area's heritage and the presence of water. These two give a resonance to the urban collage, a distinctiveness lacking either in completely new areas or in cities more fixed physically. Hence the remainder of London is too densely composed and too rigidly planned to be considered worthy of the title collage, and other cities such as Houston or Hong Kong are too recently evolved to have that historical layering essential for its development. For collage exploits both space and time in the intellectual process of city making.

The sketchy urban framework now in place will require infilling with pattern, texture and colour. Some areas are already well developed, others just an isolated monument or a forlorn new building along a length of road. The openness of Docklands will become in time a densely packed city, but the relatively chaotic structure already in place should ensure the survival of an attractive blend of idiosyncrasy, deconstruction and civic formality.

Docklands as a model of post-industrial society?

The post-industrial society represented by Docklands thrives not on products or even services but on ideas. The new class predicted by Galbraith in *The Affluent Society* resides here, and as an audience for architecture is remarkably well informed. Many have chosen the area because of its design values, not because of any sense of community or social well-being. The architectural idea – the pluralism and open-endedness of this consumer environment – has attracted a new class of people well versed in gallery books, building and theatre. They nearly all represent new wealth, not old money, and hence new tastes and values, not old ones. So they dwell in lofts, studios, attics, Dutch gabled warehouse-like houses, not the dainty flats of the West End or the Edwardian villas of Battersea. The people of this post-industrial society have learnt to love Docklands deconstructivism, not just as a clever way of explaining the dereliction and mismatch of urban parts, but as a serious attempt to become wise about their environment.

The sense that London Docklands is more design museum than designed place is appropriated by some commercial developers. No two office buildings are alike, except where Docklands merges into some of the poorer suburbs. Elsewhere the competitive forces of the market place have led to a happy jumble of colours, styles and patterns. In Docklands as elsewhere commercial architecture has perhaps been the most interesting and rewarding building type of the past decade. New approaches to the design of the commercial environment have led to many innovations both in the architecture itself and in the relationship between office buildings and the space round about. In London, Broadgate and London Bridge City have introduced exciting building types and spaces into a worn out city, and further afield suburban office campuses of which Stockley Park is the most memorable have enlivened the urban fringe. Commercial buildings have always responded directly to the whim of the market and, when the market woke up to the value of design and the imperative of the idea in the eighties, office buildings suddenly became interesting. Docklands is no exception.

A distinction has to be drawn between the city as museum and the city as art gallery. A museum consists of objects of varying technological, social or biological importance, each a distinct being set in a showcase for public enjoyment or education. An art gallery is a place where decorative objects are hung on walls, each framed in gilt and then surrounded by space. Mumford likens a museum to a concrete equivalent of a library where specimens and samples explain the complexity of our world, and he speculates that the modern metropolis is in fact a museum.[3] For Mumford, historical layering and social and technological diversity are qualities upon which the concept of the city as a museum depends. London Docklands is undoubtedly a museum in this broad sense, but it could also be called a gallery of design. For the technological and architectural diversity of Docklands, its love of colour, shape, form and construction, make the area immediately a place of learning by specimen and example. What the architecture of Docklands has done is to take almost every theory of design in the 1980s and built a monument to each. The superficiality of some of the specimens may suggest more the experience of an art gallery than the rigorous discipline of a museum, but on balance Docklands remains a fascinating place if viewed as an open-air design museum. It is a place to learn from rather than one in which to live or work, a city of spectacle and experiment.

Figure 10.5

Townscape as urban museum. Docklands is less a place than an open air museum of architecture. The specimens on display represent the values of the age, the technology of fast track building, and the sensibility of the post-industrial era (photo:LDDC)

Design in the post-industrial age has led to a new respect for individuality both in the way buildings are designed and in the whole plethora of commercial services from headed notepaper to logo printed toilet paper. The new designers have sought impact, variety and Disney-like fun where the old designers gave us monotony, conformity and good taste. It is not that Docklands had bad taste; it is rather that taste as a series of values has been subsumed within commercial targets. An indifference to traditional taste marks the commercial landscape of Docklands, just as it does in Manhattan or Dallas. The instinct amongst developers and their architects (both often North American) is to distrust taste and to place their faith in the values of the new class that Docklands itself has helped manufacture. Hence classical and avant-garde buildings sit happily alongside Hollywood enlarged versions of the Piazza San Marco from the Isle of Dogs to Tower Bridge.

London Docklands: the architecture of the Thatcher years

In October 1987, having won her third general election, Mrs Thatcher said something had to be done about Britain's decaying inner cities. That something one suspects was the transplanting of the London Docklands model into the decaying bodies of other inner city areas. By 1991 the ideological high ground of the New Right had been lost, London Docklands had proved to be less of a success than formerly claimed, and Margaret Thatcher was out of office. The moral supremacy of economic liberalism, authoritarian decentralism and anti-bureaucratic sentiment had given way to politics by consensus and urban renewal by partnership. The reorientation of municipal planning during the eighties had not been accompanied by wholesale demolition of the development plan system as some predicted. Only in areas managed by urban development corporations did the market enjoy great development freedom, and here London Docklands is undoubtedly the fullest blossoming of the New Right's experiment in environmental deregulation.

London Docklands is as much the legacy of the Thatcher years as the National Health Service is of Attlee's premiership. Both are accurate reflections of the priorities as perceived, and of the methods employed. Attlee put the health service into being after lengthy consultation; by contrast, the Tories set up the Docklands model as an experiment in the new thinking. The Conservative right had no real understanding or concern for the environment which would follow, other than the expectation of a regenerated economy. The urban consequences were not considered important; the arguments employed in support of the 1980 Act dealt with economic revival, national interests and the pace of inner city renewal.

Environmental deregulation in Docklands was only part of a wider experiment in development freedom unleashed by the Thatcher administration. The relaxation of aesthetic aspects of planning control, the shifting of historic building protection to the quango of English Heritage under its free market chairman Lord Montague of Beaulieu, the proliferation of enterprise zones, and the spread of urban development corporations, all parallel new regulatory freedoms put in place by the New Right in other fields. The deregulation of the Stock Exchange had particular benefits for Docklands, but in other fields, such as law, medicine and education, market interests were encouraged to displace the old order.

Because New Right thinking was particularly allied to the south-east of Britain and led to the emergence of a new young middle class, London Docklands became almost their area. It represents the quintessence of Thatcherism, not just because a certain type of person was attracted to the area, but because the buildings and spaces created closely reflected the new ideology. Urban community barely exists; civic building is the result of corporate wealth creation not public welfare; and the main environmental assets of the area, such as water and heritage, have been secured for private gain. Deregulation has led to wealth creation and the building of several well designed commercial enclaves, but it seems incapable of generating a broader canvas of civic well-being.

If deregulation marked the Thatcher years, so too did the moral supremacy of private interests over public ones. In Docklands this takes telling form in the dominance of the car over public transport. At the Isle of Dogs an under-scaled DLR enjoyed the same level of public subsidy as a 1.5 km length of road needed to service Canary Wharf. Roads (not streets) have enjoyed the lion's share of public subsidy, with all the corresponding problems of traffic congestion and poorly defined urban space. The value systems imposed by New Right thinking have been destructive of traditional urban qualities, just as similar economic thinking has destroyed old business customs and eroded the cosy world of the professions.

In place of old urban values like the public square, the linking street and the community park, there is in Docklands a pattern of circulating roads, open car parks, and well fortified buildings. The townscape of Docklands has been suburbanized and Americanized. Englishness survives only at the edges in quiet corners of Surrey Docks; elsewhere the Thatcher revolution has created corporate placelessness. The effects of deregulation, of a rampant modernism of town layout as well as building design, and of largely international money have made Docklands into a world market place just as

Reg Ward predicted. Professor Peter Hall's invention of the enterprise zone concept as a means of cutting the Gordian Knot of planning blight in the inner cities has been rewarded by the creation of an embryonic Los Angeles.

If the eighties marked a shift from bureaucracy to deregulation, and public welfare to private gratification, the decade also saw a decline in Britain's manufacturing base and a corresponding rise in information services and technology. Docklands is the manifestation of this change with its vast collection of newspaper offices, design studios and news agencies. It is no accident of geography to find London's Reuters office on the Isle of Dogs and the News International at Wapping. Both represent opposite extremes of the landscape of information created in a mere decade in Docklands. For all one's misgivings over architectural form and physical disjointedness, the information systems operate effectively. Perhaps the initial chaos on the ground will give way to the smoothness which characterizes the data transfer within the huge information technology factory of Docklands. For Docklands is less a series of buildings when seen in this way than an agglomeration of parts of a factory all connected by underground cables and overhead satellite dishes. These are buildings producing information to make money, creating services not goods, employing energy and imagination rather than raw materials. Perhaps the physical disjointedness and chaos are all necessary manifestations of the switch from a manufacturing economy in Docklands to a servicing one.

Figure 10.6

Corporate placelessness. The values of the Thatcher decade are well represented in this view: the dominance of the car, well fortified buildings, and a Los Angeles approach to site planning (photo: Chorley and Handford Ltd)

If the City is to remain a financial centre, then it can only do so with Docklands by its side. Whatever the architectural merits of Canary Wharf, the reality is that this development is necessary if London is not to lose out to Frankfurt as the European centre for banking. World money markets need big, efficient and well located buildings. Sadly, the reluctance of the New Right philosophy to accept a case for public transport subsidy may well have jeopardized Olympia and York's chance of rivalling Frankfurt's claims for European supremacy in world banking. The Thatcher revolution unleashed an unprecedented development boom but it failed to deliver in the areas under its own control – namely quality within the public realm, infrastructural support and social provision. Docklands is prosperous (even allowing for the recession of the early nineties) but it lacks the necessary ingredients of metropolitan well-being.

The civic failure is largely the result of political dogma. The prime task for the LDDC under the 1980 Act was to regenerate London Docklands. In development terms few would doubt the success of operations, but other measures of renewal have been neglected. The great tradition of European urbanism has been overlooked. There are no extensive lengths of riverside garden, no attractive new river bridges, no squares surrounded by buildings of mixed use and civic importance, no formal streets for public promenade. The practice of town planning has been the principal vehicle for providing a framework for these public realm elements in the past. The eschewing of the local authorities and as a consequence the discipline of town planning under the Act, and the emphasis given to questions of regeneration alone, have been the main reasons for these shortcomings. The responsibility for Docklands' civic failure lies not in professional limitations or at the door of developers (many of whom have sought to address the problems) but in government philosophy itself. Only significant public intervention can deal with that Giedion calls the 'unworkable disorder of today's great cities'.[4] It is not enough to expect private developers, no matter how enlightened, to create a civilized whole out of the collaging together of countless projects.

The political failure of Docklands manifests itself in the indifference shown to civilizing values. Future action must address the public realm, and here questions of quality are important. Governments of whatever persuasion must realize that quality in those things governments alone can do is more important than narrow definitions of cost–benefit analysis. The myth that urban quality can be created by private sector developers enjoying unprecedented levels of design freedom should be finally buried by the example of the Isle of Dogs.

In the end one is torn between the obvious failures of Docklands and the emergence of a new way of seeing cities. The public realm has suffered, but the private world has been enriched and contributes greatly towards an urban whole. The sheer pleasures of Docklands' disjointedness compensates for the neglect of traditional civic values. The disaggregation and rotation in time of objects which cubism represents is somehow paralleled by the freedoms from development or physical restraint which the Docklands model manifests. The emphasis placed upon speed, change and enterprise by the LDDC has created a new architectural culture. The formal response in its partially completed state has the virtues of collage and the failings of lost place and illegible buildings. But it may be better to exploit the new culture for expression than to seek a revival of an outmoded European urban model.

The unworkable disorder of modern cities is merely testament to the limits to control. Docklands has shown us that urban planning should go with the trends rather than oppose them, that architecture is merely a tool of corporate marketing. The predicament of texture and grain that the Isle of Dogs conspicuously expresses is perhaps preferable to authoritarian control from the left or the right. The closing of the Thatcher decade may liberate

Docklands from a doctrinaire approach to urbanism. The way ahead lies in the imposition of a public layer on to the rich base of private development already in place. The layers in the Léger painting are multiple views and conflicting geometries: Docklands now provides the opportunity not so much to reconcile private and public ambitions, but to allow the opposing visions to add richness and complexity to a distinctive landscape.

Notes

1 Lewis Mumford, *The City in History* (Penguin, 1966), p. 639.
2 J.K. Galbraith, *The Affluent Society* (Penguin 1962), p. 275–9.
3 Mumford, *The City in History*. p. 640.
4 Sigfried Giedion, *Space, Time and Architecture* (Harvard University Press, 1954), p. 725.

Appendix I
Chronology of London Docklands

	Date
St Katharine's Hospital (religious foundation) built	12th c.
Bermondsey Abbey built	1182
St Mary Overie (now Southwark Cathedral) built	c.1220
Tooley St occupied by Sir John Falstof or Falstaff (Henry IV)	14th c.
Tooley St (nearby) Rosary Palace of Edward II	13th c.
Royal Naval Victualling Yard built (by Henry VIII) at Deptford	1513
Prospect of Witby built (frequented by Samuel Pepys)	1520
Twenty legal quays established near London Bridge	1558
East India Company develops land at Blackwall	1615
Captain Christopher Jones sailed *Mayflower* from Rotherhithe via Plymouth to America	1620
Shadwell built up with shipyards and houses occupied by 10,000 (70 per cent employment in docks and river authorities)	1650
St Matthias Church, built by East India Company in Shadwell	1654
Blackwall Wet Dock built	17th c.
Howland Great Dock built at Rotherhithe by East India Company	17th c.
Wapping Marsh and Isle of Dogs drained by Dutch engineers	17th c.
St-George-in-the-East and St Anne's, Limehouse churches built by Nicholas Hawksmoor	1712–26
Greenland Dock (formerly Howland Great Dock) established as whaling trade centre	1750
Chaos, overcrowding, theft and fires commonplace in London Docklands	18th c.
Parliament acts to 'improve' Docklands	1796
London's first police force established at Wapping	1798
West India Docks open (engineers included John Rennie) at cost of £500,000 (about £100 million today)	1802
Sugar Warehouses built at North Quay, West India Docks	1802–3
Warehousing Act of 1803 which established bonded warehouses led to further building activity	1803
London Dock (Wapping) including Tobacco Dock opened	1805
East India Docks opened (as extension of Brunswick Dock)	1806
Surrey Commercial Docks built	1807
St Katharine Docks opened	1828
Victoria Dock built	1855
Hays Wharf built	1856
Brunel's *Great Eastern* iron steamship built in John Scott Russell's yard at Millwall	1858
Millwall Dock built	1868
Butlers Wharf built	c.1870
Royal Albert Dock built	1880
Great Dock Strike	1889
Tower Bridge built	1890
Rotherhithe Tunnel built	1908
Port of London Authority set up	1909
Improvements to London Docks, West India Docks, East India Docks	1914
King George V Dock opened (making the Royal Docks then the largest dock complex in the world)	1921

Heyday of London Docklands: 35 million tons of cargo handled per year worth £700 million, carried by 55,000 ship movements using 1700 wharfs, employing 100,000 dockers, stevedores, sailors etc.	1930s
25,000 bombs fell on London Docklands, destroying much of West India, St Katharine's and Surrey Docks	1939–45
Docklands rebuilt and improved	1945–60
60 million tons of cargo handled	1961
Decline of London Docklands due to containerization etc.	1965
East India Docks closed	1967
Regent's Canal Dock closed (part of Grand Union Canal which linked London Docks to Birmingham)	1967
St Katharine Docks closed	1968
London Docks closed	1968
Surrey Docks closed	1970
West India Docks closed	1980
Millwall Dock closed	1980
Royal Docks closed	1981
London Docklands Development Corporation formed to regenerate Docklands	1981
Thames Barrier opened (cost £550 million)	1982
Michael Heseltine announces plans to extend the Docklands model to the lower Thames	August 1991

Source: Chris Ellmers, Head of Museum in Docklands, from *Time and Tide* in *Guide to London Docklands*, 1987

Appendix II
Relevant Provisions of the Local Government Planning and Land Act 1980 and Action of LDDC

Urban development corporations

Objectives
Regenerate area
Bring land and buildings into effective use
Encourage the development of industry and commerce
Create an attractive environment
Ensure that housing and social facilities are available

Methods
Vesting land from local authorities and other public agencies in UDCs
Upgrading utility services
Carrying out environmental improvement
Giving grants towards the provision of amenity

Specific actions of LDDC
Rejection of urban design framework for area
Introduction of masterplans for specific pockets
Marketing as against town planning basis for forward planning
Provision of new services such as DLR
Emphasis upon environmental improvement
Rejection of social development framework
Generation of income through sale of land

Design related policies at LDDC
Use of architectural competitions to raise level of design
Attraction of 'new blood' design practices to area
Use of financial aid to promote adventurous design
LDDC acts as development catalyst on key or difficult sites

Enterprise zones

Create an environment for economic regeneration

Providing rate and tax rebates
Relaxing planning control

Attraction of flagship schemes such as Canary Wharf
Provision of new infrastructure
Promotion of climate of aesthetic freedom
Sacrificing of public amenity
Rapid exploitation of former PLA land

Attraction of US designers to area as part of the international market place
Rejection of Gosling and Cullen development framework for Isle of Dogs
Site marketing with minimum design controls

Appendix III
Three Key Interviews

Interview with Reg Ward, chief executive LDDC, March 1987

Q1. There seem to be many people like yourself working in London Docklands with extensive northern experience. Do you take the view that the expertise in urban renewal is found mostly in the north and the means to carry it out in the south?

A. It is probably accidental, though certainly northern cities have been tackling these sorts of problems much longer than the south. Many of us have cut our teeth on urban renewal problems in Scotland, especially that of industrial dereliction, where I and people like Bill Gillespie were involved in the Coatbridge Project back in the early 1970s. But I think it is largely accidental.

Q2. Do you see the success of London Docklands in development terms because of favourable geographical location, or as a result of the approach of the LDDC?

A. The evidence is there to see, it is the approach of the LDDC. We sought to change perception – to make people aware of the opportunities rather than just the problems of Docklands. It is both irritating and pleasing to hear people say it was bound to be a success because it was in London, but the fact is that nobody in London looked east of Tower Bridge as a place to invest. Our job was to reverse the development axis in London which has been going westwards for the past 200 years and to persuade institutions and others that the east had great potential. That is why we spent the first few years changing perceptions, achieving attitudinal changes if you like.

Q3. The approach at LDDC has been one of relaxing, almost deregulating town planning. Do you see this recipe likely to be applied by government in other inner city areas?

A. This reflects a very strong, personal stance: I believe our planning system inhibits thinking, inhibits opportunities, doesn't create them. It is also detached from the realities of the market place; it is no good sitting down producing beautiful urban designs, shapes and so on and waiting for thirty years because nobody wants to do it. The fact is that you have only one view of things as represented in the planning system; it is only one possibility. At LDDC we have gone for an organic approach, rather than the traditional masterplan, and if you don't react to it conceptually then you are really not for us.

Q4. It is quite remarkable that such a large area of London is being redeveloped without an urban design overview; this puts London rather outside the European tradition. This clearly doesn't worry you; you remain happy for aesthetics to be development led.

A. I think there is an urban design overview. The thing is we refuse to write it down because it then becomes inflexible, it develops a life of its own. Such plans are unresponsive to the needs of different architects, or developers or changed situations. These is an urban design overview; it is dictated by the place and that is always changing as various proposals are built.

Q5. Are you happy with the results so far, now that there are many schemes on the ground?

A.   I am very happy – I am a dreamer – but you have to be pragmatic and learn to accept second best. We have built a platform from which something greater can grow later. Everything here is a reflection of our present shift from one level of urban design to another, and schemes like Canary Wharf are a measure of changing perceptions in design terms. In between time we have had to settle for getting nicely designed but very modest buildings and creating a bit of architectural indigestion in the process, but now we look to the future.

Q6. The approach of LDDC is outside the formal tradition of urban design – the use of squares, vistas, streets and boulevards.

A.   I think you are misreading what is happening. We have some unusual boulevards and grand urban designs; the shape of the river itself is a grand boulevard, as are the water basins. We failed in the first developments to respond to the water itself; now we realize that the character of the water is a major urban statement and our present schemes use the water more imaginatively. Cullen and Gosling's earlier study of the Isle of Dogs was a good conceptual piece which I initiated and then stopped from becoming prescriptive, but the big schemes like Canary Wharf are grasping the full potential of the water structure – and this is quite unique in Europe. The water ties together the various schemes and this is far more relevant than artificial concepts like the Wren axis from Greenwich.

Q7. What do you see is the biggest threat to implementing schemes like Canary Wharf?

A.   I think it is the traditional concept of land use planning and urban design control. The biggest danger is wanting to bureaucratize, to restrict the momentum we have built up, instead of having the courage to run with it and create something beyond our beliefs.

Q8. Do you see yourself essentially as an instrument of government?

A.   No, we are merely an instrument of government approach and policy. We were created to sit, perhaps rather uncomfortably, between the governmental machine and the private sector, and a lot of the strains of operating really come from that position.

Q9. The approach of LDDC is in the Thatcherite mould – deregulation, private sector freedom etc.

A.   I'm not sure if I would label it as Thatcherite. I think it does reflect Mrs Thatcher's thinking and also the corporation's, but you do both a disservice if you trap it in that sort of political dimension. It is quite properly a way of freeing people's ideas, gaining opportunities and having aspirations which go beyond reality.

Q10. It is widely recognized that the present government has no great appetite for town planning, and the success of LDDC and its deregulating approach is likely to be applied elsewhere. Does this worry you?

A.   In this country we describe an area of activity, give a professional label to it and then it has a life of its own. One can actually put it the other way round and say that what life is about in the urban environment is total uncertainty. What the planning system, what chartered surveyors and all the conventional professions want to do is ignore that uncertainty and to create a false certainty, so that one produces plans which have nothing to do with the market's response. You get a surveyor who can't handle a piece of urban land without putting a line around it and specifying its use. What London Docklands is trying to do is to manage uncertainty, and you don't manage it by creating artificial certainties within it.

Q11. Are you concerned that US money and US architects are moving into Docklands in a big way? Do you fear a loss of Englishness in design terms?

A. I am delighted that we have created a world market place for architectural skill. The biggest challenge in a sense is how do you fuse architects drawn up in one idiom with a different perspective from outside. The problem is usually quite the reverse: the American architects like SOM and I.M. Pei are trying to be too English. The main complaint about Canary Wharf is that it is not American enough; there needs to be a far more positive assertion of an architectural language, from outside the UK. What docklands is providing is an opportunity for architects from all round the world – the best British and overseas – to work together. Hopefully, the fusion of ideas will make an exceptional place and one we couldn't possibly have described in advance; we now have I.M. Pei, SOM, Pederson, and Stirling all working on Canary Wharf. I think Docklands is a big challenge to English skills. My concern is that I have some difficulty with post-modernism, and what I see missing at the moment is a language which stands on its own – though you see it in the younger firms. The great problem in a place like Docklands is how do you allow the great talents in the smaller firms to come through and express themselves. We try to encourage developers to search out unique architectural skills, and this provides a challenge to the traditional practices to stay in competition with the new designers coming through. We have a house style of encouragement here in Docklands and that extends to architects and developers.

Q12. You have been outspoken regarding the need for effective as against purely efficient financial management. Does this view endear you to government?

A. I think it worries them. There is a tendency to see the extrovert style the corporation must have, and perhaps also my own style, as outside the mould of the routine, very secure, process minded one which governments are used to dealing with. To some extent it is a fair worry, in that we have discovered new mechanisms, we have been adaptive and ingenious – but this is all done within a very rigid framework of rules.

Q13. In financial terms, the results of Docklands are overwhelming. In Docklands for every pound of public money you are attracting seven or eight pounds of private money, whereas in cities like Glasgow every public pound attracts at most 70p of private investment. The success must appease your critics.

A. Yes, though in reality our approach could be used by other public institutions. It is largely tradition and professional attitudes which inhibit an entrepreneurial approach, not the rules as such. The skills tend to be trapped over a period of time into the organizational context in which they exist; that is why I believe people should not stay too long in an organization, particularly chief executives. The thing is you need different people at different stages in growth of any project.

Interview with Michael Heseltine, Secretary of State for the Environment, 10 July 1991

Q1. London Docklands is one of the most interesting urban experiments of the post-war period. Looking back over the past ten years of LDDC activity, what do you think is the main lesson?

A. It is, I suppose, that we had to introduce a framework flexible enough to attract developers, bearing in mind the failure of orthodox planning in inner city areas like the East End. My position at the time, and also that of Reg Ward who was very influential in the early years, was that we should seek quality in the things we controlled. The finishes are very good in Docklands and so is the urban design variety. We deliberately avoided rigid masterplans; this isn't the British way of going about urban development in the twentieth century. The single lesson concerns the importance of creating opportunities for development in the inner city, rather than imposing regulation.

Q2. But in the process of removing controls, do you not feel Docklands has grown into a disjointed place with developments in competition with each other?

A. A lot of Docklands is very good to look at and Reg Ward must take credit for this. He used every lever he could pull in order to excite people into doing things in a more appealing and design sensitive way. I don't accept the criticisms which are often lodged in the architectural press. It would not have been appropriate to lay down a single matrix and expect developers to conform to it, and to discuss the possibility now is rather like crying over spilt milk.

Q3. The 1980 Act specifically discouraged plan making. The task was to regenerate. But urban plans might have anticipated the problems we are seeing today, such as poorly defined urban space and lack of correlation between transport and development.

A. I have thought about this quite a bit myself. It is quite impossible for those who criticize us today to realize the problems we faced in 1979. We took over 5500 acres administered by a variety of public bodies and utility companies, and we had a recession on our hands. The first three years were spent on tidying up the environment and putting in some new infrastructure. We were surprised, overwhelmed if you like, by the success after 1985. No one expected the scale of development we are now seeing and, of course, we are putting in place the new transportation to service it.

Q4. Without such plans Docklands has grown into an exciting collage. Is this happy showcase of British architecture the direct result of deregulation?

A. I think Docklands will be an exciting place to live and work, but you need to probe a little bit deeper. Deregulation only really applied to the enterprise zone and here Reg Ward sought quality developments; he encouraged design competition between developers to raise standards.

Q5. The rebuilding of Docklands has run against the main flow of European urbanism over the past ten years as witnessed by Berlin, Paris and Barcelona. Regeneration on the Continent tends to be highly structured, in Britain laissez-faire.

A. It would have not been credible to have gone to colleagues in 1979 to suggest some Haussmann-like vision of the East End of London. If we had been starting in 1987 it might have been credible, but you have to remember the squalor and lack of confidence in the area at the time. That's why confidence building was so important, and grand plans are not necessarily the best way of going about this.

Q6. Docklands has really been a political experiment. Are you happy with the environmental results?

A. We were driven by the need to reverse the decline, but personally I would like to see more greenery. There are, of course, a whole lot of questions about what next – about the river corridor and extending the Docklands model further east. I am presently asking myself how to finish what we have started; the principal task now is a management one, of completing the renaissance after which the LDDC will be wound up.

Q7. A considerable amount of land remains undeveloped – perhaps as much as 15–20 per cent. Would you like to see this treated any differently, perhaps by extending the enterprise zone into the Royal Docks?

A. I am concerned to consolidate Docklands as a showcase of British achievement and urban architecture. The 1980s were a very interesting period for architecture, particularly commercial architecture. Docklands seems to me to be an achievement of which we can be proud, and when the recession ends I am sure the sites in the Royal Docks will quickly be taken up. It doesn't depend upon extending the enterprise zone.

Q8. About 100,000 jobs have been created in Docklands, but few have gone to local people. Would you like to see a technical college or university annex in Docklands to help with skill training, designed perhaps as a grand project on the French model?

A. The problem is generational as much as educational. The present generation have suffered from the closures, but one must ensure that their children are retained in the area. There is a relentless logic in the market place – a logic which requires new skills, attitudes and high quality environment. That's what we have tried to achieve in Docklands and will endeavour to finish.

Interview with Barry Shaw, former Head of Urban Design, LDDC, 15 April 1991

Q1. What do you see as the main urban design priorities of the 1990s in Docklands?

A. Completion and linkage – completion of what we have begun, especially in terms of putting back the streets and walls around the buildings, and linkage in terms of south and north Docklands. I'd like to see more bridges and better transport connections to unify the different parts of Docklands. Completion has to build upon what we have begun and may take another decade. We are reaching the hand-stitching stage where all the new development has to be darned back into the physical and social fabric of the old Dockland communities. Ideally resources need to be found to renew the physical landscape.

Q2. The LDDC is due to be wound up in 1996. Will you have solved the urban design problems by then?

A. I think we have got the main structure about right, but I am not entirely happy – that is, I suspect, in the nature of the job. The big developments like Canary Wharf are signposts for Docklands. When you look down the Thames from Charing Cross Bridge you are aware of the axial relationships of the tower of Canary Wharf – a kind of East London signpost, and when you look back to the city from the Royals there is the tower again on the axis of the big dock basins. We must complete what has been started in making Docklands a new node of economic activity in London and that means thinking about external linkage – to King's Cross, the East Thames Corridor, the Channel Tunnel Terminus and on to Northern Europe. When you look at linkages you inevitably have to address transport systems and that is where a lot of our urban design effort is now going.

Q3. It is interesting to hear you are now addressing questions of infrastructure, but didn't Docklands reverse the usual process of development in the first ten years by putting development in place before the transportation network was finalized?

A. Not really, we had to attract development in the early years and I think people were surprised at the success of our measures. Nobody really expected the scale of development we are now seeing, and of course, we have to upgrade our infrastructure to suit. But don't forget, at the Royal Docks a great deal of transportation infrastructure has been provided with little in the way of building. It is only in the Enterprise Zone that things have got rather overheated, and our powers under the 1980 Act are fairly limited in terms of plan making. Our main task was to market Docklands, to upgrade the environment and improve basic services – I think we have been successful – perhaps too successful at times for urban design. But the present shortcomings in terms of the public realm can now be addressed with a confidence beyond our imagination a decade ago. This means more planning and a return to a more traditional methodology.

Q4. We have talked about the public realm and public space, but not about public buildings. Why are there no civic buildings in Docklands?

A. That is not really a Docklands question but one for society as a whole. We are not making public buildings at the end of the 20th century. Our problem is really how to keep in use the public buildings we have inherited from the past. In Docklands a lot of effort has gone into using or adapting churches for new public uses and the offices of the old Port Authority. We have no authority to make civic architecture (with one or two minor exceptions) – our task is to concentrate upon civic space and try and relate this to private development.

Q5. Docklands will be seen as a monument to 'Thatcherism' – does it damn the age?

A. Questions like that may sell books but I don't see Docklands in these terms. I think the 'Thatcher' Tag is fashionable and dangerous – it bundles together too many arguments which are best examined individually. New Right thinking did focus effort away from the regions and back onto the South East and Docklands undoubtedly benefited. But one way of creating jobs in the 80s was to build offices. Docklands represents an important public/private partnership for the constructing of office space and the generation of employment in the inner cities. You could call this 'Thatcherism', but Docklands is more than office space – look at the housing and schools built in Surrey Docks and Wapping. Docklands is far more than the Isle of Dogs in spite of public perception to the contrary. The less well known areas are already being integrated into the local city structure.

Q6. The Royal Docks is the one area which has been masterplanned and where transport infrastructure has been of an adequate scale, but developers do not seem interested in the Royal Docks at present?

A. This had nothing to do with masterplanning. Greenland Dock was masterplanned and land was sold very profitably by the LDDC. The Royals have their own problems such as the airport and East London river crossing. Success or otherwise of the Royals may have to wait a generation, but at least we have put a framework in place. Your general question about masterplanning is valid. Docklands has raised a number of urban design issues which we – the planning and architectural profession – have to address. What benefits does a masterplan provide, how do we build flexibility into the process, what are the key qualities that a masterplan for an area like the Docklands should address. In Docklands we have had public masterplans and private masterplans – both are valid but I would not support development without urban plans and here I have to disagree with Reg Ward. But let's be realistic – what kind of masterplan can accommodate the changes we have seen at the Isle of Dogs where in less than ten years a landscape of tin sheds has given way to fifty storey office towers. It took Dallas nearly a hundred years to do this.

Q7. Do you think space exists to form a coherent network of urban space in Docklands?

A. Rapid urbanisation always creates problems – in Boston and Liverpool space was reclaimed from in front of older docks to form civic areas and we may have to do this in Docklands. To my mind the problem is one of balancing urban space and the amenity value of the water areas. As I said earlier we are into the stitching and darning stage – stitching together the spaces created often by private developers and darning the gaps between the buildings. I don't underestimate the task especially on the Isle of Dogs.

Q8. There is talk of the LDDC being wound up in 1996. Are you putting in place a long term framework for urban design in Docklands?

A.   Yes we are – city making has a far longer perspective than the framework of our existence provided under the 1980 Act. My own view is that we must establish guidelines which go beyond the timescale of the LDDC. One of the problems of this part of London is that historically there has been no vision to guide urban design. We are presently looking at what that vision might contain.

Bibliography

Aldersey-Williams, H.	'Temple to industry and commerce', *RIBA Journal*, August 1989
Aldersey-Williams, H.	'A Rogers for Reuters', *Blueprint*, November 1989
Aldous, T.	'Soft centres', *Building Design*, 22 March 1991
Al Naib, S.K.	*London Docklands: Past, Present and Future*, Thames and Hudson (1990)
Anderton, F.	'Docklands double act', *Architectural Review*, April 1989
Atha, A.	'Blue is not green', *The Observer*, 18 November 1990
Bacon, E.	*Design of Cities*, Thames and Hudson (1967)
Bar-Hillel, M.	'Going down the tube', *Building Design*, 12 October 1990
Barrick, A.	'Docklands – an urban failure', *Building Design*, 5 April 1991
Bentley, I., Alcock, A., Murrain, P., McGlynn, S. and Smith, G.	*Responsive Environments: A Manual for Designers*, Architectural Press (1985)
Blackwell, L.	'Promise for jobs boosts finance centre prospects', *Building Design*, 4 October 1985
Broadbent, G.	*Emerging Concepts of Urban Space Design*, van Nostrand Reinhold International (1990)
Buchanan, P.	'Regenerating Barcelona with parks and plazas', *Architectural Review*, June 1984
Buchanan, P.	'What city? A plea for place in the public realm', *Architectural Review*, November 1988
Buchanan, P.	'Quays to design', *Architectural Review*, April 1989
Calvocoressi, P.	*Conservation in Docklands: Old Buildings in a Changing Environment* (Docklands Forum 1990)
Coombs, A.	'City ventures', *Urban Design Quarterly*, no. 36, October 1990
Cowan, R.	'The market stalls', *Architects Journal*, 8 November 1989
Cowan, R. and Gallery, L.	'A vision for London', *Architects Journal*, 14 March 1990
Cruikshank, D.	'Modern housing', *Architects Journal*, 17 August 1988
Cruikshank, D.	'Guilt complex', *Architectural Review*, April 1989
Cruikshank, D.	'Street wise', *Architects Journal*, 16 May 1990
Cullen, G.	*The Concise Townscape*, Architectural Press (1971)
Davey, P.	'Three on the waterfront', *Architectural Review*, April 1989
Davey, P.	'What to do in the docks', *Architectural Review*, April 1989
Davidson, A.	'Special offers fail to fill Canary Wharf', *The Sunday Times*, 23 September 1990
Davies, C.	'The electronic page', *The Daily Telegraph*, 27 April 1987
Davies, C.	'*Ad hoc* in the docks', *Architectural Review*, February 1987
Docklands Consultative Committee	*The Docklands Experiment* (1990)
Edwards, B.	'Docklands: the story so far', *Building Design*, 19 June 1987
Edwards, B.	'Art of the possible', *Building Design*, 26 July 1991
Elkin, T., McLaren, D. and Hillman, M.	*Reviving the City: Towards Sustainable Urban Development*, Friends of the Earth (1991)
Evans, R.	'London Docklands', *Financial Times*, 1 October 1986
Fyson, A.	'Too late for Docklands?', *The Planner*, 12 October 1990
Giedion, S. (ed.)	*Space, Time and Architecture*, Harvard University Press (1956)
Girouard, M.	*Cities and People*, Yale University Press (1985)
Gosling, D. and Maitland, B.	*Concepts of Urban Design*, Academy Editions (1984)
Hall, P.	*The World Cities*, World University Library (1966)
Hannay, P.	'Docklands guiding light', *Architects Journal*, 8 August 1984
Hatton, B.	'The development of London's Docklands', *Lotus International* no. 67, 15 December 1990

Hollamby, E.	*Docklands: London's Backyard into Front Yard* (Docklands Forum 1990)
Hollamby, E.	'A review of the past', *Urban Design Quarterly*, June 1989
HRH The Prince of Wales	*A Vision of Britain*, Doubleday (1989)
Hughes, R.	*The Shock of the New* , BBC Publications(1980)
Jencks, C. (ed.)	*The Language of Post-Modern Architecture*, Academy Editions (1987)
Jencks, C.	*The New Moderns*, Academy Editions (1990)
Jenkins, D.	'Blue movie architecture', *Blueprint*, July 1990
Jones, S. R.	*Thames Triumphant*, The Studio Publications (1945)
Klotz, H. (ed.)	*New York Architecture 1970–90*, Prestel (1989)
Krier, R.	*Urban Space*, Academy Editions (1979)
London Docklands Development Corporation (LDDC):	*Area brochures for Isle of Dogs, Royal Docks, Surrey Docks and Wapping and Poplar* (1985–91)
	Corporate Plans (1985–90)
	Decade of Achievement 1981–91 (1991)
	Docklands Heritage: Conservation and Regeneration in London Docklands (1987)
	Greenland Dock: a Framework for Development (January 1984)
	Homes Sweet Homes (undated)
	Isle of Dogs: a Guide to Design and Development Opportunities (1982)
	London Docklands Architectural Review: Isle of Dogs (1990)
	London Docklands Transport: the Growing Network for the 1990s (1991)
	Review of Achievement (1990)
	Royal Docks: a Draft Development Framework (January 1985)
	Royal Docks: a Vision for the Future (undated)
	The Royal Docks: an International Opportunity (undated)
	Royal Victoria Dock (South) and Thames Barrier Lands: Interim Master Plan and Development Framework (1989)
	The Southwark Site Proposals for Redevelopment (November 1983)
Lynch, K.	*The Image of the City*, MIT Press (1960)
Lynch, K.	*Good City Form*, MIT Press (1981)
Melhuish, C.	'Class wharf', *Building Design* 30 November 1990
Moore, R.	'Land of lost opportunities', *Blueprint*, July 1987
Mumford, L.	*The City in History*, Penguin Books (1966)
Murray, C.	'St George and the dragon', *Architects Journal*, 28 February 1990
Nicholson-Lord, D.	'London Docklands focus', *The Times*, 18 November 1986
Olin, L.	'Singing the praises of Canary Wharf', *Landscape Design*, October 1986
Olsen, D. J.	*The City as a Work of Art: London, Paris and Vienna*, Yale University Press (1984)
Owens, R.	'Blue circle', *Architects Journal*, 17 October 1990
Pearman, H.	'A planning inquiry that missed the boat', *The Sunday Times* 11 March 1990
Petty, J.	'Fleet Street on the water', *The Daily Telegraph*, 27 April 1987
Pevsner, N.	*The Englishness of English Art*, Penguin Books (1964)
Rabeneck, A.	'The American invasion', *Architects Journal*, 28 March 1990
Randall, C.	'A glass shed rises where once shed 19 decayed', *The Daily Telegraph* 27 April 1987
Robson, D.	'Canary Wharf', *The Planner*, 12 October 1990
Rossi, A.	*The Architecture of the City*, MIT Press (1982)
Rowe, C. and Koetter, F.	*Collage City*, MIT Press (1978)
Rowlands, C.	'The Seifert concept of light and reflections', *The Daily Telegraph*, 27 April 1987
Shaw, B.	'The Journey to Docklands', *Urban Design Quarterly* June 1989
Shaw, B.	'Greenland Dock', *Architects Journal*, 14 November 1990
Shaw, B.	'London Docklands development', *Cities on Water – Waterfront Symposium*, Venice, 1991
Slessor, C.	'Current account', *Architects Journal*, 16 May 1990
Stamp, G. and Slessor, C.	'Tobacco trader', *Architects Journal*, 28 February 1990
Strong, R.	*'Rus in urbe'*, *Urban Design Quarterly*, June 1989

Summerson, J.   *Georgian London* (Barrie and Jenkins 1969)
Tabor, P.   'Boilerhouse to Bauhaus', *Architects Journal*, 16 August 1989
Tinniswood, A.   *The Thames and its Buildings*, English Heritage (1990)
Trancik, R.   *Finding Lost Space: Theories of Urban Design*, Van Nostrand Reinhold (1986)
Tyler, R.   *Canary Wharf: the Untold Story* (Olympia and York 1990)
Venturi, R.   *Complexity and Contradiction in Architecture*, Architectural Press (1966)
Venturi, R., Scott Brown, D.,
    and Izenour, S.   *Learning from Las Vegas*, MIT Press (1972)
Ward, R.   'London: the emerging Docklands city', *Built Environment*, vol. 12, no. 3
Ward, R.   'The years ahead', *The Complete Business World*, February–April 1987
Welsh, J.   'Reckoning on the riverside', *Building Design*, 4 August 1989
Welsh, J.   'Water works', *Building Design*, 27 October 1989
Williams, S.   *ADT Architecture Guide: Docklands*, Architectural Design and Technology Press (1990)
Wolmar, C.   'The new East Enders', *Weekend Guardian*, 8–9 April 1989
Wolmar, C.   'Crisis of confidence rocks Docklands dream', *The Independent*, 4 January 1990
Woodman, L.   'After decades of decay', *Landscape Design*, October 1986
Wythe, J.   'Ten years in the docks', *Landscape Design* October 1986
Young, A.   'Big Bang sets off chain reaction in Docklands', *Glasgow Herald* 16 March 1987
Zwingle, E.   'Docklands: London's new frontier', *National Geographic*, vol. 180, no. 1, July 1991

Index

(Italic type denotes illustration)